VOID

Library of
Davidson College

Regionalism and Regional Devolution in Comparative Perspective

REGIONALISM AND REGIONAL DEVOLUTION IN COMPARATIVE PERSPECTIVE

Mark O. Rousseau
and
Raphael Zariski

PRAEGER

New York
Westport, Connecticut
London

Library of Congress Cataloging-in-Publication Data

Rousseau, Mark O.
  Regionalism and regional devolution in comparative
perspective.

  Includes bibliographies and index.
  1. Decentralization in government. 2. Regionalism.
3. Comparative government. I. Zariski, Raphael.
II. Title.
JS113.R69   1987   351.007'3   87-47735
ISBN 0-275-92546-3 (alk. paper)

Copyright © 1987 by Praeger Publishers

All rights reserved. No portion of this book may
be reproduced, by any process or technique, without
the express written consent of the publisher.

Library of Congress Catalog Card Number: 87-47735
ISBN: 0-275-92546-3

First published in 1987

Praeger Publishers, One Madison Avenue, New York, NY 10010
A division of Greenwood Press, Inc.

Printed in the United States of America
∞
The paper used in this book complies with the
Permanent Paper Standard issued by the National
Information Standards Organization (Z39.48-1984).

10 9 8 7 6 5 4 3 2 1

To Marion with Affection
To Oscar, Yole, and Vera

Contents

Foreword ix

Acknowledgments xi

1 National Power and Local Governance: Problems and Perspectives
  Raphael Zariski and Mark O. Rousseau 1

2 Power and Decentralization: Concepts and Theories
  Mark O. Rousseau and Raphael Zariski 43

3 Italy: The Distributive State and the Consequences of Late Unification
  Raphael Zariski 91

4 France: The Bureaucratic State and Political Reforms
  Mark O. Rousseau 152

5 Spain: The Multinational State and the Consequences of Incomplete State Building
  Raphael Zariski 202

6 Conclusions and Interpretations
  Mark O. Rousseau and Raphael Zariski 268

Index 283

About the Authors 293

Foreword

This book approaches a given problem--political power and regional devolution--in a variety of settings. In doing so, it relies on both political and sociological perspectives, corresponding to the interests and intellectual orientations of the authors. It deals with the highest subnational decision-making territorial level of government--the region-- which is becoming increasingly important in the nonfederal systems under scrutiny. The comparative cross-cultural approach makes it possible to highlight the similarities and differences between regional structures of power in democratic societies and to compare alternative solutions to the problem of decentralization. Such problems and their proposed solutions in the United States can be better understood when the experience of other Western democracies has been analyzed.

This study is addressed to students and scholars in both political science and sociology, and utilizes concepts and theories from both disciplines. By placing the examination of centralized and decentralized structures in historical context, the authors seek to facilitate an understanding of the evolution of center-periphery problems over time and an appreciation of the ways in which reforms reflect the historical context of problem development.

Acknowledgments

We wish to thank the Research Council of the University of Nebraska-Lincoln for providing one of the authors with a travel grant in the summer of 1984--a grant that permitted us to acquire vital research materials in Italy, France, and Spain.

Invaluable assistance in typing the manuscript was provided by Lawrence M. Kenney and Kris Holliday. Valuable research assistance was furnished by the Centro Studi della Fondazione Adriano Olivetti in Rome and the Istituto per la Scienza dell' Amministrazione Pubblica in Milan.

1

National Power and Local Governance: Problems and Perspectives

Raphael Zariski
Mark O. Rousseau

THE POWER PROBLEM: DISTRIBUTION
OF POWER IN THE GOOD SOCIETY

One of the fundamental issues in the study of government and politics is the problem of political power. It is a problem with both empirical and normative facets. In order to understand the basic character of a political system, we must observe how power is distributed among the various governmental institutions and political forces. In order to grasp the dynamics of the political process in such a system, we must take note of how power is exercised and in what ways and to what degree it is restrained. The positions adopted by various actors in the political system with regard to such questions as the distribution and restriction of political power provide us with insights into the material interests involved in one of the key controversies in political philosophy.

Finally, the normative aspect of the power question can hardly be overlooked. It is impossible to speculate in a meaningful fashion about the nature of the good society and of the political system best suited for such a society without considering what values are at stake when power is wielded and what methods of distributing and checking power are most likely to advance some values while possibly neglecting or threatening others. Where power is concerned, hard choices among competing values are often inescapable.

The study of political power has often tended to confine itself to the national level, to the relationships among various functional agencies of the national government, and between those agencies and the parties and interest groups that attempt to influence their decisions. With the exception of a flourishing literature on federalism, little attention has been paid to the interaction between the central government, on the one hand, and regional and local authorities on the other. Yet this territorial, or areal, division of power has always constituted an important problem to be confronted in any democratic system--unitary or federal. It has spawned a continuing debate over the respective virtues of centralization and decentralization. This debate has waxed more intense in recent years in all modern industrial democracies; for doubts about the efficacy of central power and central decision making have become increasingly audible. Moreover, this issue has taken on strong normative overtones. The centralization-decentralization controversy is more than a disagreement over questions of efficiency and administrative capacity; it involves conflicts among certain fundamental values as well.

REGIONAL DEVOLUTION: THE TOPIC AND ITS TREATMENT

One form of decentralization is federalism, in which the constitution divides power between the national and regional levels of government and in which each level of authority retains some exclusive powers of its own. Another form is regional devolution, in which national power tends to be paramount over regional powers and in which a central government agent can intervene directly to block or appeal against regional legislation. Regional devolution is a response adopted by a number of unitary states, such as Italy, Spain, and to a lesser degree, France. It is a system that possesses both unitary and federal features.

In this chapter, we begin with a discussion of the centralization-decentralization issue in Western societies. Historical and social factors that culminated in the centralization of political power at the highest level of the national state are noted. Historical and social factors that have produced growing demands for enhanced local decision making are also examined. The ideological and empirical debates over centralized and decentralized power are surveyed, and the leading arguments for and against decentralization evaluated. We then proceed to identify the political forces that have tended to favor centralization and decentralization, respectively. The chapter closes with a brief comparative discussion of various alternatives to centralization in a unitary system: deconcentration, decentralization, and regional devolution.

Chapter 2 directs attention to some major theories regarding the exercise of power and the distribution of power between central and regional governments. Elitist theories, pluralist theories, and more recent theories dealing with center-periphery interaction are examined and compared to see what light they shed on the centralization-decentralization issue. Chapter 2 also touches on certain peripheral contributions to empirical theory in the centralization-decentralization area of comparative politics—for example, the issue of technocratic reform versus distributive welfare (Tarrow 1977) and the tension between territorial representation and functional representation (Tarrow 1978).

A comparative analysis of political decentralization and regional devolution in several major Western industrial democracies constitutes the central theme of this book. Chapters 3, 4, and 5 are devoted to the systematic treatment of processes of centralization and decentralization in Italy, France, and Spain, culminating in the currently ongoing experiments with regional devolution. Each chapter considers political centralization and decentralization in historical context and traces the steps by which the centralizing nation-state prevailed over the regional periphery. It then deals with the revival of regionalism, a tendency that (never completely suppressed) came into its own after World War II. For each nation, the main ideological issues underlying the regional movement and its pressure on the central government are noted. As a result of revived decentralizing movements, Italy, France, and Spain provided for some form of regional devolution.

In each national context, the chapter examines the institutional and social forces that promoted and resisted decentralization and devolution, and addresses the ways in which ethnic forces made use of the movement toward regional autonomy. We examine the problem of economic planning and show how such planning has been partly responsible for regional decentralization.

Each chapter describes and analyzes the decentralizing and devolutionary solutions to the problems of political power and decision making taken by each nation. The changing legal relationships between the regional and other levels of government are explored and the resulting governmental structures described. The structures and operations of regional government are surveyed, and the ways in which the various forms of regional devolution deviate from both the federal and the unitary models are noted. Decentralization and devolution are related to the political milieu, and the changing positions taken by parties and pressure groups toward regional and local issues are analyzed. In the context of a growing skepticism about the effectiveness of centralized governmental institutions in Western democracies, an attempt is made to evaluate the adequacy of contemporary decentralizing and devolutionary reforms in Italy, France, and Spain.

Chapter 6 concludes the book with a discussion of centralization, decentralization, and regional devolution as ongoing processes. A summary of the findings about regionalism and regional devolution is then presented, and the theoretical implications of the survey of regional and national power for assisting in the construction of a growing body of empirical theory on comparative politics and political power are assessed. Last, unanswered questions are suggested and patterns for future research proposed.

CENTRALIZATION OF POWER: THE NEED FOR NATIONAL UNITY

Historical and Social Factors Favoring Centralization

The origins of the centralization process in western Europe are usually traced back to the development of the European nation-state, which displaced or defeated the autonomous city, the feudal principality, the temporal claims of the Roman Catholic Church, and the confederal impotence of the Holy Roman Empire. The process of state formation in western Europe began to accelerate in the sixteenth century. In 1500, there were about 500 independent or semiindependent political units in western and central Europe. By 1900, there were approximately 25 (Tilly 1975a, p. 15).

The state formation process in western Europe was stimulated by a number of factors that also contributed to increased centralization in the expanding nation-states. First of all, expansion was often achieved through military conquest at the expense of feudal principalities bordering on the territory of the nation-building centralizing core. In order to maintain the necessary level of military strength, it was necessary for the centralizing monarch to raise and supply a large standing army. This in turn necessitated a rising rate and expanding scope of taxation, plus a powerful and skilled bureaucracy to extract the requisite fiscal resources and to administer the newly acquired territories. Thus, military conquest, and the fiscal impositions and bureaucratic aggrandizement it entailed, did much to speed the trend toward greater centralization (Badie and Birnbaum 1983; Tilly 1975a, 1975b, 1981).

Certain social and economic factors had to be present, however, in order for this process of military expansion and centralization to be feasible. By the sixteenth century, the presence in western Europe of a growing merchant class, inhabiting a network of prosperous urban commercial centers, ensured that the essential financial resources would be available for extraction. The Protestant Reformation, along with the expansion of trade and commerce, contributed to the formation of a purely secular bureaucracy, which could be trusted to assist the king in his conflict with the interests of the Church (Friedrich 1963, pp. 549-50). These developments also helped to bring about the rise of what Eisenstadt (1966) has called the centralizing middle groups--Protestants, the urban middle class, the more prosperous peasants, even some members of the aristocracy--who saw the king as an ally in the struggle for religious reform and economic progress.

The centralizing tendencies that began to gather momentum in the sixteenth century did not have an easy victory, however. There was much grass-roots resistance to the impositions from the capital, resistance that often took the form of riots and local rebellions. The Church and the landed aristocracy conducted a long and frequently successful delaying action against the reforms demanded by the centralizers. Moreover, the expansionist wars waged by the absolute monarchs posed almost unbearable financial burdens and increased the need for more taxes, which in turn generated further resistance against the national government. On the eve of the French Revolution of 1789, entrenched regional and aristocratic privileges were still alive and well in France, to say nothing of the rest of Europe.

Paradoxically enough, it was the French Revolution of 1789 and the democratic revolutions of the nineteenth century that not only ousted or neutralized the monarchy, but also speeded up the march toward greater centralization. These revolutions encouraged people to feel an overriding loyalty toward the nation, and the resulting wave of nationalism did much to undermine preexisting allegiances to villages, cities, and regions. Moreover, the democratic revolutions emphasized representative democracy, typified by the elected legislature; and this new phenomenon met the objections of those whose resistance to the centralizing absolute monarch had been based in part on an idealized nostalgia for the direct democracy of the ancient Greek city-state. Nationalism and the representative principle served to render the myth of the Greek city-state obsolete in the minds of many Western progressives (Dahl and Tufte 1973, pp. 8, 12).

Closely related to the impact of the democratic revolutions were the far-reaching effects of the industrial revolution. The political revolutions of the eighteenth and nineteenth centuries had cleared away many feudal privileges and many restraints on trade. They thus helped to stimulate massive social and economic changes. Great numbers of people moved from the countryside to the big cities, from the farm and the artisan's workbench to the factory production line. Industrial combinations drove many small entrepreneurs out of business and created an oligopolistic economy dominated by a relatively small number of corporate giants. Public educational opportunities were extended to the great majority of the people, and illiteracy rapidly declined. Improvements in transportation and communication bound the outer regions more closely to the center, creating a nationwide market and a national public opinion. In short, what occurred was a kind of national standardization process (Beer 1973; Sharpe 1979, pp. 11-13) or what Elazar (1973) has referred to as extrapolitical centralization. It is self-evident that such tendencies were bound to reenforce the centralizing trends in the political system itself.

Furthermore, industrialization led to the eventual emergence of an increasingly class-conscious proletariat and to the class cleavages that have played such a key role in European politics and elections. These class cleavages tended to crosscut center-periphery cleavages. In other words, by creating class conflict in the periphery, they divided the periphery in its confrontation with the center, providing the centralizers with grass-roots allies among lower status people who resented the economic and social advantages enjoyed by regional elites. Thus, for example, the economically dependent forestry workers and fishermen of northern Norway tended to vote for the socialist parties rather than for middle-class parties committed to the defense of regional interests (Rokkan 1967, pp. 437-38; Rokkan and Valen 1970, pp. 199-203). As a result of these crosscutting tendencies, the extension of the suffrage often had the effect of gravely weakening any purely territorial opposition against centralization (Lipset and Rokkan 1967, p. 12).

During the eighteenth, nineteenth, and early twentieth centuries, a number of self-governing political communities chose to band together to form federal systems. These federal systems are often described as alternatives to a centralized unitary system. Yet the very fact of their formation represented a centralizing tendency as opposed to the separate existence each member state or province had enjoyed prior to the creation of a "more perfect union."

A sizable body of literature has formed around the phenomenon of federalism, and a number of authors have raised the question as to what factors are responsible for the establishment of federations. In many instances, the factors cited are quite similar to those we have already mentioned as contributing to centralization. For example, one factor frequently mentioned is the desire to attain protection or a greater degree of military security against some external enemy (Birch 1966; Dikshit 1975; Riker 1964; Sawer 1969; Wheare 1964). Another attributed cause is the existence of an interdependent economy, with convenient networks of transportation and communication linking the prospective member states of the federation. This type of interdependence suggests that certain economic advantages would probably result from the establishment of a federal union (Dikshit 1975; Wheare 1964).

In the twentieth century, the growing complexity and increasingly acute problems confronting the governments of industrial and postindustrial societies, and the newly aroused appetites of the people of the former colonies in the Third World, have combined to generate additional pressures for expanding the role of the central government.

With the advent of the welfare state, there has been a steady and inexorable rise in popular expectations regarding the services governments are supposed to provide for the people under their jurisdiction (Friedrich 1974, pp. 62-63; La Palombara 1971, pp. 222-23; Sharpe 1979, pp. 14-15). This growing clamor for governmental assistance has placed public authorities under severe financial stress and has imposed weighty burdens on local and regional governments--burdens that render them increasingly dependent on central government aid in the form of grants and of direct expenditures by field agencies.

As the possessor of superior fiscal resources, particularly more broadly based powers of taxation, the central government was bound to become the primary dispenser of services and to carve out a position of apparent superiority in the field of intergovernmental relations (Beer 1973; Sawer 1969, pp. 139-45). The cost of defraying the expenses of two world wars has compelled even federal central governments to expand their tax base and to amplify their taxing powers at the expense of regional and local authorities (Livingston 1968, pp. 125-39; Sharpe 1979, pp. 15-16).

Nor have central governments simply responded to demands and pressures in furnishing services to the public. To an increasing degree, central governments have taken the initiative in formulating sets of proposed solutions to social and economic problems and have attempted to impose those solutions at the local and regional levels. Such a strategy of hierarchical imposition naturally leads to a strong operational bias in favor of centralization (Blondel 1969, pp. 285-86). Furthermore, the central government bureaucracy seeks to augment its influence and to protect the job security of its personnel by attempting to multiply the functions performed by the various agencies of the central government (Sharpe 1979, pp. 16-17).

Certain demographic and geographic factors have also tended to strengthen the center at the expense of the periphery. For example, Blondel (1969, p. 285) has pointed out that centralization is more likely to be accentuated in a small, homogeneous country without significant regional differences. For their part, Rokkan and Urwin (1983, p. 36; 1982, pp. 5-6) suggest that in many cases a monocephalous state (characterized by the predominance of one area or even one city along political, economic, and cultural dimensions) is more likely to follow a centralizing strategy.

Paris could be expected to have more ambitious goals than Bonn, according to this thesis.

As one can readily discern, a formidable combination of historical and social factors has favored the expansion of the powers of the central government over the periphery. These factors include the centralizing effects of the burgeoning bureaucracies and fiscal impositions that the military conquests of the absolute monarchs brought in their wake; the support that the monarchs obtained from a wealthy and powerful merchant class; the impact of the democratic revolutions and of the industrial revolution in its various manifestations; the advent of the welfare state; and the purposeful, self-generated initiatives of central government agencies seeking to extend their domains.

We have thus far treated centralization as if it had been a natural elemental force prevailing largely on the basis of superior power and resources. In the next section, we deal with some of the justifications offered by the centralizers to those who questioned their objectives. We also touch on some empirical arguments for centralization.

The Rationale for Centralization:
Normative and Empirical Arguments

Supporters of centralization frequently uphold the claims of the central government in the name of achieving a more rapid rate of modernization and a more far-reaching transformation of society (Pye 1971, pp. 139-41; Weiner 1971, p. 160). There is more to this claim, however, than a febrile desire for change for the sake of change: There is also an underlying normative aspiration. Change is supposed to bring about a more egalitarian distribution of goods and services. A number of authors refer to this rationale for centralization, stressing the point that, in a decentralized or federal system, economically weaker regions will be unable or unwilling to dispense the same quantity and quality of social services as the more prosperous regions. Only a centralized government has the capacity and the will to equalize the resources allocated to the various regions, giving the poorer regions a larger share of central government assistance, rather than simply allowing spending patterns to reflect existing economic disparities (Cameron and Hofferbert 1974; Fesler 1949, pp. 43-44; Smith 1980, p. 231). Some empirical confirmation of this thesis appears in a cross-national study of spending on public education. Unitary systems seem to provide a greater measure of distributive equity (Cameron and Hofferbert 1974, pp. 247-48).

Another normative defense of centralization is the Jacobin concept of the general will of the nation which should prevail over the particularistic wills of the local and functional interests of the realm (Dahl and Tufte 1973, pp. 11-12). This is a view based on a strong belief in the virtues of popular sovereignty. It questions the ability of local governments to instill a sense of meaningful participation among their citizens (Fesler 1965, pp. 547-49).

Local government may also threaten the rights of the minority in a way that only a powerful central government can redress (Crozier 1982, pp. 67-68). James Madison, one of the authors of The Federalist Papers, expressed the fear that arbitrary local majorities might pose a serious threat to republican government (Huntington 1959, pp. 188-94), and this fear was to prove all too justified in the centuries ahead. The memory of how brutally southern blacks were oppressed, in the name of states' rights, in the autonomous states of the American South is still with us. In Ulster, decentralization of power to the Parliament at Stormont enabled the Protestant majority to oppress the Catholic minority. Direct intervention, and eventual direct rule from London was required to protect the civil rights of Catholics (Smith 1980, pp. 229-30, 315). As Dahl puts it (1982, p. 104), "To shift resources away from the Center to more autonomous subsystems may prevent domination by the Center, but . . . decentralization may also allow domination within each subsystem." In the case of the United States, only federal intervention (i.e., greater centralization) could liberate the southern black from second-class citizenship.

Still another rationale for centralization is based on the natural human desire for stability and order. Writing in sixteenth-century France, at a time when the French state was still threatened by civil conflict between religious factions, Jean Bodin warned that, without a highly centralized state, domestic tranquillity could not be ensured (Davis 1978, pp. 43-47).

In modern times, a number of writers have touched on the danger that an excessive degree of autonomy for regional or local units of government might pose the threat of secession, or at any rate might jeopardize the process of creating a truly integrated nation (Tarlton 1965, pp. 872-74; Teune 1968, pp. 227-33). The experience of the United States during the nineteenth century and of Canada in recent years suggests that, in a society characterized by a very high degree of diversity among regions, the separatist temptation is hard to resist. For this reason, some advocates of centralization believe in the so-called cultural diffusion model: The Center should gradually extend its cultural supremacy over the traditionally oriented outlying regions and establish the core culture as the culture of a united nation-state (Deutsch 1961; Hechter 1975, pp. 22-25).[1]

Finally, it has been suggested, decentralization may permit an antisystem party to establish and consolidate a secure local or regional base to serve as a springboard for future expansion (Friedrich 1974, pp. 58-59). It was partly the fear of precisely such an outcome--the creation of an autonomous system-threatening "Red Belt" in north-central Italy around Bologna and Florence--that induced the Italian Christian Democratic party to resist the creation of the Italian autonomous regions for more than 20 years after the inauguration of the constitution of the Italian Republic in 1948.

With the introduction of the motif of stability, order, and public safety, we have added empirical to purely normative considerations. Another empirical justification for centralization rests on the claim that the central government can act with greater efficiency and dispatch to cope with the complex problems of a modern industrial or post-industrial society. By the same token, it is argued, the regional and local authorities are poorly equipped to deal with such problems and are too sluggish and conservative to embark on such a task. The greater efficiency of the central government is seen as based on a number of factors--for instance, its ability to coordinate and oversee the activities of lower units of government that might otherwise be reciprocally unaware of each other's policies (Dahl 1982, p. 104) and its more selectively recruited and more adequately trained personnel (Fesler 1949, pp. 29-30). Those who stress the inadequacy of the local and regional authorities point to such shortcomings as their lack of fiscal resources (Fesler 1949, pp. 26-27, 40-46); their lack

---

[1] Hechter is not an advocate of the cultural diffusion process; he simply outlines the views of its partisans.

of functional specialization, stemming from a higher proportion of generalists in the field than at the center (Fesler, 1949, pp. 66-72); and their conservatism and inflexibility, which lead them to inhibit and discourage needed reforms (Kesselman and Rosenthal 1974, pp. 29-30; Sawer 1969, pp. 25, 182-83; Schulz 1979, pp. 5-6).

THE DECENTRALIZATION OF POWER:
THE RECOGNITION OF LOCAL DIVERSITY

Historical and Social Factors Favoring
Regionalist Resistance and the Eventual
Resurgence of Decentralizing Tendencies

We have already referred to the determined resistance that the centralizing monarchs had to overcome after 1500. Deliberative assemblies, representing various established interests of the realm; peasants and artisans, hard-pressed by the escalating material impositions of the centralizers; local and regional magnates, struggling to hold on to their positions of privilege--these were the forces with which the state-building center had to contend. The great number of autonomous authorities would have been invincible had they maintained a united front, but the centralizers were able to prevail by a strategy of shifting alliances. The cost was heavy, however, both in financial outlays and in human lives. Terrible resentments were aroused by the new taxes and other contributions that the centralizing monarchs were obliged to exact to finance their expansion (Bien and Grew 1978, p. 238; Tilly 1975a, pp. 21-25, 71-75).

In some instances, the network of autonomous forces was too dense for any core area to arise and dominate its neighbors. Rokkan (1973, pp. 79, 84-94) speaks of a belt of wealthy and powerful commercial cities stretching across the European heartland from northern Italy through Germany to the North Sea. This territory could only be unified from outside; it contained no single natural urban core that could serve as a state-building force. Any attempt by a single city or principality to become such a core would promptly precipitate the formation of an invincible hostile coalition. It was not until the nineteenth century, therefore, that outside powers (Prussia and Piedmont, respectively) were able to establish unified states, including these thickly settled, polycephalous (many-centered) regions.

In some countries, the centralizing process was hampered by country-specific factors. In England, for example, the monarchy had never really developed a strong standing army or a powerful bureaucracy. Probably England's insular position, which protected the country against foreign invasion, was partly responsible for this lack of military and administrative muscle. In any event, the king had to accept and work with the existing networks of local authority (Thomas 1978, pp. 78-80). In Spain, on the other hand, the centralizing forces of Castile failed to promote socioeconomic development and progress, and had to confront the resulting upsurge of autonomist demands by the more progressive areas along the Spanish periphery (Payne 1978).

These peripheral demands were reenforced by keenly felt cultural differences and by grants of special local rights and privileges extended to the regions by the centralizing monarchs in order to disarm opposition to their state-building strategy. The cultural differences among various regions of Spain, France, and Britain were not of overriding importance in the sixteenth and seventeenth centuries, when the primary object of allegiance was the monarch. They became far more divisive after the French Revolution, when industrialization and the spread of literacy made language a vital tool for economic survival and when the erosion of feudal loyalties transformed languages and cultures into talismans of identity (Gellner 1964, ch. 7). By the same token, ancient rights and privileges granted in the late Middle Ages by the centralizing monarch, or exercised by outlying regions on the basis of customary prescription, proved to be relatively irrevocable, even in unitary states, in the modern era (Duchacek 1970, pp. 120-28). In fact, the regionalist movements of the nineteenth and twentieth centuries often reasserted these historic rights (like the Basque <u>fueros</u>).

As we can see, the historic forces affecting centralization have had a dialectical impact--every factor promoting centralization seems to have produced its own antithesis. Thus, the military, fiscal, and bureaucratic expansion undertaken by the centralizing core areas provoked obstinate and often violent regional resistance. Similarly, in the nineteenth century, the industrialization, urbanization, and widespread literacy that followed upon the democratic revolutions helped to establish the conditions under which ethnic anxieties and grievances could awaken and attract supporters.

Earlier in this chapter, we referred to the formation of federal systems in the eighteenth, nineteenth, and twentieth centuries. In one way, the coming together of a number of previously independent states or separately governed provinces could be regarded as a centralizing trend. However, the concomitant preservation of constitutionally guaranteed regional autonomy, with at least a few exclusive powers retained by the several regions, represented a clear victory for the forces of decentralization.

Why did federal institutions, rather than unitary systems, develop and survive in the cases of the United States, Switzerland, Canada, and Australia, thus salvaging an area of regional jurisdiction for the future? A number of explanations have been offered. First, federalism or accentuated regional autonomy seems to be called for when the territory to be governed is very large or is internally divided by geographic barriers (Dahl and Tufte 1973, pp. 36-40, 79). Federalism or accentuated regional autonomy seems to facilitate the coexistence of people of different languages, religions, or "races" in very heterogeneous societies in which those differences are geographically delineated (Dikshit 1975, pp. 227-28; Wheare 1964, pp. 40-42). This kind of political arrangement is also a way of mitigating the antagonisms produced by widely divergent sectional economic interests or by highly dissimilar social customs and political institutions (Dikshit 1975, pp. 227-28; Wheare 1964, pp. 40-42). Finally, the local pride engendered by a history of separate existence of the several component regions, and the presence in a single country of several competing, evenly matched, large urban centers of commercial, industrial, and cultural life, are two additional factors making for a federal compromise (Duchacek 1970, p. 314; Rokkan and Urwin 1982, pp. 5-6).

Once a federal system has been established, judicial review becomes a powerful mechanism for shifting the balance of power in a centralizing or decentralizing direction. In the United States, the Supreme Court has generally tended to uphold federal authority at the expense of states' rights, although the trend has by no means been unidirectional or uninterrupted. In Canada and Australia, on the other hand, the organs of judicial review have been far more prone to restrict national power and uphold the jurisdictional demands of the provinces and states (Livingston 1968, pp. 115-25).

It may be noted that some of the centrifugal factors, making for federalism or a high degree of regional autonomy to accommodate diversity, are in contrast with some of the centripetal factors that encourage several territories to come together to form a federal system. Size and geographic barriers do not seem entirely consistent with an interdependent economy, with convenient transportation and communications links between regions. Some federal systems possess common languages and similar political institutions in each component region, yet continue to maintain federal institutions. Other federal systems are internally divided by linguistic differences and by sharp institutional divergences separating the regions, yet continue to maintain the integrity of the state. These inconsistencies illustrate the multifaceted nature of the federal phenomenon and the difficulty of formulating universally applicable propositions with regard to that phenomenon.

We have seen how the advent of the welfare state has fostered the growth of the central government and the expansion of its activities. Once again, we must note the curious paradox; for this historical development, too, has in some ways helped to bring about some measure of decentralization. The growth of central functions and central spending has stimulated the development of local, provincial, and regional lobbies representing elected and appointed government officials at each of these levels. Every Western democracy has its counterpart of what Beer (1977, pp. 11-15) described in the United States as "the intergovernmental lobby." These interests have generally pressed for unconditional categorical grants and revenue sharing on the part of the central government in place of the much more restrictive grants-in-aid. As a result of these activities, local and regional interests in numerous democracies have been successful in increasing the proportion of nonbinding unconditional grant money allocated to local and regional authorities by the center. At the same time, naturally enough, the proportion of conditional-grant money has decreased. Also, subnational public spending has increased even more than national public spending (Tarrow 1978, pp. 8-16).

The growth of functional specialization and technocracy at the national level has been increasingly offset by the recruitment of skilled technocratic elites at the regional and local levels. These elites have begun to act as spokesmen for the regions and cities whose interests they represent. They have also cemented professional and personal ties with their technocratic colleagues in the central government ministries and, above all, in the field offices of those ministries. As a result of these linkages, the relation between central and regional/local officials in the same area of functional specialization is often one of alliance and collaboration. In place of central-regional confrontation, there are contests between various central-regional-local functional groupings (Tarrow 1978, pp. 12-16). Functional conflicts overshadow territorial rivalries.

The uneven rate of economic growth in modern democracies has become increasingly evident since the mid-nineteenth century. This factor has been partly responsible for the demands posed by those regions or sections that have lagged behind in the economic race. Such areas as the French "desert" in the south and west, the Italian south, and the north of England and western Scotland have become aware of their economically disadvantaged status. They have, in many instances, demanded more of a say in their economic destinies. The establishment of regions in Italy and France and the abortive move toward Scottish devolution may be seen in part as an attempt by the embattled central governments to assuage the economic grievances of the depressed periphery (Smith 1980, p. 210).

Finally, the social, economic, and cultural centralization that was ushered in by the industrial revolution and further accentuated by the rise of the multitentacled welfare state has also bred a decentralist reaction. Ethnic groups in the outlying regions see the immigration of industrial workers and summer vacationers from the core areas as threatening their cultural survival. Economically underdeveloped regions within a given country regard an insufficiently sympathetic central government as being partly responsible for their plight. The growing complexity and ambiguity of class cleavages in postindustrial society focus more attention on primordial religious and ethnic loyalties. In short, economic and social progress creates imbalances and fears that lead to new demands for decentralization (Sharpe 1979, ch. 1).

We have described some of the grass-roots responses to centralizing trends. However, decentralization has not only resulted from challenges emanating from below. To a considerable degree, recent decentralizing trends have come about because of initiatives from above (Duchacek 1970, pp. 351-52). Central authorities have tried to encourage greater initiative and flexibility at the local level. They have done this by relying more heavily on local authorities to interpret and administer national programs. Hope has been expressed that locally managed programs would be more efficient and realistic programs. Enlisting the aid and participation of regional and local officials has also been seen as a way of generating public support for nationally formulated programs (Beer 1973, pp. 85-87). Furthermore, unitary governments have discovered that decentralizing certain hard decisions to the grass roots is an excellent way to get those issues out of the national political arena.

Central planning has been a post-World War II adjunct of the welfare state. Its ultimate result has been to develop a national economic plan--a series of educated and informed forecasts about national economic trends. On the surface this appears to represent a strong force for further centralization. Again, however, central planning has led to some unforeseen decentralizing outcomes. In order for, say, the French central plan to be realistic, it had to be related to the prospects and requirements of various subnational areas. The necessary information could hardly be processed and evaluated in Paris without overloading the system. Consequently, the French regions were originally created for the purpose of facilitating the planning process by drawing up a series of regional plans, which could then be sorted out in Paris. So central planning, at least in France, was the precursor of decentralization (Smith 1980, p. 210; Ullmo 1975, pp. 49-50).

We have traced a number of historical and social factors that have worked on behalf of decentralization. In one sense, as we have seen, decentralizing tendencies have been a form of reaction fueled by fear and resentment--resentment of military aggression, higher taxes, and bureaucratic encroachments; fear of economic stagnation, cultural extinction, and enforced uniformity. In another sense, however, the drive toward greater decentralization has appeared as a series of rather sophisticated adaptations to the needs of a complex industrial or postindustrial society. Decentralization has, to some extent, acquired the halo of efficiency that was once attributed to the central government alone. Rather than nostalgia for a vanished past, decentralizing tendencies increasingly appear to be expressing a more realistic view of the future, of the adjustments necessary to control a postindustrial society. Also—and this is a theme to which we shall return—advocates of decentralization have found allies in unexpected places: in the national capital and in national field agencies. This suggests that the centralization-decentralization controversy may be a false dichotomy, oversimplifying a complex reality.

The Rationale for Decentralization: Normative and Empirical Arguments

Perhaps the most powerful argument for decentralization is its alleged contribution to increasing citizen participation in public affairs. Participation is important for a number of reasons. It enables the citizen to have more meaningful control over policy decisions that relate to vital interests (Dahl and Tufte 1973, pp. 20-22). In a broader sense, it provides a means for individual and group self-expression. It thus contributes to the development of the full potentialities of the human personality, to the release and constructive utilization of spontaneous human energies (Crozier 1982, pp. 99-122), and to the consequent development of a sense of mutual respect and trust between the governors and the governed (Hoffmann 1959, pp. 124-29[2]). In a complex modern society, it preserves some of the traditional advantages of community life by enhancing communication and mutual trust among the citizens (Elazar 1973, pp. 283-98). It thus instills in many participants a subjective feeling of political efficacy, raising the level of support for the system.

There is a good deal of testimony to the effect that decentralization really leads to greater citizen participation. Elazar (1973, pp. 273-83) points to the success of federalism in overcoming new forms of <u>political</u> distance resulting from population growth. The growing size of the public can actually serve as a formidable barrier to participation and communication; decentralization, by reducing political distance, lessens the barrier. Ylvisaker (1959, pp. 30-34) states that decentralization provides the individual citizen and the local group with more points of access, pressure, and control in their dealings with the

---

[2] Hoffmann was discussing the ideas of Alexis de Tocqueville.

political system and makes government more responsive to the people. Finally, Schulz (1979, pp. 6-7) addresses the centralizers' assertion that people are not really interested in local politics. As the evidence she submits indicates, the assertion holds true only in the absence of vigorous competition and/or significant concrete issues.

What seems to emerge from this array of pleas for greater participation through decentralization is a certain underlying normative consensus. Federalism and other forms of decentralization result in greater freedom for those being governed and also, by expanding participation, help to promote political and social unity (Teune 1968, pp. 220-33).

Another normative consideration raised by the advocates of decentralization is the need to restrain abuses of power by the central government. Thomas Jefferson regarded local self-government as an essential bulwark against corruption and tyranny (Huntington 1959, pp. 173-79; Tarlton 1965, pp. 864-65). Others have elaborated on this thesis, pointing to the desirability of providing minorities with local and regional power bases as a means of establishing a countervailing force at the subnational level to check central encroachments on human liberty (Ylvisaker 1959, pp. 30-34). Nor are the dangers of centralization limited to the political sphere. Some observers have noted that extrapolitical centralization poses a threat to small entrepreneurs and to small communications media and educational enterprises. In order to help control the vast and intricate complex of public and private enterprises at the national level, it is desirable to have concentrations of public power at the subnational levels as well (Elazar 1973, pp. 260-67).

Even when the central government shows great respect for individual liberties and minority rights and abstains from committing serious abuses of power, the interests of minority groups may still be seriously threatened by the mere fact of majority rule at the national level. In a highly centralized political system, smaller and/or economically less powerful groups may find it difficult to obtain access to the conventional channels of decision making in the executive branch. A restricted number of decision-making agencies may choose to deal with a restricted number of lobbies and to ignore marginal or fringe groups, even when those groups represent substantial local or regional interests (Watson 1975, pp. 473, 480-81). The experience of democratic corporatism in Scandinavia suggests that such overcentralization can result in serious rank-and-file alienation.

Vital sectional or regional interests may be menaced by majority rule even when there is meticulous adherence to democratic procedures. In the United States, it was the apparent Northern threat to the South's slaveholding interests that led John C. Calhoun to propound the doctrine of the concurrent majority. Under the terms of this doctrine, federal bills affecting sectional interests could become law only if each major section gave its approval (Sawer 1969, pp. 21-22). This doctrine, in the form of the mutual veto, has been revived in some consociational democracies like Belgium, where the approval of the parliamentary caucus of each linguistic community is required before a bill affecting cultural matters is allowed to receive approval of the full parliament.

However, the most substantially threatened minority interest to be considered is that of minority ethnic or linguistic groups that have an important stake in maintaining a distinctive identity and lifestyle. In this type of situation, a minority's vital interests may be undermined even by a central government policy of benign neglect. This is particularly true for linguistic minorities. How are their languages, their cultures, and their primordial customs to be preserved unless they can control their own educational systems and write their own laws regulating family and personal property issues? How can they enjoy equal opportunities for obtaining employment unless some form of bilingual or multilingual arrangement and a system of communal representation (an ethnic quota system) in the bureaucracy are established? The peculiar problems faced by the French in Canada, the Catalans and Basques in Spain, and the Germans in Italy's South Tyrol can only be resolved by either federalism or some other form of accentuated decentralization (Friedrich 1968, pp. 4-7, 30-35, 52-57; Friedrich 1963, pp. 543-45; Sharpe 1979, pp. 38-63).

It is interesting to note in passing that the protection of minority rights is a professed goal of both centralizers and decentralizers. Both are correct, of course, in their respective claims to protect hapless minorities against neglect or outright oppression. For an ethnic or religious minority may be dominant in a given region, in which case its grievances can only involve its relations with the central government; or it may be a minority group within the region, in which case it may regard the regional capital as posing a greater threat to its interests than the national capital. The periphery may confront more than one center, in other words, and circumstances determine which center represents a bigger problem for the rights of a given minority group.

Decentralization is often defended on the ground that it recognizes and encourages diversity at the grass roots (Cameron and Hofferbert 1974, pp. 230-31). This makes for an administrative system more attuned to local customs and traditions and, consequently, more realistic in formulating and implementing decisions. It also makes for a more interesting and livelier society in which a secure pride in regional diversity can actually reenforce feelings of national unity. Above all, local and regional governments in a decentralized system can experiment with new solutions to their problems, learn from each other's diverse experiences, and eventually act as channels for political innovation and change (Kesselman and Rosenthal 1974, pp. 30-31). Again, this claim strikes a familiar note: Do not the advocates of centralization see their mission as partly one of societal transformation?

Finally, there is a down-to-earth empirical defense of decentralization: It is simply a sound approach to getting the job done. This view of decentralization as ensuring greater efficiency and more satisfactory performance helps to account for the fact that even Communist systems frequently go through periods of decentralizing their adminministrative apparatus. It is often claimed that decentralization facilitates the performance of specialized functional tasks by utilizing local resources and services (thus relieving the pressure on the central government) and by enlisting the cooperation and support of local authorities (Friedrich 1968, pp. 4-7, 72-73). There is more assurance that demands will be heard and acted upon within a reasonable time frame, that government--acting as a neighbor rather than as a distant receiver of petitions--will perform its duties more efficiently and with more regard for the public it serves (Ylvisaker 1959, pp. 30-34). In reply to those who disparage the professionalism and functional expertise of regional and local officials, Ashford (1976, p. 51) asserts that regional and local subunits of government often set higher administrative standards than does the central government itself.

There is a more compelling reason why decentralization may be regarded as essential to improving efficiency and performance: the danger of system breakdown in the event that overcentralization clogs the arteries of the system. It has been pointed out, for example, that a highly centralized system of control requires a centralized system of communication. Such a centralized system of administrative communication may easily jam through overload or result in the transmission of distorted and inaccurate messages (Crozier 1982, pp. 79-80; Dahl 1982, p. 103). When all or most major decisions must be referred to the center, delays become interminable, costs mount, and vital services cannot be performed (Blondel 1969, pp. 300-301; Smith 1980, p. 206). As we can see, then, the empirical claims of the centralizers have also not gone unchallenged. Centralization is not only seen as violating important values; it is also condemned as standing in the way of progress and adequate performance.

CENTRALIZATION AND DECENTRALIZATION: A DYNAMIC EQUILIBRIUM

Forces Favoring Centralization

We turn now to a survey of the forces favoring centralization in a given society. These forces include (1) certain traditions of a legal, cultural, or institutional character; (2) central officials and the agencies they serve; (3) certain national, regional, local, or functional vested interests; (4) reformist policy commitments of the government of the day; and (5) associational interest groups and political parties.

The importance of established cultural attitudes and traditions in promoting centralization or helping to hold back decentralization can hardly be ignored or downgraded. A legal tradition of supporting federal expansion at the expense of the states has the effect of generating court decisions that, in turn, authorize the federal government to act, state objections notwithstanding. Such a legal tradition has prevailed, by and large, in the United States (Tarlton 1965, pp. 862-63). A given administrative forma mentis, entailing an established manner of conducting public business, may incline policy makers to approach questions of decentralization with a preconceived negative bias. For example, the strong tradition of centralized administration in a country like Britain has been a significant obstacle to the adoption of a political system based on federalism or regional devolution (Smith 1980, p. 235). Similarly, the prefectoral tradition of a fused hierarchy (in which the centrally appointed prefect acts simultaneously as director of central government activities at the local level and supervisor of local governments in his bailiwick) tends to stand in the way of genuine decentralization of power to local authorities in prefectoral unitary systems (Smith 1980, pp. 233-34).

Certain attitudes prevalent in the political culture--attitudes toward authority, toward the state, toward cultural differentiation for ethnic minorities, toward regional and local traditions--may also help to promote centralizing tendencies in a political system or encourage strong opposition to decentralization. Some of the literature stressing the importance of such attitudes is surveyed by Gourevitch (1980, pp. 37-41). He refers to Michel Crozier's view that a fear of face-to-face relations makes it difficult for French officials to work easily with their superiors and inferiors in the hierarchy. He also cites the French Jacobin tradition of regarding pluralism and decentralization with extreme suspicion as potential threats to republican institutions and popular sovereignty.

The interests and working habits of central government officials and of their agencies may represent another significant force hostile to decentralization, although these interests and customary working procedures are by no means uniform or unidirectional in their orientations. Central government agencies and officials may oppose decentralization for a number of reasons that have nothing to do with normative considerations or cultural traditions. For one thing, no official normally likes to relinquish power and control, particularly if he or she is imbued with a strong sense of professional pride and is confident of doing a good job. Central government officials may seek to stave off delegations of functions to field offices or to subnational governments on the ground that the field agencies or the local authorities are allegedly less competent to carry out certain specialized tasks. Consequently, they may fear (often with good reason) that serious administrative errors or omissions will be the by-products of decentralization. Or, on the other hand, they may prefer to postpone decentralization because it would entail serious problems of adjustment and retraining and create unfamiliar relationships with the field agencies and local governments, thus disrupting the customary routines of the central office (Fesler 1949, pp. 66-72).

Vested interests of a functional or territorial nature can feel seriously threatened by decentralizing tendencies, as we have just noted in the stand often adopted by central government ministries and their officials. Functional interest groups and centralized parties operating in a unitary system may harbor a legitimate anxiety that decentralization may compel them to undertake a complete revamping of their internal structure and modus operandi to conform to the new organization of public services. They may also suspect that their established clientela ties with central government agencies may be rendered relatively ineffective. Moreover, any functional interest group (labor union, farm organization, or the like) or class-based party has a much easier time maintaining its internal unity, cohesion, and discipline if territorial cleavages are not allowed to cross-cut its homogeneous functional structure.

Ironically, continued centralization is often championed by significant forces on the periphery. Local elites may have close ties with national regime elites, ties based on the local distribution of national patronage and appropriations to favored agents at the grass roots. This kind of situation can create a quasi-colonial relationship that either prevents decentralization altogether or robs it of all meaning (Schulz 1979, pp. 7-8). Even in the absence of such a pork barrel relationship, local mayors may prefer to deal with a remote national capital or with a relatively neutral prefect rather than with elected politicians in a traditionally unfriendly regional capital (Crozier 1973, pp. 83-84). Then again, ruling classes at the regional or local level may fear that regional or local autonomy might deprive them of the central protection they need in order to hold on to their power and privileges (Wright 1979, pp. 211-12; Zariski 1983, pp. 14-15).

A central government with a strongly reformist orientation may feel compelled to assume a centralizing posture. Here centralization is supported not by central bureaucrats protecting their administrative turf, but by central politicians with a mission to perform. When the goals of such a government are so far-reaching as to have a major impact on social relationships, the early stages of the radical reform may require centralized supervision to deal with local resistance (Blondel 1969, pp. 285-87). In some cases, a central government may be attempting "to make society more democratic by reducing the dominance of local interests" (Grew 1978, p. 21). This kind of centrally based subversion of local oligarchies again requires a considerable degree of centralization to ensure its initial success.

We have already referred to the likelihood that centralized parties and functional interest groups would find a centralized political structure to be more in harmony with their organizational structures, functional clienteles, and customary lobbying techniques, and would therefore be averse to the introduction of the territorially divisive motif of decentralization. We have suggested that this proposition also holds true for parties that reflect cleavages based on class interests.

The Norwegian case furnishes a convenient illustration of this point (Rokkan 1967, pp. 437-38; Rokkan and Valen 1970, pp. 195-96, 218-20). In the late nineteenth century, the Norwegian Labor party and the Norwegian Conservative party had their main strongholds in the big cities, in the industrializing communities of the eastern countryside, and in the highly stratified forestry and fishery towns of the north, where class divisions were keenly felt. Only in the relatively egalitarian farming areas of the south and west did socialism and conservatism fail to dominate the scene. Consequently, these parties never took a strong interest in the center-periphery issue of territorial defense against central hegemony—an issue that loomed very large indeed in southern and western Norway. More recently, the Socialists and the Conservatives, along with big business and the highly centralized Norwegian labor confederation, vigorously backed the proposed Norwegian entry into the European Common Market, whereas the parties of territorial defense successfully argued against this new form of centralization. Thus, it may be proposed that class stratification and the resulting class-based parties are likely to work in favor of centralizing tendencies, since territorial distinctions tend to undermine functional unity.

Parties that advocate redistributive policies are apt to favor centralization and consolidation of local jurisdictions as a means of overcoming local obstacles to those policies. For example, in Great Britain, the Labour party took a relatively centralizing line on the issue of local government reform. It proposed merging local governments into relatively large units in order to absorb and neutralize small, wealthy enclaves that might prefer to keep their tax bases for themselves. The Conservatives, on the other hand, preferred to have the central government deal with a larger number and variety of local authorities, thus ensuring greater local autonomy and diversification and protecting the distinctive identities and material interests of small, prosperous communities (Ashford 1976, p. 21).

Yet we must not be tempted to oversimplify the relationship between centralized structure, class-based party composition, and redistributive goals, on the one hand, and centralizing proclivities on the other. As we shall see in the French and Italian experiences, leftist parties that are excluded from access to power at the center are apt to become fervid supporters of local and regional autonomy. In a very real sense, a party's attitudes on the centralization-decentralization controversy are likely to follow the election returns.

Forces Favoring Decentralization

The traditions and actors favoring decentralization fall under much the same categories that we utilized above. Like the forces favoring centralization, they do not always operate as predictably as one might imagine.

Cultural traditions may serve to sustain decentralizing tendencies. For instance, in France, the United States, and India, the political culture is characterized by strong traditions of loyalty to local interests. In France, this support for localism coexists in incongruous juxtaposition with the Jacobin tradition of national sovereignty. In all three countries, a national government that neglects local interests does so at its peril. When an emotional attachment to local interests plays a key role in the political culture, even highly centralized legal structures can become malleable (Kesselman and Rosenthal 1974, pp. 17-19, 36-37).

Habitual political recruitment patterns in France and elsewhere also contribute to local autonomy. It is customary for many French national legislators to retain their positions as mayors, thus enhancing their ability to look out for the interests of their home town. It is also customary in France and some other democracies for local elective office to be a stepping-stone to national elective office, even if one does not wish to take advantage of the cumul des mandats and occupy both offices simultaneously (Kesselman and Rosenthal 1974, pp. 24-25). This habitual recruitment pattern has the effect of bestowing much more importance on the local governments than their formal legal powers would appear to suggest.

Officials of regional and local governments may be expected, out of professional self-interest, to demand a higher degree of decision-making autonomy (Sawer 1969, pp. 135-36). In fact, the "intergovernmental lobby" to which Beer (1977, pp. 11-15) refers--an array of local and state government officials who negotiate with the functional agencies of the central government in order to protect state and local interests--is to be found in European countries as well. We have already noted, however, that the attitudes of officials, both elected and appointed, at the periphery are not that easy to pin down. The periphery, like the center, is by no means united. Many small-town mayors in France would prefer to do business with a centrally appointed prefect than with an elected regional government (Wright 1979, pp. 211-12). Lacking the expertise and technical staff of big-city mayors who can deal directly with Paris, they would rather entrust themselves to the protection of a nonpolitical figure who has no particular local ax to grind.

At the same time, the central bureaucracy is not united in opposition to decentralization. When the issue of establishing some sort of regional devolution arose in France in 1969, the proposed reform had the support of some officials in the General Planning Commission in Paris and in other central agencies (Wright 1979, pp. 201-24). As Duchacek (1970, pp. 351-52) points out, central officials are often likely to propose decentralization as a means of achieving greater efficiency and responsibility in the field. As for the centrally appointed prefect, that official may be against regional devolution but often contracts alliances with mayors and other local officials, and almost acts as their agent in their dealings with Paris. By forming such alliances, by becoming identified with local interests, the prefect is expanding the de facto autonomy of the communes and departments under his or her jurisdiction (Milch 1974, p. 159). Thus, both central planning and the centralization implied by the prefectoral system have tended to encourage the development of a form of decentralization from above, designed to share the burdens of the central government with administrators at the grass roots and to elicit local and regional cooperation with central projects.

Important vested interests at the local and regional levels are among the strongest supporters of decentralization. As noted, however, not all regional and local interests support the cause of subnational autonomy. The centralizers have many allies at the grass roots. In the final analysis, material self-interest and local traditions may be compelling motivations for forming an alliance with the central government and its agents.

We have already referred to the opposition of outlying areas against the centralizing pretensions of the core area. With the decline of feudalism and of the landed aristocracy, such resistance has come mostly from peasant communities. However, these are peasant communities of a special type. They tend to be made up primarily of small and medium-sized family farmers, and do not normally contain great numbers of tenants and farm laborers. In short, peasant reaction against centralization tends to be most militant and single-minded in relatively egalitarian rural regions where the class struggle does not divide the forces of territorial defense (Lipset and Rokkan 1967, pp. 12-13, 20-21, 45; Rokkan 1967, pp. 368-425, 437; Rokkan and Valen 1970, pp. 197-203, 206-20).

Where great socioeconomic differences among regions have manifested themselves, the more backward regions in a unitary state will frequently demand some measure of control over economic decisions affecting their destiny. Such areas as Brittany in France, Andalusia in Spain, and Sicily and Sardinia in Italy generate far-reaching demands. Some of these demands relate to cultural defense, which we shall touch upon later. Many of the regionalist grievances, however, are based on a sense of economic deprivation, of being relegated to the role of "an economic backwater" (Smith 1980, pp. 210, 235).

However, the other kind of asymmetry can also lead to strong local or regional claims to have more control over their own affairs. Regions that are more prosperous or well endowed than the rest of the country—like Catalonia in Spain or Croatia in Yugoslavia—may object to having to pump a large share of their resources into aid programs for their less fortunate neighbors. Thus, those local authorities that prefer the status quo are likely to resist the exactions that greater central control may bring, whereas local authorities that regard themselves as hard-pressed financially may conceivably see control over their own fiscal resources as a way out of their dilemma (to be sure, many such governments react to their plight by demanding _more_ central government assistance and supervision).

Finally, local elites who oppose the effective performance of a regulatory or service function, who feel threatened by policies of social or territorial redistribution directed by the central government, and who want to keep their fiscal resources for their own use will react very negatively to central intervention and will demand full local autonomy. Here, again, as in the case of wealthier towns and regions, the haves prefer not to accept the price of redistributive centralization: a more equitable sharing with the have-nots (Fesler 1949, pp. 31-32).

The most insistent and passionate demands for regional autonomy have been coming from regionally concentrated minority ethnic groups, particularly those that have languages or distinctive dialects of their own. Such groups as the Scotch, the Welsh, and the Northern Irish in the United Kingdom; the Bretons and Corsicans in France; the South Tyrolese and, more recently, the Sardinians in Italy; and the Basques and Catalans in Spain have been increasingly vociferous over the past two or three decades. Their motives vary, ranging from primarily economic grievances to fear of cultural extinction. They all agree, however, in demanding greater control over their own affairs (Mughan 1979; Sharpe 1979).

Is it possible to make any broadly applicable statements about the types of pressure groups and parties that seek a greater degree of regional and local autonomy? With regard to group pressures, we have already cited the natural decentralizing propensities of associations of local and provincial government officials. However, as we shall see, they do not constitute a united front; conflicts of interest divide even those associations that claim to speak for territorial concerns. In France and elsewhere, pressure groups representing the economic and/or cultural interests of certain regions or of certain regionally based ethnic groups have pressed for decentralization. Also in France, much of the pressure for the creation of regional units of government has come from new economic elites created by industrialization and urbanization--the so-called _forces vives de la nation_ (Wright 1979, pp. 215-24). However, these economic regionalizers were really pressing for the consolidation of départements into regions for planning purposes--a kind of regional centralization.

Evidence from Scandinavia indicates that small landholders and fishermen have been most antagonistic to centralization in the form of Norwegian membership in the European Economic Community; but in this case, economic considerations may have far outweighed the centralization-decentralization issue (Rokkan 1967, pp. 437-38; Rokkan and Valen 1970, pp. 218-20). It does appear probable, however, on the basis of Rokkan's evidence, that small farmers and small businesspeople in predominantly rural regions are more likely to be swayed by territorial considerations, since class cleavages do not represent much of an issue in such regions.

Political parties also fail to present a clear and unequivocal picture. Such rural middle-class parties as the Liberals, the agrarian Centre party, and the Christian People's party have generally spoken out for the cultural rights and religious fundamentalism of the southern and western Norwegian hinterlands. These parties have expressed the demands and grievances of the economic groups cited previously (Rokkan and Valen 1970, pp. 195-96, 218-20). Weakly organized, decentralized parties often appear to favor governmental decentralization (Livingston 1968, pp. 135-38; Riker 1964, pp. 133-40). In this case, to be sure, one might argue that decentralization has been the cause, rather than the effect, of this particular type of party structure.

Moderate rightist parties, which are relatively cool to the idea of large-scale redistributive policies, might be expected to oppose major increases in the power of the central government. By checking centralization, they seek to restrain that level of government that is best equipped to disrupt the socioeconomic status quo. Thus, for example, the British Conservatives have tried to resist the trend toward the consolidation of local government units into a relatively small number of extensive, heterogeneous jurisdictions (Ashford 1976, p. 21). They rightly calculated that such jurisdictions would be better equipped and more inclined to engage in share-the-wealth policies at the local level. A number of scholars subscribe to the view that parties sympathetic to private enterprise, and suspicious of welfare programs, are more likely to favor federalism or some other form of decentralization (Sawer 1969, pp. 146-47). Yet there is contrary evidence as well: As we shall see, a number of French rightist forces have been generally opposed to decentralization.

Parties influenced by the doctrines of political Catholicism are also somewhat inclined to favor grass-roots autonomy. This attitude is not born out of an opposition to social reform measures, but rather out of a pluralistic view of society as a network of groups and associations that shield the individual from oppression on the part of the centralized state and also give him or her an alternative to a meaningless and frightening existence as an isolated atom in a complex universe (Gourevitch 1980, pp. 193-95).

However, it would be a gross oversimplification to engage in facile and premature labeling of the Left as favorable to centralization, while classifying the Center, the Christian Democrats, and the moderate Right as invariably supporting grass-roots autonomy as a means of preserving entrenched privileges or associational life. Experience has shown that, as soon as a decentralizing party achieves a position of power in the national capital, its devotion to local and regional autonomy becomes noticeably less ardent. The Italian Christian Democrats are a case in point. Conversely, a party that has always defended the right of the central government to dominate the periphery in the name of popular sovereignty becomes remarkably solicitous about the preservation of local and provincial rights after it has been excluded from the national government for a number of years (Gourevitch 1980). This change of heart seems most likely to occur in the case of a party (like the Italian Communist party) that has attained considerable power at the regional, provincial, and local levels.

ALTERNATIVES TO CENTRALIZATION

Before concluding this survey of the centralization-decentralization issue, we briefly delineate the main alternatives to centralization. These include federalism and various forms of decentralization practiced by unitary political systems: deconcentration, decentralization of functions to local and provincial authorities, and regional devolution. These are, of course, all subtypes of the same phenomenon: the location of a number of powers and/or functions at the grass roots rather than at the center.

Federal Systems

There has been a great deal of disagreement over the proper definition of a federal system (Dikshit 1975; Duchacek 1970; Riker 1964; Wheare 1964), but some basic characteristics have been isolated. We have already spoken about two common features of a federal system: The constitution explicitly divides power between the central government and the regional units of government, and each of these two levels of authority possesses some exclusive powers of its own. Other aspects to be observed in most federal systems include (1) a constitutional guarantee of the continued existence and territorial integrity of the regional units of government; (2) an upper house of parliament, normally elected directly or indirectly by the people of the several regions, which represents the regions and which has some power to block or delay legislation originating in the lower house; (3) possession by the regions of some measure of discretion in shaping and regulating their respective systems of local government; and (4) the exercise of some control over central-regional relations by a constitutional court wielding the power of judicial review. Federal systems are generally recognized as existing in the United States, Canada, Australia, West Germany, and Switzerland, where all or most of the above conditions hold true. They are also alleged to exist in a number of other countries by those who adopt a looser, less demanding definition of federalism (Riker 1964).

Decentralization in Unitary Systems

One form of decentralization of authority emanates from above and is designed to serve the convenience and greater efficiency of the central government. This is _deconcentration_: the "delegation of authority from one level of the administrative hierarchy to a lower one which is spatially remote from the center" (Smith 1980, p. 207). This procedure simply entails the transfer of functions to field agencies of a central government department (Sherwood 1969, pp. 65-66). The central ministry may retain complete legal and administrative oversight over the carrying out of these functions, but in practice, the field agencies tend to acquire considerable freedom of action in carrying out their assigned duties.

Decentralization, in its narrower sense, involves devolution of powers to local governments. These powers are defined and granted by central laws and decrees, not by the constitution. They may turn out to be quite broad and substantial, if the central government chooses to be generous in its devolution of authority. However, they are not original powers, based on constitutional provisions, like the powers possessed by the regions under a federal system. The central government has conferred them on the local authorities; legally speaking, the central government is free to take them away. Nor is the existence of the respective local governments guaranteed by any kind of fundamental law--witness the recent extensive reform and consolidation of the British system of local government, including the extinction of the county borough.

Regional devolution, the type of decentralization that represents the principal focus of this work, needs to be distinguished from the limited devolution of power to local authorities discussed by Sherwood (1969, pp. 66-69) and Smith (1980, p. 207). For one thing, it bears some intriguing similarities to federalism. The constitution, for example, may guarantee, or at least recognize and define, the existence of the regional governments. The powers of the regions are frequently enumerated in the constitution, although the regions usually possess no exclusive powers of their own, but only concurrent powers that may have to give way to central occupancy of the field. Furthermore, a constitutional court exercises the power of judicial review over central-regional relations, playing the role of referee much like a constitutional court in a federal system. Finally, the regions not only have an elected parliament and a cabinet responsible to that parliament, but also those organs of regional government may not be dissolved or suspended by a central government official like the French or Italian prefect. This immunity distinguishes them from the legally precarious position of local legislative and executive organs in a unitary prefectoral system.

On the other hand, regional devolution falls somewhat short of the federal model. As we have seen, the regions normally lack exclusive powers. Second, they are not usually represented as regions in the upper house of the national parliament. Third, they are not normally allowed to construct their own structure of local and provincial governments, free from central advice and control. Fourth, they have nowhere near the degree of fiscal autonomy, especially with regard to taxation, that is enjoyed by regional units of government in a federal system. Fifth, a central government agent can block the enforcement of regional legislation pending an appeal to the constitutional court. In sum, despite the considerable degree of autonomy allowed to the regions by a system of regional devolution, the central government enjoys a status of greater superiority vis-à-vis the regions than it does under a truly federal system.

CONCLUSIONS

We have provided the reader with a fairly lengthy chronicle of the historical development of centralizing tendencies since the late Middle Ages and of the resistance aroused by those tendencies. We have also discussed the underlying normative and empirical rationales for centralization and for decentralization and the forces and actors that seem to favor each of these two alternatives. Some tentative conclusions emerge from our analysis.

1. There appears to be a dialectic relationship between centralization and decentralization. Since the Middle Ages, every centralizing trend appears to have produced a countervailing force in the form of regional resistance, a growth in regional expertise, regional pressures exerted at the center, and so on.
2. Centralizing forces eventually tend to advocate a certain degree of decentralization in order to increase the efficiency of the center or gain allies at the periphery.
3. The center and the periphery are both internally divided, with some important forces at the center demanding decentralization and some important interests at the grass roots pressing for more central control. The center-periphery model gives a somewhat misleading picture of the struggle for power in central-regional-local relations.
4. While the centralization-decentralization controversy is often discussed in normative terms, empirical considerations (material interest, power, efficiency) will often determine the position adopted by a given party or pressure group. Moreover, the position will change with the shifting distance between the organization in question and the actual possession of access to power in the government. A party that comes to power may abandon its

decentralizing posture and become a strong advocate of centralization.

5. Given points 1 through 4, it would appear that the centralization-decentralization controversy sets up a false dichotomy, a deceptive picture of a struggle between two united and stable coalitions. Elazar's concept of "non-centralization" may be a more fruitful and realistic device for viewing central-local relations (1976). Instead of seeing power as a simple pyramid, Elazar postulates a complex matrix with no single center of power and influence. Instead of a precise vertical allocation among various levels in a hierarchy, there is an uneven, vaguely defined, ever-shifting horizontal distribution among various power centers.

REFERENCES

Andrews, William G. 1974. "The Politics of Regionalization in France." In Politics in Europe: Structures and Processes in Some Postindustrial Democracies, edited by Martin O. Heisler, pp. 293-322. New York: David McKay.

Ashford, Douglas E. 1976. "Democracy, Decentralization, and Decisions in Subnational Politics." Sage Professional Papers in Comparative Politics, vol. 5. Beverly Hills, Calif.: Sage.

Badie, Bertrand, and Pierre Birnbaum. 1983. The Sociology of the State, trans. by Arthur Goldhammer. Chicago: University of Chicago Press.

Bastianini, Attilio, and Giuliano Urbani. 1975. "Land-Use Planning in Italy." In Planning, Politics and Public Policy: The British, French, and Italian Experience, edited by Jack Hayward and Michael Watson, pp. 358-77. London: Cambridge University Press.

Beer, Samuel H. 1977. "Political Overload and Federalism." Polity 10 (Fall): 5-17.

─────. 1973. "The Modernization of American Federalism." Publius 3 (Fall): 49-95.

Bien, David D., and Raymond Grew. 1978. "France." In *Crises of Political Development in Europe and the United States*, edited by Raymond Grew, pp. 219-70. Princeton, N.J.: Princeton University Press.

Birch, Anthony H. 1966. "Approaches to the Study of Federalism." *Political Studies* 14 (February): 15-33.

Blondel, Jean. 1969. *An Introduction to Comparative Government*, ch. 16. New York: Praeger.

Cameron, David R., and Richard J. Hofferbert. 1974. "The Impact of Federalism on Education Finance: A Comparative Analysis." *European Journal of Political Research* 2 (September): 225-58.

Clark, Terry N. 1974. "Community Autonomy in the National System: Federalism, Localism, and Decentralization." In *Comparative Community Politics*, edited by Terry N. Clark, pp. 21-51. New York: Wiley.

Crozier, Michel. 1982. *Strategies for Change: The Future of French Society*, trans. by William R. Beer. Cambridge, Mass.: MIT Press.

———. 1973. *The Stalled Society*, trans. by Viking Press. New York: Viking Press.

Dahl, Robert A. 1982. *Dilemmas of Pluralist Democracy: Autonomy vs. Control*. New Haven, Conn.: Yale University Press.

Dahl, Robert A., and Edward R. Tufte. 1973. *Size and Democracy*. Stanford, Calif.: Stanford University Press.

Davis, S. Rufus. 1978. *The Federal Principle: A Journey Through Time in Quest of a Meaning*. Berkeley: University of California Press.

Deutsch, Karl W. 1961. "Social Mobilization and Political Development." *American Political Science Review* 55 (September): 493-514.

Dikshit, Ramesh Dutta. 1975. *The Political Geography of Federalism: An Inquiry into Origins and Stability*. New York: Wiley.

Duchacek, Ivo D. 1970. *Comparative Federalism: The Territorial Dimension of Politics*. New York: Holt, Rinehart & Winston.

Eisenstadt, Shmuel Noah. 1966. *Modernization, Protest, and Change*. Englewood Cliffs, N.J.: Prentice-Hall.

Elazar, Daniel J. 1976. "Federalism vs. Decentralization: The Drift from Authenticity." *Publius* 6 (Fall): 9-19.

———. 1973. "Cursed by Bigness or Toward a Post-Technocratic Federalism?" *Publius* 3 (Fall): 239-98.

Fesler, James W. 1965. "Approaches to the Understanding of Decentralization." *Journal of Politics* 27 (August): 536-66.

———. 1949. *Area and Administration*. Birmingham: University of Alabama Press.

Friedrich, Carl J. 1974. *Limited Government: A Comparison*, ch. 5. Englewood Cliffs, N.J.: Prentice-Hall.

———. 1968. *Trends of Federalism in Theory and Practice*. New York: Praeger.

———. 1963. *Man and His Government: An Empirical Theory of Politics*. New York: McGraw-Hill.

Gellner, Ernest. 1964. *Thought and Change*. Chicago: University of Chicago Press.

Gourevitch, Peter A. 1980. *Paris and the Provinces: The Politics of Local Government Reform in France*. Berkeley: University of California Press.

Grew, Raymond. 1978. "The Crises and Their Sequences." In *Crises of Political Development in Europe and the United States*, edited by Raymond Grew, pp. 3-39. Princeton, N.J.: Princeton University Press.

Hansen, Tore, and Francesco Kjellberg. 1976. "Municipal Expenditures in Norway: Autonomy and Constraints in Local Government Activity." Policy and Politics 4 (March): 25-50.

Hechter, Michael. 1975. Internal Colonialism: The Celtic Fringe in British National Development, 1536-1966. Berkeley: University of California Press.

Hoffmann, Stanley. 1959. "The Areal Division of Powers in the Writings of French Political Thinkers." In Area and Power, edited by Arthur Maass, pp. 113-49. Glencoe, Ill.: Free Press.

Hueglin, Thomas O. 1986. "Regionalism in Western Europe: Conceptual Problems of a New Political Perspective." Comparative Politics 18 (July): 439-58.

Huntington, Samuel P. 1959. "The Founding Fathers and the Division of Powers." In Area and Power, edited by Arthur Maass, pp. 150-205. Glencoe, Ill.: Free Press.

Kesselman, Mark, and Donald Rosenthal. 1974. "Local Power and Comparative Politics." Sage Professional Papers in Comparative Politics, vol. 5. Beverly Hills, Calif.: Sage.

King, Preston. 1982. Federalism and Federation. Baltimore: Johns Hopkins University Press.

La Palombara, Joseph. 1971. "Penetration: A Crisis of Governmental Capacity." In Crises and Sequences in Political Development, by Leonard Binder et al., pp. 205-32. Princeton, N.J.: Princeton University Press.

Lipset, Seymour M., and Stein Rokkan. 1967. "Cleavage Structures, Party Systems, and Voter Alignments: An Introduction." In Party Systems and Voter Alignments: Cross-National Perspectives, edited by Seymour M. Lipset and Stein Rokkan, pp. 1-64. New York: Free Press.

Livingston, William S. 1968. "Canada, Australia, and the United States: Variations on a Theme." In Federalism: Infinite Variety in Theory and Practice, edited by Valerie Earle, pp. 94-141. Itasca, Ill.: Peacock.

McBeath, Gerald A., and Andrea R. C. Helms. 1983. "Alternate Routes to Autonomy in Federal and Quasi-Federal Systems." Publius 13 (Fall): 21-41.

Merkl, Peter H. 1970. Modern Comparative Politics. New York: Holt, Rinehart & Winston.

Milch, Jerome E. 1974. "Influence as Power: French Local Government Reconsidered." British Journal of Political Science 4 (April): 139-62.

Mughan, Anthony. 1979. "Modernization and Regional Relative Deprivation: Towards a Theory of Ethnic Conflict." In Decentralist Trends in Western Democracies, edited by L. J. Sharpe, pp. 279-312. Beverly Hills, Calif.: Sage.

Payne, Stanley G. 1978. "Spain and Portugal." In Crises of Political Development in Europe and the United States, edited by Raymond Grew, pp. 197-218. Princeton, N.J.: Princeton University Press.

Pennock, J. Roland. 1959. "Federal and Unitary Government—Disharmony and Frustration." Behavioral Science 4 (April): 147-57.

Pye, Lucian W. 1971. "The Legitimacy Crisis." In Crises and Sequences in Political Development, by Leonard Binder et al., pp. 135-58. Princeton, N.J.: Princeton University Press.

Riker, William H. 1975. "Federalism." In Handbook of Political Science, vol. 5, Governmental Institutions and Processes, edited by Fred I. Greenstein and Nelson W. Polsby, ch. 2. Reading, Mass.: Addison-Wesley.

———. 1969. "Six Books in Search of a Subject or Does Federalism Exist and Does It Matter?" Comparative Politics 2 (October): 135-46.

———. 1964. Federalism: Origin, Operation, Significance. Boston: Little, Brown.

Rokkan, Stein. 1975. "Dimensions of State Formation and Nation-Building: A Possible Paradigm for Research on Variations Within Europe." In *The Formation of National States in Western Europe*, edited by Charles Tilly, pp. 562-600. Princeton, N.J.: Princeton University Press.

---. 1973. "Cities, States, and Nations: A Dimensional Model for the Study of Contrasts in Development." In *Building States and Nations: Models and Data Resources*, edited by Shmuel N. Eisenstadt and Stein Rokkan, vol. 1, pp. 73-97. Beverly Hills, Calif.: Sage.

---. 1967. "Geography, Religion, and Social Class: Crosscutting Cleavages in Norwegian Politics." In *Party Systems and Voter Alignments: Cross-National Perspectives*, edited by Seymour M. Lipset and Stein Rokkan, pp. 367-444. New York: Free Press.

Rokkan, Stein, and Derek W. Urwin. 1983. *Economy, Territory, Identity: Politics of West European Peripheries*. London: Sage.

---. 1982. "Introduction: Centres and Peripheries in Western Europe." In *The Politics of Territorial Identity: Studies in European Regionalism*, edited by Stein Rokkan and Derek W. Urwin, pp. 1-17. London: Sage.

Rokkan, Stein, and Henry Valen. 1970. "Regional Contrasts in Norwegian Politics." In *Mass Politics: Studies in Political Sociology*, edited by Erik Allardt and Stein Rokkan, pp. 190-247. New York: Free Press.

Sawer, Geoffrey. 1969. *Modern Federalism*. London: Watts.

Schulz, Ann. 1979. *Local Politics and Nation-States: Case Studies in Politics and Policy*. Santa Barbara, Calif.: Clio Books.

Sharpe, L. J. 1979. "Decentralist Trends in Western Democracies: A First Appraisal." In *Decentralist*

Trends in Western Democracies, edited by L. J. Sharpe, pp. 9-79. Beverly Hills, Calif.: Sage.

Sherwood, Frank P. 1969. "Devolution as a Problem of Organization Strategy." In Comparative Urban Research: The Administration and Politics of Cities, edited by Robert T. Daland, pp. 60-87. Beverly Hills, Calif.: Sage.

Smith, Gordon. 1980. Politics in Western Europe: A Comparative Analysis, 3rd ed. New York: Holmes & Meier.

Tarlton, Charles D. 1965. "Symmetry and Asymmetry as Elements of Federalism: A Theoretical Speculation." Journal of Politics 27 (November): 861-74.

Tarrow, Sidney. 1978. "Introduction." In Territorial Politics in Industrial Nations, edited by Sidney Tarrow, Peter J. Katzenstein, and Luigi Graziano, pp. 1-27. New York: Praeger.

———. 1977. Between Center and Periphery: Grassroots Politicians in Italy and France. New Haven, Conn.: Yale University Press.

Teune, Henry. 1968. "The Future of Federalism: Federalism and Political Integration." In Federalism: Infinite Variety in Theory and Practice, edited by Valerie Earle, pp. 213-33. Itasca, Ill.: Peacock.

Thomas, Keith. 1978. "The United Kingdom." In Crises of Political Development in Europe and the United States, edited by Raymond Grew, pp. 41-97. Princeton, N.J.: Princeton University Press.

Tilly, Charles. 1981. "Sinews of War." In Mobilization Center-Periphery Structures and Nation-Building, edited by Per Torsvik, pp. 108-26. Oslo: Universitetsforlaget.

———. 1975a. "Reflections on the History of European State-Making." In The Formation of National States in Western Europe, edited by Charles Tilly, pp. 3-83. Princeton, N.J.: Princeton University Press.

———. 1975b. "Western State-Making and Theories of Political Transformation." In *The Formation of National States in Western Europe*, edited by Charles Tilly, pp. 601-38. Princeton, N.J.: Princeton University Press.

Ullmo, Yves. 1975. "France." In *Planning, Politics, and Public Policy: The British, French, and Italian Experience*, edited by Jack Hayward and Michael Watson, pp. 22-51. London: Cambridge University Press.

Watson, Michael. 1975. "Conclusion: A Comparative Evaluation of Planning Practice in the Liberal Democratic State." In *Planning, Politics, and Public Policy: The British, French, and Italian Experience*, edited by Jack Hayward and Michael Watson, pp. 445-83. London: Cambridge University Press.

Weiner, Myron. 1971. "Political Participation: Crisis of the Political Process." In *Crises and Sequences in Political Development*, by Leonard Binder et al., pp. 159-204. Princeton, N.J.: Princeton University Press.

Wheare, Kenneth C. 1964. *Federal Government*, 4th ed. New York: Oxford University Press.

Worms, Jean-Pierre. 1966. "Le préfet et ses notables." *Sociologie du Travail* 3 (July-September): 249-75.

Wright, Vincent. 1979. "Decentralization Under the French Fifth Republic: The Triumph of the Functional Approach." In *Decentralist Trends in Western Democracies*, edited by L. J. Sharpe, pp. 193-234. Beverly Hills, Calif.: Sage.

Ylvisaker, Paul. 1959. "Criteria for a 'Proper' Areal Division of Powers." In *Area and Power*, edited by Arthur Maass, ch. 2. Glencoe Ill.: Free Press.

Zariski, Raphael. 1983. "The Establishment of the Kingdom of Italy as a Unitary State: A Case Study in Regime Formation." *Publius* 13 (Fall): 1-19.

2

Power and Decentralization: Concepts and Theories

Mark O. Rousseau
Raphael Zariski

EXPLANATIONS OF POWER: INTELLECTUAL
ROOTS AND CONTEMPORARY INTERPRETATIONS

Understanding and interpreting national structures of power is a major undertaking in the social sciences. The significant theoretical and empirical problems in studying regional devolution involve explaining political and economic power in modern societies. The challenge is to obtain a meaningful conceptual perspective that aids our comprehension of political devolution. How are we to make this complex phenomenon understandable?

To assist our understanding, we review varied perceptions of power based on different theoretical assumptions. Over the years scholars have examined political and economic power from a variety of perspectives. We wish to consider the utility of this intellectual heritage for understanding political decentralization. We focus on sometimes conflicting explanations of power that help us understand our topic. As we examine the insights obtained from elitist, pluralist, and center-periphery theorists, we want to be alert to sensitizing concepts that help us interpret political decentralization. Sensitizing concepts call our attention to important institutions, positions, decision makers, and processes that influence the development of regional government. As we review theorists who typify opposing perspectives, the assumptions about political and economic power made by each should be noted. Our discussion will point these out and suggest how these ideas are related to understanding regional decentralization.

We approach our analysis assuming that in modern societies power is lodged in primary political and economic institutions whose leaders are key decision makers. Political decentralization changes the structure of institutional arrangements and thus changes the structure of political power. The meaning of decentralization is found in the theoretical interpretations one applies to it. Let us now consider several differing interpretations.

CLASSICAL ELITISM

The first set of theorists we examine are the classical elitists. Writing in the late nineteenth and early twentieth centuries, these theorists were responding to the major political and social issues of their day, a period of rapid political and economic change in Europe. These changes resulted in evolutionary and sometimes revolutionary change in the governments of many nations. These scholars were concerned about the unfamiliar directions such changes portended and particularly their influence on existing structures of political and economic power.

The classical elitists believed political and economic power were relatively concentrated, discerning few institutional and personal power centers (Putnam 1976, pp. 3-4). They suggested power derived from the control of dominant political institutions as well as the personal characteristics of power holders. As a group, the classical elitists assumed that some concentration or centralization of political power was inevitable, and several of them believed it to be desirable. In their view, elite rule or rule by a few is inevitable and possibly beneficial.[1] We shall see

---

[1] The classical elitists in part developed their arguments as a refutation of the work of Marx and Engels and their followers. In our analysis of the contributions of political and economic elites to regional devolution, we have refrained from examining the Marxian perspective. We do this because we believe that in the strong unitary states that we are considering, political elites are not subordinate to economic elites and the state exercises considerable power and autonomy. Further, the abstract assumptions and complex arguments developed by Marxian analysts cannot be adequately treated in a work of this kind.

why this is the case as we examine several elitist theorists, beginning with the work of Pareto.

Pareto

Vilfredo Pareto, an Italian aristocrat, was appointed professor of political economics at the University of Lausanne in 1893, where he taught courses in political science, economics, and sociology. Pareto (1966) hoped to develop a scientific, value-free science of society, and his theory places great emphasis on individual behavior and the instincts and emotions that motivate it. In Pareto's sociology, individual residues and derivations explain not only human behavior but the direction of entire societies as well.

Pareto applied the term "social heterogeneity" to the inevitable division between elites and masses. Elites appear in all societies and constitute the small class of persons who exhibit superior levels of capacity in every area of human endeavor--economic, political, religious, and so on. Pareto was concerned with the political elite, or what he called the governing class, because this elite controls power in society. The governing elite consists of those who play a role in government and thereby control and direct political power. Governing elites are the most important elites in society. The majority of society, the masses, consists of those not in the elite. Pareto saw the state as the most important source of power in society since only the state possesses the ultimate resort of force. Those with access to the state exercise primary power in society.

Because elites tend to stagnate and deteriorate over time, Pareto believed a circulation of elites was inevitable. Ruling elites are characterized by residues of intellect, and Pareto referred to them as foxes because they rule by guile and cunning. Since elites decay and new forces well up among the masses, no governing class can perpetuate its rule forever. Pareto termed this process the circulation of elites. As the foxes deteriorate, lions obtain power by displacing them through force. The cycle continues as the new lions begin to rule by intellect and evolve into foxes. At this point, another set of lions emerges, and the cycle goes on. As lions emerge, they may be absorbed into the ruling class, and the rate of social change is slow. When foxes resist incorporating lions into their ranks, revolution may occur, and the pace of change is rapid.

It is important to understand that, in Pareto's perspective, concentrated elite rule is inevitable regardless of type of government or society. Human beings are characterized by certain psychological predispositions that do not change. The elites who rule society are always driven by personal interest and a desire for power. Elites may change, but all societies will always be governed by a small, concentrated elite. For Pareto, elite rule is not only inevitable but also desirable. The masses are disorganized and incapable of governing themselves. Rule by a strong elite is necessary to preserve stability and give direction to society. Governing elites set goals for the society and make social order possible.

How useful is Pareto's theory of elites? On the positive side, his work calls attention to the important role that elites play in society. Yet much of his theory is problematic. Pareto's theory essentially rests on unprovable assumptions about human nature and largely neglects the role of social forces and institutions in societal change. Pareto's focus on national political power and concentrated national elites leads to a neglect of local elites. He omitted the powerful role of economic institutions and the elites who head them. Pareto assumed that the sovereign state is the only important source of power and governing elites exercise power only by virtue of their political position in the state. In his view, the wealthy are not members of the governing elite unless they hold political office. Pareto believed elite rule is inevitable and governing elites are basically alike because all elites are driven by sentiments of self-interest. Little attention was paid to differences in the goals and purposes that governing elites may pursue, and thus Pareto neglected to place elites in historical context.

Finally we note that Pareto was a man of strong passions and dislikes. In spite of his claim to have developed an objective science of human society, his personal biases and emotions deeply influenced his scholarship. This is perhaps one reason Pareto has so few intellectual heirs today.

Mosca

Gaetano Mosca (1939) developed a theory of elitism that is richer and more detailed in its attention to social and political forces than the theory of Pareto. Mosca himself participated in political activity and was a deputy in the Italian parliament at the turn of the century. Mosca's theory of power gives primacy to the key role played by the dominant political elites or ruling class. He saw the state as independent or autonomous and the salient institution of power in modern societies.

Mosca's theory of political power and governance rests on the fundamental assumption that concentrated elite rule is always inevitable. He believed that all societies are composed of two classes of people, a class that rules and a class that is ruled. For Mosca, the ruling class is the class that possesses political power and attempts to perpetuate itself in power. Like Pareto, Mosca attributed superior personal traits to members of the ruling class. Unlike Pareto, Mosca believed the inevitability of elitism lay in social forces and political processes.

Mosca suggested that an organized minority united by common interests will prevail over an unorganized majority. He argued that the small, organized ruling class learns the art of governance and the qualities and activities necessary for the maintenance of power. In his view, offspring of the ruling class are naturally more favored with advantages than offspring of the masses. Mosca's explanation of political inequality rests in part on the political formula that consists of the justifications used by every ruling class to vindicate its rule. All ruling classes invoke moral principles, such as divine right or majority rule, to justify their monopoly of power.

While ruling classes attempt to perpetuate themselves in power, as social conditions change, new elites may emerge to challenge their rule. New sources of wealth or expertise may provide previously excluded groups an opportunity to seize political power. The ascent of various sections of the ruling class to the pinnacle of political power depends on the social forces prevailing at a particular time. Though prior elites may be displaced, new ruling classes always emerge since elite rule is inevitable. Like their predecessors, newly arrived ruling classes attempt to consolidate and perpetuate power. Mosca saw continuity within change; the certainty of elite rule remains constant. Mosca was himself untroubled by elite rule since opposing the inevitable would be pointless. He believed concentrated elite rule was ultimately beneficial because the masses are always disorganized and elites provide order and continuity. Further, the political formula furnishes a set of common values that help make society cohesive.

We note several insights and limitations of Mosca's elitist view. Unlike Pareto, Mosca recognized more clearly the role social forces and political processes play in power. He called attention to the regular occurrence of elite rule, even in parliamentary democracies, and his theory helps us see that when social conditions change new elites may emerge. Some of our criticisms of Pareto apply likewise to Mosca. He assumed that elite rule was inevitable and attributed a psychological drive to domination and power to all members of the ruling class. Like Pareto, Mosca's argument rests on untestable assumptions about human nature. Another difficulty in Mosca's work concerns his supposition that at all times there exists only one ruling class with a cohesive and unitary common interest. He excluded the possibility of concurrent multiple elites or competing elites, except for the tendency of some in the masses to replace existing elites. This perspective resulted from Mosca's belief that state political power is the only important source of power in society. Thus, he neglected local elites and economic institutions as significant sources of power, foreclosing the possibility that economic elites might vie with political elites for power. Like Pareto, Mosca believed wealth is not a source of power in its own right but only as it provides access to political leadership. To his credit, Mosca recognized that new elites might spring up as sources of wealth changed. We turn now to a more influential elitist than Pareto and Mosca, Robert Michels.

Michels

Robert Michels (1962) remains one of the most important elitist theorists. Though influenced by Pareto and Mosca, he developed his insights further than his two predecessors. His approach to power is closer to the traditions of twentieth-century scholarship because he gathered empirical data from observations of the ongoing social world.

As a good social scientist, Michels searched for negative evidence to disprove his thesis that all organizations have inherent tendencies toward oligarchy, rule by a small elite. He looked for oligarchic trends where they might be least expected, in socialist political parties. Michels reasoned that socialist parties, having ideologies of equality, ought to be nonoligarchic. He assumed that if socialist parties were oligarchic, then all organizations were likely to be so. Studying socialist parties in Italy and Germany, Michels discovered that power in those parties became increasingly concentrated in the hands of the leadership to the exclusion of the followers. Michels referred to this process as the iron law of oligarchy. His frequently quoted maxim summarizes his observations: "Who says organization, says oligarchy" (1962, p. 365).

What is the iron law of oligarchy, and how does it come about? Michels developed two explanations for the trend toward oligarchy in complex organizations. Following Pareto and Mosca, he argued that all humans crave power and act in their self-interest. Since leaders use power to further their interests, organizations inevitably tend toward oligarchy.

His more creative explanation concerns the nature of organizational processes themselves. Michels viewed complex organizations as ongoing social entities characterized by certain processes and tendencies. These very organizational characteristics make oligarchy inevitable. He maintained that genuine democracy and egalitarian decision making are possible only in small groups. When organizations increase in size and scale, division of labor becomes necessary. Leaders become experts in the pursuit of particular organizational goals. Experts are necessary to mobilize the organization in pursuit of the resources needed for goal accomplishment. This means that hierarchies of expertise and authority inevitably develop, creating distance between leaders and led. Increasingly, the professionalism of leaders separates them from the mass of followers and leaders develop interests of their own. Leaders develop lifetime careers and a desire to stay in office-- and an interest in maintaining their power.

The leaders Michels studied were frequently successful in maintaining power. By virtue of their position at the top, leaders enjoy various resources not available to the masses. Leaders possess detailed knowledge concerning the workings of the organization and its relationship to other organizations. They also control the structure of power and communication within the organization. In addition, leaders control leadership recruitment. Capable but rebellious members may be brought into positions where they begin to take on identities as leaders. Finally, Michels suggested, leaders make up a small group with cohesive and similar interests. For this cohesive group to pursue its shared interests is easier than for the masses to pursue their diverse interests. For these varied reasons, Michels concluded that all organizations tend toward oligarchic rule by the few. Concentration of power in the hands of leaders is inevitable.

What can we say about Michels' work? On the positive side, his empirical method and search for negative cases places him within the traditions of twentieth-century scholarship. Michels' observations forcefully attune us to many of the characteristics and consequences of political bureaucracies. His iron law implies the possibility that oligarchy may occur even in decentralized governmental structures, as federal governmental systems or unitary governments with devolved regional assemblies. Federalism or devolution may, in Michels' view, simply result in numerous smaller oligarchies. Michels' ideas alert us to perils from which even democratic organizations and governments may not be exempt. His work highlights the potential contradiction between democratic intentions and oligarchic realities.

There are difficulties and limitations in Michels' work, however. Little evidence exists to support Michels' assertion that all humans crave power. Further, while Michels' conclusions about oligarchy seem plausible, we do not believe he has conclusively shown it to be inevitable. We might reasonably ask why there is not greater oligarchy in democratic governments than we presently find. Critics such as Gouldner (1955) have raised the possibility of an iron law of democracy. We might ask why democratic organizations have remained as open and nonoligarchic as they have. Are there not some countervailing processes limiting concentrated elite rule? Pluralist theorists raise this possibility and reject the elitist conclusion that oligarchy must occur in all governments and organizations. Michels' failure to distinguish clearly oligarchy from leadership leaves him open to criticism on these grounds. In part this raises a problem of interpretation. When is leadership oligarchic and when is it not? Clearly, different observers utilizing different perspectives will answer this question differently.

Finally, we note that Michels, like many other elitist theorists, essentially distinguished only two levels of power in organizations and societies: elite and masses. Many complex organizations and governments, as we shall observe in our analysis of governmental power structures, are characterized by more than two levels of power. Indeed, many complex organizations, such as corporations, universities, and political parties, exhibit multiple levels of power and decision making. We shall return to this question of power levels and their multiple interpretations. We now examine the most theoretically sophisticated and influential elitist theorist, Max Weber.

Weber

Much of the work of Max Weber is consistent with the elitist perspective (Gerth and Mills 1958; Bendix 1962). Though influenced by Michels and Marx, Weber developed his own complex and sophisticated interpretation of power. Weber's complex and varied scholarship reflected his consuming interest in the character of Western civilization and its institutions. He was dedicated to understanding how particular historical processes shaped the development of rationality in Western political and economic institutions.

We focus on three of Weber's ideas that are helpful for understanding political power and regional devolution: social stratification, power and authority, and bureaucracy. Weber argued that stratification and inequality in modern societies have multiple dimensions—including class, status, and party—all of which are related to the distribution of power within society. A class comprises a collection of persons whose economic interests and income opportunities are similar. Unlike classes, status groups are communities with a conscious and shared sense of identity, though sometimes amorphous. Ethnic, religious, and racial groups are examples of status groups. While class and status membership may overlap, they need not. Parties, the third dimension of stratification, are formal organizations for the collective pursuit of power by persons sharing common class or status interests. Parties may include political parties, special interest groups, or lobbies and be organized around class or status interests or both.

Weber's three-dimensional characterization of political and social inequality is important for several reasons. It suggests the existence of multiple bases for collective cooperation and conflict in modern societies. Weber recognized the complex interplay of political and economic cooperation and conflict. Collectivities may share interests at times and not at other times. The aphorism that politics makes strange bedfellows recognizes this. Thus, we might expect that in such complicated activities as regional devolution, complex and varied political and economic interests are at stake.

Weber's second helpful conceptualization concerns the nature of power and authority. While power consists of the ability of a group to achieve its interests even in the face of opposition, authority involves power acknowledged to be legitimate or right by both superordinate and subordinate. Weber argued that three general principles of legitimation have existed historically--traditional, charismatic, and rational-legal authority. The power or domination of superordinates over subordinates is legitimated by a shared belief in one of these types of authority. Traditional authority derives from a shared belief in the validity and sacred nature of long-standing tradition. Charismatic authority results from a shared belief in the worth of particular qualities exhibited by a magnetic personality.

Weber's third principle of legitimation, rational-legal authority, is important in modern societies. It is based on a willing submission to formally and explicitly defined rules and takes the form of bureaucratic social organization. The modern state and a large economic enterprise represent the purest examples of rational-legal authority. Participants in bureaucratic organizations willingly submit to the rules that define the operation of the bureaucracy because they believe in their legitimacy and validity. Examples of rational-legal authority include paying taxes, obeying traffic laws, and completing work assigned by one's supervisor. In rational-legal organizations, orders are not capricious but derive from rationally developed and interpreted rules. In modern states, the constitution is the highest set of rules.

Weber's genius was to analyze the pervasive nature of rational-legal bureaucracies in the modern world. He showed that seemingly different organizations share numerous characteristics in common (Gerth and Mills 1958, pp. 196 ff.). Weber persuasively argued that rational bureaucratic principles of work organization were indispensable and inevitable in modern societies. The growing complexity of civilization requires increasingly centralized administration, resulting in increasingly bureaucratic forms of social organization. The growing complexity of tasks undertaken by government, such as urban planning, maintenance of public works, criminal and civil law, and other tasks, has increased the need for centralized government. This does not mean that bureaucracies are entirely rational or approach the pure ideal. Bureaucracy remains, nonetheless, the most rational and efficient organizational form for the achievement of complex goals requiring the collective endeavor of many individuals. For this reason, Weber believed, increasing bureaucratic growth is inevitable in the modern world.

Because bureaucratic organization is pervasive, all are caught up as subordinates or superordinates in hierarchies of power and control. Bureaucracies function as organizations of power and domination within democratic societies as well as authoritarian ones. Political and economic organizations develop into centralized bureaucracies that make tremendous power available for the political and economic interests of those who head them. Because class and status groups compete for scarce resources and varied ends, conflict occurs over the direction and purposes of bureaucratic goals. Since administrative concentration and centralization are indigenous processes, Weber argued that centralized governmental domination could be constrained only by bureaucratically centralized class and status interests. We confront the inevitable growth of bureaucracy, or what Weber called the iron cage. The monolithic central state can only be checked by other centralized organizations that become sources of bureaucratic domination, such as giant multinational corporations.

Weber stands as one of the towering intellectual figures of the twentieth century. His analysis of power and bureaucracy is particularly useful for understanding political centralization and regional devolution in that it sensitizes us to the importance of political and economic power and how bureaucratic organizations structure power in complex societies. He recognized the consequences of the bureaucratic concentration of political and economic administration. Weber saw that class and status groups organize bureaucratically to influence both state and economy in pursuit of their political and economic interests. Political and economic institutions become arenas for conflict and cooperation. Weber characterized the ways in which cooperation and conflict became bureaucratically organized. Bureaucracy is today the primary vehicle of organization for the pursuit of political and economic power. Weber helps us see how regional devolution changes the structure of organized government and the role that varied class and status interests may play in the process. For example, we shall see how the status interests of ethnic groups influence devolution and how the state becomes an important arena for the rational resolution of conflict. Weber helps us recognize that power in democratic societies is unequally distributed and that bureaucracies inevitably create political and economic elites. We shall be alert to the ways varied interest groups exercise greater or lesser political power and how they attempt to influence the state bureaucracy for the achievement of their goals.

Weber's analysis of bureaucracy forces us to think in particular about the very nature of political centralization and decentralization. We must ask what decentralization and devolution imply for bureaucratic political organization. To what extent do decentralized forms of government actually reduce or increase bureaucratic organization? If Weber was correct that bureaucracy continuously grows, then are regional devolution and decentralization exceptions to the rule or merely centralized bureaucratic power in somewhat altered form? We shall discuss these issues in greater detail.

CONTEMPORARY ELITISM

The contemporary elitists reflect the traditions of the classical elitists but with important modifications. Modern elitists largely reject the social-psychological assumptions of Pareto and Mosca and the view of the state as the sole institution of power. Contemporary elitists have been principally influenced by Michels and particularly Weber and their emphasis on the empirical measurement of power. Contemporary elitists deemphasize the personal characteristics of power holders and emphasize the positional and institutional bases of power. They assert that individuals exercise power because of the positions they hold in dominant political and economic institutions, and examine the interrelationships between political and economic power holders. Like the classical elitists, contemporary elitists believe that power is concentrated in the hands of a few key power holders in dominant political and economic institutions and not dispersed as suggested by pluralist theorists.

Recent empirical approaches to the study of power have largely employed one of three measurement methods (Bonjean and Olson 1964; Domhoff 1978, ch. 4; Bonjean and Grimes 1974). These three approaches to power measurement include the reputational, the positional, and the decision making. We shall briefly outline these three approaches here and more fully illustrate them in our discussion of their respective elitist and pluralist advocates.

The reputational approach to power, examined in our discussion of the work of Floyd Hunter, consists of asking questions of key informants about principal decision makers in the community and how they exercise power. This approach assumes that the researcher can initially identify important decision makers, that they can be approached by him, and that the observations of informants are valid. This approach has been criticized for various reasons that we shall shortly consider. The positional approach to power, exemplified in our discussion of the work of C. Wright Mills, rests on the researcher's ability to identify important organizations and institutions of power in national and local communities. The researcher examines the characteristics of those who head these institutions and the ways they make and implement decisions. This approach assumes that the researcher has correctly identified important institutions of power and those who head them. The decision-making approach to power was developed by those critical of the reputational and positional approaches. Decision-making researchers examine how actual decisions occur and who participates in the process. This approach was initially developed by Robert Dahl and is discussed in our analysis of contemporary pluralism.

Each of these three approaches to power measurement has its advantages and disadvantages, and the debates among their proponents are long-standing. Rather than adopting one or another of these positions, we take the view that political power is a complex phenomenon, and open-minded, multiple approaches to it are in order. We suggest that the debates among advocates of these positions are ideological as well as empirical (Walton 1966; Marger 1981, pp. 4-5, 247-51; Dye 1983, pp. 6-11; Domhoff 1978, pp. 151-52). Those favoring a pluralist approach to power are inclined toward the decision-making approach and tend to find multiple, competing centers of power rather than a concentrated power elite. Elitists are partial to the reputational or positional approach and typically find power concentrated within specific political and economic elites. Yet both pluralist and elitist theorists observe that the exercise of extensive political and economic power is a privilege shared by a few. Pluralists maintain that multiple elites compete for power, whereas elitists discern a closed and concentrated power elite in which a few individuals exercise power.

While the differences in these conclusions reflect real empirical and theoretical differences, we should not forget that both positions recognize that political and economic power are unequally distributed. Therefore, we do not wish to be unduly distracted by refined ideological debate and empirical disagreements as we move toward our analysis of political decentralization and devolution.

Hunter

The measurement of power from an elitist perspective developed with the early work of Floyd Hunter (1953, 1959), who pioneered the reputational approach to power. He interviewed informants in Atlanta, Georgia, who were presumably informed about decision makers in the major organizations of that city and asked them about the principal movers and shapers in the community. From this information he compiled a list of persons said to exercise power. He then interviewed them, asking their opinions about the major leaders in the political and economic institutions of Atlanta. Hunter concluded that power in Atlanta was held by a number of leadership cliques, although business leaders predominated in making major economic and political decisions. Somewhat similar patterns of concentrated power were found by Hunter in his examination of power nationally.

Hunter's innovative reputational approach was lauded by many researchers because it seemed to get behind the visible scenes and uncover the true holders of power. His method recognizes the possibility that those who exercise power actually may not hold high political or business positions. Conversely, Hunter was criticized by many for taking a subjective approach to the study of power based on opinion and hearsay. Critics (Bonjean and Grimes 1974) argued that Hunter did not truly measure power but only one's reputation for it and that the results depended heavily on the selection of persons interviewed. While the controversy and discussion raised by Hunter's reputational and elitist view of power had not yet quieted, a more influential analysis of national power from a different elitist perspective suddenly burst onto the scene.

Mills

In 1956, C. Wright Mills published his controversial and influential study The Power Elite, in which he developed a positional approach to national power. Prior to Mills, most positional studies of power focused on government, assuming that power was exercised by persons holding elective public office. This unsophisticated positional view supposed that elected leaders are the only persons to exercise power and make policy.

Mills was much influenced by Weber's view that power is structured and bureaucratic in nature. Mills believed that individuals exercise power because of their positions in dominant political and economic institutions. The truly powerful are those whose positions permit them to make decisions having consequences for many people. He enumerated the principal institutions in society and the persons holding leadership positions in them. Mills found that three dominant institutions shape U.S. society—large private corporations, the executive branch of the federal government, and the military. He suggested that each of these institutions is tightly organized and centrally controlled, and collectively their leaders make decisions that determine the destiny of the nation and its people.

Mills found three levels of power in the United States. At the top, a small, relatively concentrated power elite shaped major decisions. This elite of top economic, political, and military leaders possessed not only great power but also wealth and prestige. The power elite came from privileged family backgrounds, most of them from the top third or higher levels of the income and occupational hierarchies. Almost all were college graduates, many from Ivy League colleges and exclusive preparatory schools. Mills argued that this shared background and common experience provided a basis for social cohesion and cooperative policies among these three institutional elites. He found that top corporate, political, and military leaders shared similar political and social outlooks and consciously worked together to promote their common interests. Mills called the U.S. economy a military capitalism in which the parallel interests of corporate, military, and political leaders fashioned political and economic decisions.

Below the top level, Mills detected a middle level of power visible in the halls of Congress where interest groups lobbied for policies benefiting their interests. Mills described this middle level as a semiorganized stalemate in which no one group or groups dominated and shifting coalitions occurred. Only within this rather ineffective middle level was power somewhat pluralist and less concentrated, Mills believed. The bulk of the citizenry made up the bottom level of the power hierarchy. Relatively disorganized and powerless, they lived by the political and economic policies made by the concentrated power elite.

Mills's elitist view differs from the classical perspectives of Mosca and Pareto because Mills believed a concentrated power elite was neither necessary nor desirable. Mills's approach calls attention to the interlocking networks of cohesion and interest that power holders share and helps us recognize the institutional and organizational nature of political and economic power. One exercises power in modern society not by force of tradition or personality but as a consequence of organizational position.

Dye and Domhoff

Mills's seminal work influenced a number of investigations of political and economic power employing his conceptual paradigm. Scholars in the Millsian tradition assume that power is concentrated in the top positions of dominant political and economic institutions. The exact nature and extent of power concentration and its inevitability are issues about which they disagree, however (Kerbo and Della Fave 1979). Dye (1983) and Domhoff (1983, 1980, 1979) are representative of the similarities and contrasts in contemporary elitist perspectives.

Thomas Dye, following Michels, assumes that concentrated elite rule is inevitable due to the structural characteristics of social institutions. Dye argues that power elites have the capacity to make decisions affecting others because of their high positions of authority in dominant political and economic institutions. He suggests that elite rule is unavoidable since all organizations require leadership. Examining the top positions of formal authority in twelve major institutional sectors in the United States—including the corporate, governmental, legal, educational, communications, and civic sectors, Dye found that about 6,000 persons occupy these top positions of power. Further, large corporations have many interlocking directors with other corporations, banks, utilities, and insurance companies. Concentrations of financial and industrial power seem to be dominated by a handful of large commercial banks. At the same time, many of these power holders occupy only one top post, although many also hold secondary-level positions in other organizations. Dye finds that many of these top position holders migrate over time among the corporate, governmental, and legal sectors.

Economic assets tend to be concentrated as well. The 100 largest manufacturing firms control fifty-five percent of all manufacturing assets. Like Mills, Dye finds that members of this power elite overwhelmingly come from upper- and upper-middle-class origins. He suggests that this concentrated elite largely determines the national agenda of economic and social policy, although implementation of specific details may involve bargaining among proximate policy makers in Congress and the special interest groups. Dye believes that elite members share a fundamental value consensus, although conflict may occur within the confines of the overall agreement.

In spite of his evidence of concentrated and coordinated political and economic power, Dye remains reluctant to commit himself to a pluralist or elitist interpretation. He argues that both empirical and theoretical evidence of hierarchy and polyarchy occur within the American power structure, making interpretation difficult and ambiguous.

Though he shares some of Dye's fundamental assumptions about institutional power in America, William Domhoff differs in certain key respects. Domhoff believes that although concentrated elite rule is likely, it is not a preordained given. This leads him to suggest that, while positional measures of power are necessary, they are insufficient. One must also examine conflict resolution and decision making and who benefits from them. Domhoff argues that analyzing the consequences of political and economic decisions sheds light on who holds power and how decisions are realized.

He maintains that a cohesive ruling class, largely recruited from the upper class, rules the nation's major economic and political institutions while a power elite functions as the leadership arm of the ruling class. Like Dye, Domhoff submits that although disagreements and dissensus occur within the ruling class, overall agreement on basic values and goals obtains.

Domhoff places great importance on the role such organizations as the Council for Foreign Relations and the Committee for Economic Development play in developing value consensus and cohesion among the top ruling elite. These policy planning organizations make it possible for the ruling class to dominate national policy making. This process, combined with the nonideological two-party political system and the relative impotence of local elites on the national level, results in the ideological hegemony of the ruling class and the effective suppression of opposing points of view. While Domhoff mounts persuasive evidence for his concentrated power thesis, it is roundly criticized by opponents, particularly pluralist theorists.

Suleiman and Birnbaum

Suleiman and Birnbaum illustrate the application of a contemporary elitist perspective to political power in European unitary states, in this instance, France.

Ezra Suleiman (1978, 1974) defines elitism as the creation and maintenance of a small number of restrictive institutions that give lifelong membership to their constituents. He asserts that all societies are governed by concentrated institutional elites and that elite rule is inescapable. According to Suleiman, two singular French institutions, the grandes écoles and the grands corps, produce in France a unique, state-created political power elite. These two institutions make up the state's institutional base for political elitism and centralized political power. The grandes écoles are the state-sponsored elite educational institutions that train the preeminent technocrats and bureaucrats who command the high administration of the state. These unique and privileged state educational institutions give the state a monopoly on the creation, certification, and legitimation of the highest levels of competence and excellence. The grands corps are the top-echelon state administrative agencies that direct the vast organizational apparatus of the central government. From the time of Napoleon, these twin state institutions have grown in prestige and power, making successful graduation from a grande école a virtual prerequisite to any position in the grands corps.

These institutions constitute the foundation of the personal privilege and vast political power that redound to the benefit of the political and economic elite. Writing in 1978, Suleiman asserted that neither the political parties of the Left nor the Right would alter these institutions that benefit them personally and collectively in the pursuit of power and privilege. As we shall see in Chapter 4, however, the socialist government in France has embarked on an ambitious program of political decentralization and regional devolution. In that chapter we examine several lines of evidence that bear on Suleiman's concentrated elite perspective.

Pierre Birnbaum, a contemporary French theorist who analyzes political power from an elitist perspective, addresses temporal changes in the structures of political power in France (1982). He carefully traces historical shifts in the composition of the French power elite and the interests and coalitions of which it is composed.

Birnbaum defines the governing elite as the top politicians and bureaucrats who direct the actions of the state. He is concerned with the extent to which this ruling elite shows signs of unity or disunity over time and the implications of this for the functional autonomy of the state. Birnbaum proposes that temporal alterations in the homogeneity and heterogeneity of the governing elite affect the cohesion of the state and the degree of its autonomy from powerful economic interests. During periods of relative elite heterogeneity (or pluralism), state autonomy is enhanced, whereas during periods of relative elite homogeneity (or elitism), state autonomy is diminished. Birnbaum (1982, p. 138) writes, "the idea of the state is translated into reality in the form of specific institutions controlled by various groups within the ruling class. . . . As a result, conflicts within the social system inevitably have immediate repercussions on the machinery of government."

Birnbaum characterizes four principal centers of power: the economic interests, the central bureaucracy, the parliament, and the government (president, prime minister, and the cabinet). Birnbaum suggests that when unity exists in the political and administrative spheres, but not the economic, state independence increases. Conversely, during periods of total unification of political, administrative, and economic interests, state claims to independence are nonsense. Birnbaum observes changes in the role and composition of these various groups over an extended series of historical periods. He characterizes the July Monarchy (1830-1848) and the recent presidency of Giscard d'Estaing as times of elite unity in which the state had little autonomy of its own. Conversely, the de Gaulle presidency is viewed as a period of political and administrative unity from which economic interests were directly excluded, resulting in new claims for the functional independence of the state.

While the finer points of his thesis are debatable, Birnbaum's analysis sensitizes us to the potential for shifts in the social composition of power over time and changes in its relative degree of concentration or dispersion. We must, therefore, remain conscious of avoiding time-bound analyses of political power. In succeeding chapters, we examine Birnbaum's thesis in greater detail, as well as the implications of the socialist political decentralization program for his theory.

To sum up, the work of contemporary elitist theorists alerts us to the institutional nature of power in modern societies. The holders of top positions in the dominant political and economic institutions play major roles in the development of social policies. In the unitary states of Western Europe, the role of political leaders is a particularly important and powerful one. In our analyses we call attention to the institutions and positions that are instrumental in the development of public policies like decentralization, noting how the organizational structure and membership composition of these institutions have changed over long historical periods. At the same time, we must recognize that contradictory theoretical and empirical interpretations of political and economic power have been offered by theorists operating from different conceptual perspectives. While pluralists recognize the institutional basis of political and economic power, they also raise important questions about the degree to which such power is concentrated. To these issues we now turn.

CLASSICAL PLURALISM

Understanding and analyzing political power is not an easy task. The structures and processes of power are many and complex, open to multiple interpretations and understandings. We now examine power from a conceptual and theoretical perspective, employing a different set of assumptions from the elitist perspective. Like elitism, pluralism has its intellectual roots in the political and theoretical issues of the nineteenth century. We commence our consideration of the pluralist perspective with an influential nineteenth-century theorist, Alexis de Tocqueville; following this discussion we consider the perspectives of several contemporary pluralist theorists.

Tocqueville

Alexis de Tocqueville (1969, 1955) was a French aristocrat living in a time of turbulent political and economic change. A keen student of society, he wished to understand the political and social transformations that were shaping modern Europe and the United States. Tocqueville was interested in the revolutionary political movements of his day, particularly democracy as a new form of government. While Europe continued to be governed by monarchies, the United States embodied the bold and revolutionary democratic movement that Tocqueville believed would eventually come to Europe. Though an aristocrat, he was both an advocate and a student of democracy. In 1831, Tocqueville and a colleague were sent to America to study the prison system. Tocqueville's prison report was written shortly after his return to France, but his <u>Democracy in America</u> (1835/1969) remains his enduring work.

For Tocqueville, democracy represents that form of government in which the people participate in their own governance. He maintained that compared to aristocracies, democracies exhibit a growing trend toward equality, in which such ascriptive characteristics as social background yield to individual achievement. Equality of condition does not mean all citizens are equal in intellectual endowment or economic well-being, but that all have equal opportunity to compete and achieve. He did not believe economic inequality caused political inequality and assumed that as democracy matured, economic inequality would diminish.

While democracy is a desirable form of government, it carries potential risks and dangers, Tocqueville believed. Chief among these are the possibilities of a tyranny of the majority and a corresponding tendency toward administrative centralization. The tyranny of the majority includes not only the oppression of a numerical minority by a majority but also the tyranny of the majority over itself. Tocqueville discussed the exploitation of black slaves by white slave owners as an example of minority oppression. More complex and subtle was his concern for the tyranny of the majority over itself. Tocqueville feared that democracies promote this tyranny through conformity in values, tastes, intellectual views, political beliefs, and the like. Democratic citizens feel pressure not to deviate from accepted norms of conventional thought and behavior. Fear of publicly speaking in favor of legal rights for homosexuals or other devalued minorities constitutes an example of conformity to majority thought in Tocqueville's meaning of the term. In this manner democracies tend to promote a leveling of behaviors and beliefs in which creativity and originality may be stifled, one of the potentially harmful side effects of democracy.

Tocqueville made a distinction, important for the study of regional devolution, between governmental centralization and administrative centralization. Governmental centralization involves concentration in the central government of political interests and decisions common to every part of the nation, such as foreign affairs and monetary policies. Administrative centralization encompasses the central concentration of political interests and decisions that are of concern only to local areas of the nation, such as decisions about public schools, community hospitals, and the like. Tocqueville observed that because of increasing social and technological complexity, modern nations require a high degree of governmental centralization. At the same time, he opposed administrative centralization because it unnecessarily removes decision making from the proximate control of the people, thereby diminishing their participation in the political process. Administrative centralization is therefore contradictory to democratic governance. While democratic government made administrative decentralization and citizen participation possible, Tocqueville feared that certain trends in democracy would produce centralized administration. Because democratic citizens see themselves as the ultimate source of political power, they are unafraid of letting decision making flow to the central administration. Tocqueville believed this to be a mistake because the citizenry will ultimately lose control of their government.

While Tocqueville expressed concern for the possible undesirable consequences of democracy, he believed that democracy also embodied beneficial social and political processes that act as correctives. These countervailing tendencies safeguard democracy and aid the preservation of individual liberty. Democratic legal and normative processes produce pluralist institutions that ensure political power remains decentralized in multiple centers, avoiding the abuses of concentrated power. Tocqueville admired the federal system of the United States with its constitutional division of powers among federal, state, and local governments and its separation of powers among executive, legislative, and judicial branches of government. Tocqueville believed that the separation and division of powers, contrasted with the unitary, centralized government of France, helped enhance democratic pluralism and deterred administrative centralization.

Tocqueville also found a major source of pluralism in the propensity of Americans to create and join various voluntary organizations. Freedom of association encouraged individuals with common interests to work collectively for their goals. Constitutional provisions for freedom of association, freedom of the press, and freedom of speech created the legal foundation for pluralistic voluntarism. Voluntarism, Tocqueville believed, created political competition in which the multiplicity of groups prevented the concentration of power in any one group. This pluralistic diversity helped to inhibit conformity and to check the administrative centralization of power.

In sum, while Tocqueville admired democracy, he nonetheless articulated several reservations about it. Democracies were vulnerable to the tyranny of the majority and administrative centralization. Yet he recognized that alternative social and political processes occurred, mitigating these undesirable outcomes. What contributions does Tocqueville make to our understanding of decentralization and regional devolution? As with other theorists we see merits and limitations in his arguments.

Although his impressionistic observational methods do not meet the intellectual canons of contemporary social science, he did empirically observe political and social processes to marshal facts in support of his arguments. Tocqueville was among the first to develop an explicit political and social theory of democratic pluralism, at the same time recognizing the possibilities for abusive centralization that democratic societies make possible. He noted institutional sources of countervailing pluralistic tendencies that retarded despotism and helped ensure democratic liberties. Tocqueville's emphasis on voluntarism and local government suggests that political power in democratic societies need not be monolithic. As we suggest in later chapters, the particularistic concerns of localism and ethnicity have been driving forces in the resurgence of regionalism in Europe.

On the negative side, Tocqueville constructed rather abstract theories from limited facts. His subjective advocacy sometimes influenced his theoretical conclusions. More important, we note several substantive limitations in his analysis. Paradoxically, while he expressed concern for administrative centralization, his principal apprehension was directed toward the tyranny of the majority. Tocqueville minimized the danger of a tyranny of the minority, domination by political and economic elites, because he assumed democracy promoted social and political equality. He underestimated the powers of national political elites and virtually ignored the emergence of powerful economic elites (Zeitlin 1971).

Tocqueville minimized the inequality of wealth created by industrial capitalism and failed to see its potential contradiction with political equality. While he recognized the role influential interest groups play in democratic regimes, he neglected the relationships between economic inequality and political inequality. He failed to understand that inequality of wealth can create inequality of political participation and power, even in democratic societies—a result of his erroneous assumption that as democracy developed, inequalities of wealth would diminish. We have previously noted that concentrations of wealth and control have increased, not decreased, since Tocqueville's time. More fundamentally, Tocqueville assigned causal primacy to democratic political processes over economic processes and neglected the relationships of centralized economic elites to political elites.

In spite of these limitations, Tocqueville's work sensitizes us to possible consequences of political centralization in democratic societies while simultaneously alerting us to voluntarism and localism as sources of pluralistic institutions and processes. Tocqueville's reflections on political pluralism and its sources have influenced a number of contemporary scholars whose ideas we now examine.

CONTEMPORARY PLURALISM

Although Tocqueville's theory of political power in democratic societies remains a starting point for contemporary pluralism, modern pluralist theorists recognize that democratic governments and societies are considerably more complex than in Tocqueville's time. Contemporary pluralists acknowledge that mass society makes equal political participation by all citizens impossible. Interest group leaders exercise greater power than members, and interest groups vary in power. In the populous mass democratic societies of today, both individuals and groups exercise quite varying degrees of political power and participation (Putnam 1976).

The pluralist perspective on power, like the elitist, has evolved through time in response to these changed realities. Contemporary pluralists have developed a perspective known as elite pluralism. Elite pluralists recognize that most large organizations are headed by leadership elites and great differences exist both in the power of individuals and of organized interests. In spite of these features, however, elite pluralists maintain that competition among elites and their organizations prevents undue concentrations of political and economic power. Contemporary pluralists have also produced more explicit conceptual formulations consistent with the use of more scientific measurement methods in the attempt to collect empirical data about power and power relationships. These refinements will become apparent as we examine the contemporary pluralists.

We have already noted some similarities between contemporary elitism and contemporary elite pluralism. While the differences between these two perspectives are substantial, both perspectives recognize that in contemporary society political and economic power are concentrated in the hands of a few. The perspectives differ in their interpretations of the nature and extent to which power is concentrated. Elitists emphasize coordination and consensus among a cohesive power elite, arguing that power is highly concentrated in a few key institutions. Elite pluralists emphasize the considerable differences of purpose and interest among organizational leaders, as well as the broad institutional dispersion of political and economic power.

As Putnam (1976) notes, there exist multiple dimensions within which elites may or may not be integrated, and pluralists and elitists disagree on the actual extent of integration among these dimensions. Putnam avoids taking sides in this debate, noting that there are many unresolved conceptual and empirical issues. He does point out that both pluralists and elitists recognize that as elite integration increases, the likelihood of oligarchy also increases and the ability of citizens to participate actively in the political process decreases. Putnam speaks of a trade-off between the positive benefits of political stability that elite integration produces and the resulting negative consequences of oligarchy. The theoretical explanations and normative consequences of elitist and pluralist perspectives will become clearer as we examine the work of several contemporary elite pluralists.

Keller

Suzanne Keller (1963) is sympathetic to the original insights of Tocqueville; however, her formal conceptual framework derives from the theory of social institutions known as functionalism. The functional theory of society analyzes the structures and consequences of political and social institutions. Functionalists emphasize the positive contributions of particular institutions to the maintenance of the whole society as an ongoing social system. Functional systems theory supposes societies have basic requirements that must be met, that individuals and institutions fulfill these requirements, and that all this is possible because of agreement on shared values and ends.

As a functionalist, Keller emphasizes the positive functions that leadership elites play in modern society. In her view, elite rule is both inevitable and desirable. The increasing economic and occupational complexity of modern societies makes rule by a few unavoidable. This is desirable because a variety of multiple strategic elites possess the expertise and knowledge required to make our complex political and economic institutions function smoothly. Keller's functional orientation is seen in her definition of elites as those individuals who are designated to serve society in socially valued ways. In her view, strategic elites are responsible for achieving the major social goals that make the continuation of social order possible (1963, p. 4).

Keller's perspective assumes that contemporary society is composed of various political and social institutions, each headed by its respective leadership elite. Strategic elites comprise the sum total of leaders in the various institutional sectors, and it is their decisions and actions that have important consequences for societal members. Strategic elites include political, economic, military, moral, cultural, and scientific leaders. Keller asserts that the classical elitists failed to distinguish between the personal and selfish motives of individual leaders and the social roles that elite leaders play in the smooth functioning and maintenance of social order. She elaborates a pluralist view of political and economic power based on functional assumptions about the nature and consequences of these multiple strategic elites, which are not to be confused with social classes based on hierarchies of wealth and prestige.

As societies become technologically and socially more complex, populous, and specialized, national elites displace local and regional elites in importance. The profusion and specialization of elite leadership at the national level develop hand in hand with the manifold social functions modern societies must accomplish. Drawing on the functional theory of Parsons (1951), Keller elaborates a classification embracing four types of elite roles and their positive social functions. The function of political elites is to achieve national goals; economic, military, diplomatic, and scientific elites help society to adapt to changing opportunities for the achievement of economic growth and political stability; integrative elites such as the clergy, philosophers, and educators define and clarify the beliefs and behaviors appropriate to the moral and ethical traditions of society; finally, such elites as artists, writers, entertainers, and media personalities promote social solidarity and morale through tension management and release. The proliferation of strategic elites protects society against despotic concentrations of political and economic power since the functions and duties of each elite are specialized and limited. In

Keller's view, power in modern industrial societies is increasingly dispersed among various strategic elites and their institutions and is hence less centralized, capricious, and personal. The functionally specialized nature of power prevents its monolithic concentration. She writes: "Today, no single strategic elite has absolute power or priority, none can hold power forever, and none determines the patterns of selection and recruitment for the rest" (1963, p. 277).

Utilizing structural functional postulates, Keller elaborates a theoretically complex view of elite pluralism. Let us assess her arguments. Keller's perspective on leadership elites should not be confused with that of the elitist theorists. While both pluralist and elitist theorists recognize the existence of elites, they differ in their interpretation of them. Elitist theorists emphasize concentration, coordination, and elite circulation as major defining properties of the power elite. Keller accentuates the unique and specialized character of multiple strategic elites who, because of their expertise and specialization, are unable to concentrate their power or readily exchange positions. Additionally, she calls attention to the beneficial functional contribution of leadership elites to the successful functioning of the whole society.

Keller's functional pluralism attunes us to the interdependent nature of social institutions and processes. We see how the activities of leaders in a particular institutional sector may have positive consequences for the entire society. Keller's attention to the functions of varied institutions helps us comprehend the multiple social foundations of distinct sources of power. Her work suggests sources of countervailing power other than those observed by Tocqueville. We infer from her analysis that complex political events such as regional devolution result from the activities of numerous groups and have wide-ranging consequences. We should, therefore, be alert to the contributions nonpolitical actors make to political decentralization.

We also note several limitations and ambiguities in Keller's analysis. Her classification of elites by social function appears abstract and arbitrary. We wonder how professional athletes function as tension management elites, for example. More important, we believe Keller does not analyze concentrated or pluralistic power, per se, but rather the social functions of elite leaders. We previously defined power as the ability to realize one's will even in the face of opposition. Keller's evaluation of elites does not embrace this conceptualization of power relationships. This results from her belief that society is characterized by basic value consensus and shared goals. Because of these assumptions, she ignores the question of who does and does not benefit from the decisions made by political and economic elites. Keller disavows any important linkage between social origins and the exercise of power, although she notes that most elites come from favored backgrounds. Paradoxically, she argues that elites sharing similar privileged backgrounds lack the value consensus making concentrated power possible, yet also proposes that elite decisions benefit all since society shares basic values.

Riesman

Unlike Keller's attention to the social functions of elites, David Riesman's (1953) concerns are closer to the intellectual traditions of Tocqueville and his interpretation of voluntary organizations in democratic societies. Drawing on Tocqueville's insights, Riesman describes what he calls the theory of veto groups.

In Riesman's perspective, modern democracies such as the United States are composed of a plethora of organized interest groups that mobilize around the particular concerns of their members. These concerns might include economic, political, educational, medical, ethnic, racial, or other issues. Each group enters the political process to achieve the goals that are fundamental to it. Riesman suggests that interest groups exercise power and influence only on very specific, limited issues. While interest groups are unequal in power, none is strong enough to exercise hegemonic power; the ability to achieve goals is divided among many conflicting interest groups. Riesman characterizes interest groups as veto groups because their principal strength lies in their ability to prevent or alter outcomes rather than to initiate them. Even the most powerful of groups has only limited ability to initiate and complete its specific goals. This characterization of veto groups leads Riesman to conclude that power in the United States is amorphous.

Since political and economic power is widely dispersed among veto groups, a concentrated power elite no longer exists. This contrasts with earlier periods in U.S. history when a clearly defined ruling class exercised concentrated power. Given the absence of powerful leadership and the prevalence of multiple veto groups, political and economic power is pluralistic in nature. Riesman writes, "The vaster number of veto groups, and their greater power, mean that no one man or small group of men can amass the power nationally. . . . Rather, power on the national scene must be viewed in terms of issues" (1953, p. 256). Riesman argues that economic wealth no longer provides access to political power. With the passing of once-powerful economic and political leaders, power is shared among small business persons, professional people, military people, business managers, labor leaders, blacks, whites, Poles, Italians, Jews, and any other special interest group that organizes to have its interests represented. The ascendancy of the veto group produces situational and mercurial power, not sustained, structured, and centralized power. Riesman maintains that once political and economic systems are running, little leadership is required to keep them in motion.

Given this characterization of power, Riesman states that the power perspectives of Pareto, Mosca, Weber, and others are relics of the past; their answers to power questions no longer obtain. The contrast between Riesman and the classical and contemporary elitists could not be clearer. Since he concludes that veto groups vary in influence and leaders exercise greater power than followers, we may classify Riesman as an elite pluralist. He develops an extreme form of pluralism in which pluralistic power dispersion takes explanatory dominance over organized leadership. For Riesman, the pluralism in elite pluralism is considerably more important than the elite component.

What may we say of Riesman's analysis? On the positive side, his approach calls our attention to the prominent role special interest groups play in making political and economic policy. In our analyses of regional devolution we must be attuned to the activities of various organized interests.

Riesman's conceptualization of power contains several problems. Notably, he does not provide systematic empirical data to support his conclusions. His generalizations derive from casual, impressionistic observations about various historical periods. The random character of his data results in a failure to develop a clear and adequate definition of power. While Riesman frequently refers to power and its uses, he employs the term in varied contexts and neglects a measurable definition of it. Perhaps because he sees power as amorphous and diffuse, he believes a formal definition is unnecessary. We are troubled by Riesman's near-anarchic outlook on the nature and functions of political and economic power. If we believe Riesman, complex political and economic organizations simply run undirected. In his perspective, events occur but no one makes decisions. If this is indeed the case, we wonder how difficult decisions such as the allocation of scarce and desirable resources can be made without producing marked social conflict.

At bottom, Riesman's view is extreme and unbalanced. He accords scant recognition to organized structures of power and their relationship to political and economic resources. We believe a more balanced view of power in complex societies is necessary. While we find Riesman's view interesting, we do not subscribe to it, presenting it merely as an example of an extreme form of the pluralist perspective.

Crozier

Michel Crozier (1982, 1974, 1964) illustrates the application of a contemporary pluralist perspective to political power in unitary states, in this case, France. Crozier believes the French state to be overly bureaucratized and centralized, making it inflexible and maladapted to political and social change, blocking communication and stalling progress. His multiple work centers on the analysis of organizational structures and mechanisms that create blockages in evolutionary change. He develops a comparative perspective to advance the argument that overly centralized governmental administrations would benefit from a pluralistic decentralization of power and decision making.

Crozier asserts that the state's power elite is the primary source of blockage, creating stalemate in technical, administrative, and political systems. He argues that France and other Western democracies face an explosion in the complexity of human relationships and institutions that overwhelms the smooth functioning of outmoded institutional structures. For France, the essential problem is the structure of power in the state bureaucracy. Excessive hierarchical power stratification, exacerbated in centralized unitary states, encourages a pattern of noncommunication that paralyzes effective functioning. Since social institutions are interdependent, system blockage or stalemate in one institutional sector produces dysfunctional consequences in other institutional sectors. Crozier identifies three primary sources of bureaucratic stalemate or blockage in France: the system of state public administration, the system of leadership recruitment, and the educational system. He asserts that the political parties of both the Left and Right attempt to impose reform from above by decree and that this fundamental strategy is unworkable. Crozier criticizes the Right and its emphasis on technocratic administration and the Left and its emphasis on revolutionary political slogans. He believes the entire strategy of change must be rethought. Neither technocracy nor revolution represents a key to change.

Crozier also advocates positive strategies for pluralistic, decentralized change. He sees the political and administrative power structure as both the source of the problem and the lever of needed change. He believes that France, like other modern societies, cannot be changed by administrative fiat. As a result, he advocates a series of tactical, middle-level changes that rely on investments in knowledge, human resources, and social experiments. Crozier favors moderate, nonsweeping reforms that stand some chance of long-term success. He desires reforms that can build on themselves as continuing sources of change. Experiments initiated at the bottom of the social structure will face less organized opposition and a better chance of success. This is Crozier's solution to the paradox that the state administration oversees all change in France, yet is itself nearly impervious to change. This is why Crozier adopts his strategy of moderate reform from the bottom. To decentralize the French administration, he advocates the transfer of political power to locally elected regional bodies (This process began in France with the socialist decentralization of 1981, which we analyze in Chapter 4.) Crozier would tackle the problem of leadership recruitment by reforming the <u>grandes écoles</u>, the elite French institutions that train the high administration. The educational system requires changes in the structure of basic research that would reorder the system of knowledge production and dissemination.

As an academic activist, Crozier steers a centrist political course, rejecting both the technocratic solutions

of the Right and the revolutionary utopias of the Left. He
remains a continuing critic of centralized political systems
that concentrate power at the highest levels of the national
state. As a pluralist, he actively advocates decentralized
structures of power, believing they hold the key to unlock-
ing existing hierarchical power structures. While Crozier's
critiques and prescriptions for change have received some
attention from political and academic centrists, they have
not had major influence on the political programs of parties
of the Left or Right.

Dahl

   Robert Dahl (1978, 1971, 1967, 1958) emerged in the
late 1950s as an influential pluralist theorist. He pioneered a new method for measuring power that marshaled
firmer data for the pluralist perspective than had hitherto
been the case. For this reason, Dahl's work has enjoyed
greater influence than that of Keller or Riesman.
   Dahl, dissatisfied with elitist approaches to power
measurement, wished to develop a method congruent with
the assumptions of pluralist theory. He evolved the decision-making method for the measurement of community
power. Since then, pluralist analysts of power have preferred his method over the elitist positional approach. As
discussed earlier, pluralists and elitists have engaged in
a long and continuing debate over the advantages and disadvantages of each approach. The decision-making perspective views power as a social process and observes the
ways in which specific decisions are made. The method
entails selection of a particular issue, such as a school
bond proposal or the location of public housing, and traces
out the individuals and procedures important in reaching
the final result. The researcher analyzes power by observing this process over some period of time. Dahl advocated
this method because he believed it examined decision making
as an overt, deliberative process rather than as a covert,
unknown process.
   Dahl investigated urban renewal in New Haven, Connecticut, the home of Yale University. Through examination
of assorted written documents and interviews with major
participants, he developed a picture of the decisions taken
and the results produced. Careful analysis of his empirical findings led Dahl to conclude that no one group domi-

nated decision making. Rather, he found that a plurality of power clusters, including economic, political, and social elites, were influential in New Haven. Among the leadership elites operating there, he discovered political leaders to be the most important. Elected officials, such as the mayor, played leading roles in urban renewal, while the contributions of business leaders were surprisingly minimal. Economic leaders were influential on some issues, but their participation in urban renewal was largely secondary and lacked major direct influence, said Dahl. In his view, the business community was passive and divided rather than active and cohesive. Further, Dahl's work suggested that access to political office was relatively open, and becoming a political leader was not difficult. Because political leaders are elected, Dahl argued, real political power ultimately resides with the citizenry.

Dahl painted an elite pluralist portrait of New Haven. No one class or interest group continuously monopolized power. Rather, numerous elites competed for leadership on various issues, because consensus on various issues of substance was lacking among elites. Since no group exercised power continuously, decision making required considerable negotiation and compromise. His characterization of multiple, competing elites fits well with the elite pluralist view of dispersed, nonconcentrated political and economic power. Dahl used the term "polyarchy" to describe these multiple power centers.

Dahl maintained that the decision-making process and power arrangements he discovered in New Haven are typical, asserting that most local communities possess similar elite pluralist power structures. Since local communities are but a microcosm of the nation, Dahl concluded that the United States is appropriately characterized as a pluralist, polyarchic society. Many interest groups and organizations vie for power and influence nationally, while no one of them exercises hegemony. Thus Republicans oppose Democrats, labor bargains with management, geographic regions vie for public works, and the like. Since many groups contend for power and electors choose political leaders, power is decentralized at the national level just as it is at the community level.

In appraising Dahl's characterization of power and his development of the decision-making method, we laud his creative approach to the problem. He originated a method that conceptualizes power as an ongoing political and social process rather than a static structure. Dahl's renown as a leading pluralist derives in part from his development of the approach that gave pluralist theorists a firmer empirical base for their work. His characterization of polyarchy in the United States alerts us to the possible contributions of multiple groups to the evolution of regional government in Western Europe.

There has been much criticism of the decision-making approach and Dahl's pluralist characterization of power, particularly by elitist theorists.[2] They point out that findings resulting from this method depend on the particular issue examined by the researcher. Further, conceptualizing power as a decision-making process can work only when the decisions made and results reached are visible. Decisions in the public political arena are considerably more observable than decisions in the private corporate arena. Since Dahl examined urban renewal, his conclusion that politicians and public figures are most influential in decision making is not surprising. Decisions made in the corporate boardroom simply cannot be measured with Dahl's method, although they may influence the public policy agenda. Additionally, not all decisions made in the public arena are always apparent, as the many revelations of duplicity by public officials suggest. Finally, the decision-making method is difficult to use in the study of national power structures. Unless one assumes that all important national decisions are made within the visible portion of the political arena, this approach tends to result in a built-in bias. Since decision-making researchers observe only visible public decisions, the method leads almost invariably to decentralized interpretations of national power and misses national influences on local decision making.

Let us now examine a third perspective on power, that of center-periphery interaction. After we look at several examples of this perspective, we summarize and evaluate the evidence and arguments we have discussed.

---

[2] See Domhoff (1978) for a quite different elitist interpretation of power in New Haven.

CENTER-PERIPHERY INTERACTION

Center-Periphery Relations and the Crises of Development

A number of political development theorists reject both elitism and pluralism as unsatisfactory explanations for the exercise of power. They tend to emphasize the emergence and development of entire political systems rather than limit their perspective to political elites or to interest groups and their influence on political institutions and processes. These scholars, representing a relatively recent stage in the evolution of political development theory approach political development in terms of certain crises (critical changes) that each political system will encounter and the sequences in which these crises occur (Binder 1971; Grew 1978; La Palombara 1971; Weiner 1971). The crises in question are labeled the crisis of identity, involving the development of a sense of membership in a political community; the crisis of legitimacy, involving the emergence and survival of a sense of obligation toward the political system and its institutions; the crisis of penetration, entailing the extension of the central government's control over its territory, including outlying areas; the crisis of participation, raising the question of the extension of power to broader masses of the population; and the crisis of distribution, brought on by demands for increased material benefits extended to a higher proportion of the population.

It is evident that some of these crises are related to the centralization-decentralization issue discussed in Chapter 1. The crisis of penetration has to do with the changes wrought or attempted by centralizing states. The crises of identity and participation are frequently precipitated by reactions to the central government's penetration of the periphery. On the other hand, penetration requires legitimacy in order to be successful, and the centralizers may themselves encourage broader participation in order to enhance their own legitimacy. These crises are interrelated, then, and these interrelationships need to be examined in each political system. There is apparently no uniform rule as yet for the nature of these relationships and for the order in which they occur.

Center-Periphery Relations:
Cooperation and Competition

Sidney Tarrow (1977) provides an interesting and useful analysis of the relationship between the center (the political, and perhaps the economic and cultural, capital) and the hinterland or periphery. He discusses a number of models of center-periphery relations, one example being the diffusion-isolation model, according to which the administrative and political elites at the center seek to extend their area of social control over isolated, culturally backward peripheral areas. A second model analyzed by Tarrow is the dependency-marginality model. This model views the center as exercising economic hegemony over the countryside in a kind of colonial relationship. In fact, the term "internal colonialism" is often used to describe this relationship, thus linking subnational politics to the proliferating body of dependency theory, which claims to portray the economic and political ties between the West and the Third World.

Tarrow devises a more complex and flexible synthetic model of center-periphery relations (1977, ch. 1). According to his scheme, the administrative elite does indeed try to achieve cultural and economic dominance over the periphery. However, it cannot do so unaided; it needs allies at the periphery in order to build a coherent ruling coalition. Only with such a coalition, enjoying some measure of support from the grass roots, can the center hope to extract resources from the periphery and achieve its policy goals.

In modern market economies, according to Tarrow, the administrative elites at the center may have any one of three types of policy objectives vis-à-vis the periphery. First of all, they may aim at ensuring normative equality--equality of access to education and to legal protection. This kind of goal is regarded by Tarrow as prevalent mostly in pure market economies and in federal systems. Second, the central elites may pursue a policy of technocratic reformism, as in France. Under this kind of guideline, central aid would be directed toward the more productive peripheral areas, and a "productive alliance" is formed with the more productive groups on the periphery (the more efficient businessmen and farmers). Presumably, less developed areas would be left to wither on the vine. Third, the central elite may follow a policy of distributive welfare, as in Italy. Under this dominant orientation, patronage benefits and subsidies are dispensed to the grass roots with very little concern for considerations of efficiency or productivity. In fact, the neediest, least competitive areas are apt to get the lion's share of central support. The kind of coalition formed under a distributive-welfare type of policy is the so-called "populist alliance" with peasants, artisans, and petty bourgeoisie, especially in the less developed areas like the Italian south.

Tarrow's model of center-periphery relations is less simplistic than the dichotomous models he discusses. It recognizes the possibility of several different kinds of relationships between center and periphery, depending on elite ideologies and the social context. Above all, it demonstrates the likelihood that competing alliances between elements at the center and elements at the periphery will play a more important role in the decision-making process than a crude confrontation between a united center and a united countryside.

Center-Periphery Relations: Territorial versus Functional Representation

Having effectively demolished the notion of a simple center-periphery dichotomy, Tarrow goes on to question the alleged dichotomy between functional representation at the center and territorial representation at the grass roots (1978). According to this view of the world, central government agencies represent the expertise of professional experts, whereas local agencies tend to speak for the traditional values and intuitive judgments of grass-roots democracy. In this kind of dichotomous model, the technical skills of the centralizers are bound to prevail over the emotional objections and standpat attitudes of provincial and local officials. Technocracy conquers politics.

Tarrow's objection to this kind of interpretation is based on his awareness of the growth of technical expertise at the grass roots. To an increasing extent, local and provincial governments are becoming agencies for implementing central government policies and for helping the central government to perform its planning functions. This is happening, not only because the central government is overloaded and needs help, not only because local governments can help mobilize consent and cooperation for programs in which they participate, but also because the local and provincial governments are developing their own corps of technical experts. Thus, a new localism has developed, not so much in opposition to the center, but rather in favor of an increasing local input into centrally determined programs. Once again, as Tarrow shows, we have more than a simple confrontation between the territorial unit of government and the functional agency; rather, we have competing alliances in which central specialists and local specialists may find themselves on the same side of the policy issue fence. It is hardly surprising, under the circumstances, that "peripheral energies and aspirations were not infrequently channelled and exploited by those elements which most favored modernization . . ." (Mény and Wright 1985, p. 3). According to Mény and Wright, there appears to have been as much reciprocal stimulation as conflict in the relationship between center and periphery (1985, pp. 7-8).

The insights of Tarrow and of other scholars have raised some serious doubts about the utility of both the center-periphery approach and the functional-territorial dichotomy. It is possible, for example, to view power in terms of relationships among governmental organizations without introducing territorial criteria, by focusing on the number of organizations involved, the distribution of power among them, and the type of interaction that takes place. Thus, Richard Rose (1985, pp. 22-24) distinguishes between a hierarchy, with one dominant organization; an oligopoly, with power unevenly distributed among a few important organizations; and the intergovernmental model, in which power is widely distributed among a great number of autonomous organizations, linked only by a bargaining relationship. Another suggested alternative to the center-periphery approach is the matrix model, which views the American system as <u>noncentralized</u> rather than <u>decentralized</u>, and conceives of power as being distributed among multiple centers in a matrix rather than handed down from a single center in a pyramid (Elazar 1976, pp. 11-14).

These various ways of viewing intergovernmental and intragovernmental power relationships reject the notion of a rigid separation between center and periphery in the struggle for power. By the same token, they do not view the center and the periphery as preordained antagonists. They call for more complex and more realistic analyses of power alignments, on the ground that the center-periphery approach gives a distorted picture of the real world.

POWER AND DECENTRALIZATION:
A COMPARATIVE APPROACH

What may we conclude from our review of elitist, pluralist, and center-periphery perspectives on political power? The individual and collective work of these diverse theorists results in a degree of theoretical ambiguity. In some respects, these schools of thought stand in opposition to one another, offering different conceptual frameworks for interpreting political decentralization and regional devolution. Additionally, the varied ideas of each theorist often contain within themselves multiple emphases leading in different theoretical directions.

While Tocqueville posited the dangers of administrative centralization and a tyranny of the majority, he also suggested that distinctions of status diversity and regional localism promote voluntarism and pluralism. A primary emphasis on one or the other of these distinct threads can lead to different interpretations of power. Weber, too, underlined the growth of centralized administration and its potential for domination in the rational-legal bureaucracies of the modern era. Yet he also suggested that class and status interests constitute organizing bases for the pursuit of diverse political and economic interests. The multiple insights in Weber's work likewise lend themselves to both pluralist and elitist interpretations of power, although the latter tendency is paramount.

Dye (1983, pp. 266-69) succinctly captures the duality of this theoretical tradition. He suggests that both classical and contemporary theorists of power postulate both hierarchy and polyarchy in political and economic institutions. Weber, Durkheim, and Tocqueville argued that socioeconomic development led to increasing functional differentiation, implying specialized and deconcentrated centers of expertise and power. At the same time, these theorists postulated that specialization required coordination, suggesting the need for hierarchies of authority and the concentration of power. Dye writes, "Because social theory suggests both convergence and differentiation among institutional elites, it is possible to develop competing theoretical models of the social system--models which emphasize either hierarchy or polyarchy" (1983, p. 268). Elitist theorists emphasize that hierarchy requires coordination and results in concentrations of power. Pluralist theorists believe positional and institutional differentiation produces specialization that confines power within relatively narrow institutional limits. Tarrow, for his part, believes that specialization and expertise can actually strengthen local interests, as well as national interests.

What are we to make of these differing theoretical traditions and the ongoing debate about the utility of various perspectives on power? We take the position that because power is a complex phenomenon, no one point of view is entirely correct or erroneous. Each of these positions has strengths and contributions to make to our understanding of political and economic power, as well as weaknesses and conceptual and empirical limitations. Because of this, we believe that a comparative theoretical perspective on political decentralization and regional devolution can provide us with multiple insights. As we have seen, it is possible to interpret data from the empirical world in varied ways. Theoretical diversity and competition are intellectually healthy. They prevent us from relying on conventional generalizations and stereotyped thinking while forcing us to be alert to the complexities and varied meanings of our data. The question of theoretical interpretation is partly an ideological issue as well. Value commitments and ideological biases shape one's theoretical assumptions, choice of methods, and interpretations of results. While a comparative theoretical approach does not remove all biases, it helps one become aware of them, thereby enhancing objectivity.

A comparative perspective also aids our ability to recognize the commonalities as well as the diversities in theories of power. In spite of differing emphases and interpretations, we observe that elitists, pluralists, and center-periphery theorists share in common certain broad assumptions. Our review of work from these three traditions leads us to conclude that in modern societies government and business constitute major institutions of power. An adequate understanding of decentralization and devolution requires us to take these institutions and their leaders, especially political leaders, into account. It is clear that while elitists have long emphasized the consequences of concentrated power, pluralist theorists have moved a bit closer to elements of this position. Elite pluralists acknowledge that institutions and organizations vary in power, just as do individuals, and the elite pluralist perspective suggests a point of convergence among these differing theorists. The observation that power is concentrated to a greater or lesser degree offers a key to our own conceptualization of power. Rather than characterizing power as a dichotomy that is either concentrated or dispersed, it makes greater sense to view it as a continuum. Given multiple interpretations of power, and the empirical reality that structures of power change over time, it is more reasonable to conceptualize power as a continuing series of gradations, from less to more concentrated, than as a simple dispersed versus concentrated dichotomy. Characterizing power as a continuum allows for empirical changes over time in state and local power structures as well as for multiple theoretical interpretations.

In our analyses of decentralization and devolution, we indicate how changing political and economic institutions have led both to dispersed and concentrated structures of power at different points in time. Our fluid conceptual model is congruent with the evolving historical reality of the West European political power structures that have alternated from revolution to reaction over the past two centuries. Our characterization helps us comprehend power as a social process rather than a static structure. It permits us to consider power from multiple approaches and to recognize that power structures and processes vary from nation to nation and time to time.

In spite of recent political movements toward regional devolution, some evidence suggests that a long-term trend toward increasing concentration and centralization of political power may be occurring (Badie and Birnbaum 1983). Population growth and increased organizational size, combined with the complex political and economic issues that modern governments must address, suggest the likelihood of continuing political centralization at both national and international levels over the longer term future. While it is worthwhile to keep such speculative generalizations in mind as we examine our data, we can evaluate them more fully after we observe the detailed workings of regional decentralization. We shall return to the interpretation and evaluation of our theoretical perspectives after examining the political realities of decentralization in the succeeding three chapters. In Chapter 6 we assess the implications of our survey of regional and national power for the construction of an integrated empirical theory of comparative politics and political power.

Our comparative theoretical approach is complemented by our comparative empirical analysis of political processes in major Western democracies. Our cross-cultural approach makes it possible to highlight similarities and differences among regional power structures and to compare alternative solutions to common problems of centralization. Examining political power and regionalism in several nations helps to avoid erroneous generalizations based on one unique set of governmental structures. While comparative political analysis will not resolve all problems, it is a powerful analytical tool. Let us begin with Italy.

REFERENCES

Armstrong, John A. 1973. The European Administrative Elite. Princeton, N.J.: Princeton University Press.

Bachrach, Peter. 1967. The Theory of Democratic Elitism: A Critique. Boston: Little, Brown.

Bachrach, Peter, and Morton S. Baratz. 1962. "Two Faces of Power." American Political Science Review 56 (December): 947-52.

Badie, Bertrand, and Pierre Birnbaum. 1983. The Sociology of the State, trans. by Arthur Goldhammer. Chicago: University of Chicago Press.

Bendix, Reinhard. 1962. Max Weber: An Intellectual Portrait. Garden City, N.Y.: Anchor Books.

Bill, James A., and Robert L. Hardgrave, Jr. 1973. Comparative Politics: The Quest for Theory, ch. 5. Columbus, Ohio: Charles A. Merrill.

Binder, Leonard. 1971. "Crises of Political Development." In Crises and Sequences in Political Development, by Leonard Binder et al., pp. 3-72. Princeton, N.J.: Princeton University Press.

Birnbaum, Pierre. 1982. The Heights of Power: An Essay on the Power Elite in France, trans. by Arthur Goldhammer. Chicago: University of Chicago Press.

Bonjean, Charles M., and Michael D. Grimes. 1974. "Community Power: Issues and Findings." In Social

Stratification: A Reader, edited by Joseph Lopreato and Lionel S. Lewis, pp. 377-90. New York: Harper & Row.

Bonjean, Charles M., and David M. Olson. 1964. "Community Leadership: Directions of Research." Administrative Science Quarterly 9 (December): 278-300.

Bottomore, Tom. 1979. Political Sociology. New York: Harper & Row.

──────. 1964. Elites and Society. New York: Basic Books.

Crozier, Michel. 1982. Strategies for Change: The Future of French Society, trans. by William R. Beer. Cambridge, Mass.: MIT Press.

──────. 1974. The Stalled Society, trans. by Rupert Swyer. New York: Viking Press.

──────. 1964. The Bureaucratic Phenomenon, trans. by Michel Crozier. Chicago: University of Chicago Press.

Dahl, Robert A. 1978. "Pluralism Revisited." Comparative Politics 10 (January): 191-203.

──────. 1971. Polyarchy: Participation and Opposition. New Haven, Conn.: Yale University Press.

──────. 1967. Pluralist Democracy in the United States: Conflict and Consensus. Chicago: Rand McNally.

──────. 1961. Who Governs? Democracy and Power in an American City. New Haven, Conn.: Yale University Press.

──────. 1958. "A Critique of the Ruling Elite Model." American Political Science Review 52 (June): 463-69.

Domhoff, G. William. 1983. Who Rules America Now? A View for the '80s. Englewood Cliffs, N.J.: Prentice-Hall.

_____. 1979. *The Powers That Be: Processes of Ruling Class Domination in America*. New York: Vintage Books.

_____. 1978. *Who Really Rules? New Haven and Community Power Reexamined*. Santa Monica, Calif.: Goodyear Publishing Co.

_____, ed. 1980. *Power Structure Research*. Beverly Hills, Calif.: Sage.

Dye, Thomas. 1983. *Who's Running America? The Reagan Years*. Englewood Cliffs, N.J.: Prentice-Hall.

Elazar, Daniel J. 1976. "Federalism vs. Decentralization: The Drift from Authority." *Publius* 6 (Fall): 9-19.

Gerth, H. H., and C. Wright Mills. 1958. *From Max Weber: Essays in Sociology*. New York: Oxford University Press.

Gouldner, Alvin S. 1955. "Metaphysical Pathos and the Theory of Bureaucracy." *American Political Science Review* 49 (June): 496-507.

Grew, Raymond. 1978. "The Crises and Their Sequences." In *Crises of Political Development in Europe and the United States*, edited by Raymond Grew, pp. 3-37. Princeton, N.J.: Princeton University Press.

Hunter, Floyd. 1959. *Top Leadership USA*. Chapel Hill: University of North Carolina Press.

_____. 1953. *Community Power Structure*. Chapel Hill: University of North Carolina Press.

Kadushin, Charles. 1968. "Power, Influence, and Social Circles: A New Methodology for Studying Opinion Making." *American Sociological Review* 33 (October): 685-99.

Keller, Suzanne I. 1963. *Beyond the Ruling Class: Strategic Elites in Modern Society*. New York: Random House.

Kerbo, Harold, and L. Richard Della Fave. 1979. "The Empirical Side of the Power Elite Debate: An Assessment and Critique of Recent Research." *Sociological Quarterly* 20 (October): 5-22.

La Palombara, Joseph. 1971. "Penetration: A Crisis of Governmental Capacity." In *Crises and Sequences in Political Development*, by Leonard Binder et al., pp. 205-32. Princeton, N.J.: Princeton University Press.

Marger, Martin N. 1981. *Elites and Masses: An Introduction to Political Sociology*. New York: Van Nostrand.

Meisel, James H. 1962. *The Myth of the Ruling Class: Gaetano Mosca and the "Elite."* Ann Arbor: University of Michigan Press.

Mény, Yves, and Vincent Wright. 1985. "Introduction." In *Centre-Periphery Relations in Western Europe*, edited by Yves Mény and Vincent Wright, pp. 1-9. London: Allen & Unwin.

Merritt, Richard L. 1970. *Systematic Approaches to Comparative Politics*, ch. 4. Chicago: Rand McNally.

Michels, Robert. 1962. *Political Parties*, trans. by Eden and Cedar Paul. New York: Free Press.

Mills, C. Wright. 1956. *The Power Elite*. New York: Oxford University Press.

Mosca, Gaetano. 1939. *The Ruling Class*, trans. by Hannah D. Kuhn. New York: McGraw-Hill.

Paige, Glenn D., ed. 1972. *Political Leadership*. New York: Free Press.

Pareto, Vilfredo. 1966. *Vilfredo Pareto: Sociological Writings*, trans. by Derick Mirfin. New York: Praeger.

Parry, Geraint. 1969. *Political Elites*. New York: Praeger.

Parsons, Talcott. 1951. *The Social System*. Glencoe, Ill.: Free Press.

Putnam, Robert D. 1976. *The Comparative Study of Political Elites*. Englewood Cliffs, N.J.: Prentice-Hall.

Riesman, David, with Nathan Glazer and Reuel Denney. 1953. *The Lonely Crowd: A Study of the Changing American Character*. Garden City, N.Y.: Doubleday.

Rose, Richard. 1985. "From Government at the Center to Nationwide Government." In *Centre-Periphery Relations in Western Europe*, edited by Yves Mény and Vincent Wright, pp. 13-32. London: Allen & Unwin.

Suleiman, Ezra N. 1978. *Elites in French Society: The Politics of Survival*. Princeton, N.J.: Princeton University Press.

―――. 1974. *Politics, Power, and Bureaucracy in France: The Administrative Elite*. Princeton, N.J.: Princeton University Press.

Tarrow, Sidney. 1978. "Introduction." In *Territorial Politics in Industrial Nations*, edited by Sidney Tarrow, Peter J. Katzenstein, and Luigi Graziano, pp. 1-27. New York: Praeger.

―――. 1977. *Between Center and Periphery: Grassroots Politicians in Italy and France*. New Haven, Conn.: Yale University Press.

Tocqueville, Alexis de. 1969. *Democracy in America*, trans. by George Lawrence. Garden City, N.Y.: Doubleday.

―――. 1955. *The Old Regime and the French Revolution*, trans. by Stuart Gilbert. Garden City, N.Y.: Doubleday.

Von der Muhll, George. 1977. "Robert A. Dahl and the Study of Contemporary Democracy." *American Political Science Review* 71 (September): 1070-96.

Walton, John. 1966. "Discipline, Method and Community Power: A Note on the Sociology of Knowledge." *American Sociological Review* 31 (October): 684-89.

Weiner, Myron. 1971. "Political Participation: Crisis of the Political Process." In *Crises and Sequences in Political Development*, by Leonard Binder et al., pp. 159-204. Princeton, N.J.: Princeton University Press.

Zeitlin, Irving M. 1971. *Liberty, Equality and Revolution in Alexis de Tocqueville*. Boston: Little, Brown.

3

Italy: The Distributive State and the Consequences of Late Unification

Raphael Zariski

Italy was the first country in Western Europe to adopt a nationwide scheme for regional devolution: The Italian constitution of 1948, providing for self-governing regions, preceded the Spanish and French experiments with regional autonomy by approximately three decades. Then, too, Italy has had a much longer period in which to observe and evaluate the actual operation and consequences of regional devolution. Most of Italy's regions were established by enabling legislation in 1970; a few were set up in the late 1940s; all were created before their Spanish and French counterparts.[1] Finally, regional devolution in Italy has had to overcome particularly formidable obstacles; for the long delay in the process of national unification created a strong distrust of the centrifugal tendencies that regional autonomy was perceived to embody. For these reasons, the Italian case is of particular interest to those who wish to examine regional devolution as a possible solution to the centralization-decentralization controversy.

---

[1] To be sure, Catalonia and the Basque country enjoyed a short-lived autonomy under the Second Spanish Republic (1931-1939).

HISTORICAL BACKGROUND: THE RISORGIMENTO AND ITS AFTERMATH

Italy Before 1789: A Divided Nation in Embryo

By the end of the eighteenth century, the state formation process (discussed in Chapter 1) had made little or no headway in Italy. Part of Italy was under Austrian rule, and the remainder was divided into a number of sovereign principalities. A number of historical reasons were responsible for the inordinate delay in Italy's political unification. First of all, northern Italy was a many-centered region with numerous prosperous commercial cities, none of which was clearly dominant over the rest. Such polycephalous areas are notoriously hard to unify (Rokkan and Urwin 1983, pp. 11, 35-41). Second, the Papal States in central Italy--the temporal domain of the pope--had always viewed any effort to construct a united Italy as a threat to its own interests and to those of the Church as well. A third causal factor was the profound difference between the historical traditions of northern Italy, which had been under Germanic domination, and those of the continental and insular south, which had known Byzantine, Moorish, Norman, and Spanish rule (Zariski 1972, pp. 10-13).

Revolution and Restoration, 1789-1848-- The Rise of Italian Nationalist Tendencies

The French Revolution of 1789 was followed by a series of French invasions of Italy and by a prolonged French occupation of large parts of the Italian peninsula. The two decades of French domination had a profound effect on Italian political development. First of all, the French were able to impose a uniform set of administrative institutions on those parts of Italy they controlled. Second, many traditional local privileges dating back to the feudal period were eliminated, as were any vestiges of local autonomy. And finally, by reshuffling state boundaries with bewildering frequency, the French undermined the legitimacy of the pre-1789 Italian state system and of the ruling dynasties that governed Italy's independent principalities. By creating larger territorial units with centralized institutions and more efficient administrations, the French helped to broaden the vistas of many Italians and thus contributed to the rise of Italian nationalism (Fried 1963, pp. 17, 20; Grew 1978, p. 275; Rotelli 1978, pp. 13-14, 52-53, 56-58, 97-99, 101; Tarrow 1977, pp. 59-60; Zariski 1972, p. 13).

After the defeat of Napoleon, the Congress of Vienna divided Italy into a number of kingdoms and principalities. In all of these territories, the traditional elites of the anciens régimes were returned to power, and many of the reforms introduced by the French were abrogated. However, it proved impossible to turn the clock back completely. Most of the Italian states decided to retain the Napoleonic model of local administration, characterized by the abolition of special local privileges based on custom and usage and by the imposition of a highly centralized system of decision making (Fried 1963, pp. 61-65; Rotelli 1978, p. 87; Sabetti 1982, pp. 68-69; Zariski 1972, p. 13). During the years of the Restoration after 1815, a number of Italian advocates of a unified Italy began to debate the form such a political entity should assume. These included Giuseppe Mazzini, who favored a unitary republic with a strong central government; Vincenzo Gioberti, who proposed a loose confederation of Italian states presided over by the pope; Cesare Balbo, who argued for a secularized confederation and customs union; and Carlo Cattaneo, who called for a truly federal system based partly on the American and Swiss models and partly on the Lombard experience with local and regional self-government (Sabetti 1982, pp. 70-74).

The Risorgimento, 1848-1870--The Building
of the Italian State and the Suppression
of Regionalist Aspirations

The period 1789-1848 had witnessed the germination and dissemination of Italian nationalist ideas among the educated classes. The years of 1848-1870 were marked by struggle and upheaval, culminating in the seizure of Rome by Italian troops in 1870. Unification had to be achieved largely through military conquest, although skilled diplomacy also played a role. Moreover, given the polycephalous character of the northern and central Italian heartland, the process of unification had to be spearheaded by a virtual outside power: Piedmont, the Italian equivalent of Prussia, on the northwest fringe of Italy. Finally, the Risorgimento (the movement of resurgence that animated the unification process) had its principal base of support in the urban areas and was actually opposed by most of the clergy, a large segment of the peasantry, and a sizable proportion of the landed aristocracy (Zariski 1972, pp. 16-18).

It should be noted that the ultimate outcome of the Risorgimento reflected the interests of Piedmont and the conservative ideas of the Piedmontese Prime Minister Camillo Benso di Cavour, rather than the theories of Mazzini, Gioberti, Balbo, or Cattaneo. Rather than a democratic republic, a Catholic confederacy, or a federal state, Italy was to become a highly centralized constitutional monarchy with a very restricted suffrage.

Moreover, the system of local government adopted by the newly formed Kingdom of Italy was to reflect the power realities of that revolution from above which Piedmont had engineered. A modified version of the Piedmontese system of local government--a system that had, in turn, been influenced by the French prefectoral model--was adopted by decree-law in 1859 and extended first to Lombardy and then to other territories annexed by the expanding Piedmontese state. To be sure, the Piedmontese prefectoral system provided for somewhat more local autonomy than the Napoleonic model; for example, local and provincial councils were to be elected by local taxpayers. However, most of the annexed regions found the new system more centralized than the institutions to which they had been accustomed (Fried 1963, pp. 64-72; Rotelli 1978, pp. 78-83, 86). In 1865, the Italian parliament passed the Provincial and Communal Act, which superseded the interim measures cited above and established a highly centralized unitary structure of government for the Italian state. It was clear, by this time, that the federalist recommendations of men like Cattaneo had been rejected in favor of a centralizing course.

The reasons for the triumph of the centralized unitary formula, and for the rejection of even a relatively modest variety of regional decentralization, have been widely discussed. First of all, the mutual distrust and antagonism that divided the rulers of the various Italian states during the early years of the Risorgimento seemed to rule out a federal bargain. Second, many feared that a decentralized system would breed separatist tendencies and invite foreign intervention into the affairs of the newly unified state (Sabetti 1982, pp. 74-75; Zariski 1983, pp. 7-8, 12-13).

Italy / 95

There were also some powerful domestic motivations. The backwardness of the south and the hostility of the clergy and the peasantry at the grass roots aroused the suspicion that decentralization might lead either to a complete breakdown of law and order or to a reactionary legitimist revival, either of which would threaten the existence of the new state (Fried 1963, pp. 92-93; Zariski 1983, pp. 8, 11-12). Moreover, once unification was achieved, the Piedmontese centralizers found allies all over Italy as landowners came to view a strong central government as the only way to control peasant unrest (Zariski 1983, pp. 8-10). Some scholars have touched on other exploitative rationales: an alliance between northern merchants and bankers and southern bourgeois landowners to repress the peasant masses of the south (Rotelli 1978, pp. 251-57), or a deliberate decision on the part of the Italian ruling classes to foster northern economic growth while temporarily neglecting or exploiting the south (D'Amico 1982, p. 42). Finally, there are some purely political explanations of a pragmatic nature: The party in power generally seems to favor more centralization of authority, whatever its position may have been in the past (D'Amico 1982, p. 40; Rotelli 1978, pp. 258-59).

Some of the motives animating the drive for a centralized unitary state strike a familiar chord in that they recall the rationales for centralization discussed in Chapter 1. The fear that local or regional governments might threaten minority rights applied, in the Italian case, to property-holding minorities. The desire for stability and order, the perceived need to avert secessionist threats, and the concern over the possibility that antisystem forces might use a decentralized system as a means of taking over control of regional strongholds--all of these underlying attitudes are to be found in the literature on the Italian state formation process.

Centralizing Tendencies and Decentralizing
Pressures Under the Constitutional Monarchy,
1871-1922

After 1871, Italy experienced half a century of constitutional monarchy, with an elected parliament, but with a very restricted electorate that did not undergo major expansion until 1913. Some centralizing trends were clearly visible during this half-century of parliamentary rule. The prefect possessed extensive control over the local and provincial governments and was increasingly relied on by the national government to manipulate local and parliamentary elections through patronage and other, less savory techniques (Fried 1963, pp. 122-27, 134, 149-51; Rotelli 1978, pp. 148-50). Moreover, on repeated occasions, the parties or factions in power in Rome would embrace and advocate the cause of centralization as serving their immediate interests (Rotelli 1978, p. 258) and would use the prefects as their agents.

Yet, despite the seeming triumph of centralization, decentralizing forces and tendencies were by no means to be dismissed out of hand. At the end of World War 1, the Popular (Christian Democratic) party of Don Sturzo advocated regional autonomy as part of a program designed to appeal to the Catholic masses, especially in rural areas and small towns (D'Amico 1982, p. 41; Gras and Gras 1982, p. 111). Another decentralizing phenomenon that marked the post-World War 1 period was the emergence of a number of ethnic movements demanding autonomy for their respective regions: the German-speaking Tyrolese in Bolzano Province, the French speakers of Val d'Aosta, and the Sardinian Action party (Gras and Gras 1982, pp. 111-12; Pristinger 1980, pp. 154-55).

Local autonomy and participation in local politics were also enhanced by the massive expansion of suffrage enacted in 1912 and 1919 and by the marked tendency of opposition parties, excluded from power in Rome, to take up the cudgels for greater regional, provincial, and local rights (Rotelli 1967, p. 18).

An unexpected side effect of overcentralization was the transformation of parliament into an arena for bargaining over local interests. Local elites could not take their problems to the prefect; for the Italian prefect, unlike the French, had no control over the field agencies of the central government. So, in order to obtain satisfaction for their socioeconomic demands, local elites formed clientelistic networks centering around their deputy in parliament, who was in effect employed as their ambassador to Rome. By thus invading, penetrating, and pervading the center, the periphery helped to trivialize and overload the national decision-making process (Rotelli 1978, pp. 131, 137; Tarrow 1979, pp. 243-45; Tarrow 1977, pp. 64-65).

All in all, during the period 1870-1922, local autonomy had chalked up some gains, and decentralizing forces had maintained and even at times improved their strength. The cause of regional autonomy, however, had made relatively little real progress.

Centralizing Tendencies Under Fascism, 1922-1943

The Fascist era (1922-1943) was marked by a sharp swing in the direction of centralization. A series of laws culminating in the Provincial and Communal Law of 1934 abolished all elected local and provincial authorities and replaced them with state appointees. The elected mayor was replaced by an appointed podestà advised by an appointed council (consulta) (Fried 1963, pp. 203-11). The position of the prefect in local government was enormously strengthened, although he was checked somewhat by the party bureaucracy and the police agencies (Fried 1963, pp. 205-206, 210-11). It must be borne in mind, however, that Fascist centralization did not represent a sharp break with the liberal past; rather, it simply accentuated the centralizing tendencies already present in the liberal constitutional monarchy of 1871-1922 (Rotelli 1978, pp. 231, 268).

In one respect, the Fascist regime did blaze new trails. It attempted to repress the ethnic minority movements that had begun to raise their voices after World War 1. In both Val d'Aosta and Bolzano Province, the regime embarked on a program of forced Italianization, outlawing the use of French and German, respectively, in the schools, suppressing German schools in Bolzano, and requiring the use of Italian in government offices and public places. In Bolzano, it promoted massive industrialization, designed to attract many Italian migrants and to change the demographic makeup of the province. With these draconian measures, the Fascist regime succeeded only in arousing resentment and eventual resistance. Such resistance became increasingly overt in Val d'Aosta, in the South Tyrol (Bolzano Province), and in Sardinia, where the Sardinian Action party had been alienated by Fascist intolerance and persecution (Gras and Gras 1982, pp. 148-52; Pristinger 1980, pp. 156-58). In a sense, by carrying the centralizing tendencies of the pre-1922 liberal state to ridiculous extremes, fascism prepared the way for the regionalist resurgence that was to manifest itself after the Liberation.

POSTWAR CHANGE AND ADAPTATION

The Establishment of the Italian Republic, 1946-1948

The Revival of Regionalism. During the last two years of World War II, an active Resistance movement had been formed behind the German lines in northern and north-central Italy. The Resistance, governed by a network of local, provincial, and regional Committees of National Liberation (CLNs), had waged active warfare against both the Germans and the Italian Fascists of the northern satellite Italian Social Republic. Operating pretty much on their own, without a great deal of help or guidance from the Italian government in the Allied-occupied center-south, the CLNs acquired a prestigious and patriotic aura that helped to bring about the great revival of regionalist feeling after World War II (Fried 1963, pp. 218-24; Rotelli 1978, p. 261; Rotelli 1967, pp. 15, 17-26, 36-40; Zariski 1972, p. 34). The sense of regional self-sufficiency engendered by the circumstances of wartime decision making helped to account for the insistence of many CLN spokesmen that the CLN structure be retained as the postwar political structure of the Italian state and that CLN-appointed prefects replace the regular career prefects (Fried 1963, pp. 220-24; Rotelli 1978, pp. 261-62).

Other reasons accounting for the new popularity of regionalism may be briefly summarized. First of all, there was a universal reaction against the centralization that had characterized both the Fascist regime and the constitutional monarchy, which had failed to block the advent of fascism to power (Rotelli 1967, p. 15; Zariski 1972, p. 134). Second, regional autonomy was visualized as a means of achieving a complete restructuring of the Italian state (Crisafulli 1982, p. 497). Third, there no longer seemed to be any real danger that the old Italian states of the nineteenth century would be revived (Bartole 1984, pp. 411-12). Fourth, throughout the Resistance period, the most dynamic and progressive parts of the country had been cut off from Rome and had thus been enabled to escape central control--by the Italian government or by the central headquarters of Italian political parties—over local political activities (Rotelli 1967, pp. 20-25). Finally, as noted earlier, there was a solid historical and ideological regionalist tradition on which to build.

The Early Establishment of the "Special Regions." With regard to five special regions along the fringes of Italy—Val d'Aosta on the French frontier, the province of Bolzano on the Austrian border, the territory around Trieste and Gorizia on the disputed border with Yugoslavia, and the islands of Sicily and Sardinia—events dictated particularly speedy action to cope with increasingly critical situations. In Sicily, there was an active separatist movement, led by Finocchiaro Aprile. In Sardinia, the Sardinian Action party also seemed to be emerging as a formidable force (Gras and Gras 1982, pp. 186-88). In Val d'Aosta, French troops had actually entered the French-speaking valley in late April and early May of 1945 and were giving active encouragement to secessionist elements (Rotelli 1978, pp. 292-300). In Bolzano Province, a German-speaking majority was demanding either a substantial measure of autonomy or the right to join Austria. Finally, in the northeast, Trieste and Gorizia Provinces contained Slovenian minorities and were claimed by Yugoslavia (Gras and Gras 1982, pp. 186-88; Rotelli 1967, pp. 74-84). To ward off the very real possibility that these outlying regions might seek to break away, they were accorded the status of "special" regions and were granted regional autonomy long before autonomy was actually extended to the other 15 regions—the so-called "ordinary" regions.

In February 1948, the Constituent Assembly approved four constitutional laws, creating the Special Regions of Val d'Aosta, Trentino-Alto Adige (Bolzano and Trento Provinces), Sicily, and Sardinia. In 1963, after differences with Yugoslavia and among the component provinces had been resolved, the Region of Friuli-Venezia Giulia (Udine, Trieste, Gorizia, and Pordenone Provinces) was proclaimed (Fried 1963, p. 229). Not until 1970 were the ordinary regions established.

The Constitutional Debate over Regionalism—Contending Forces. On June 2, 1946, the Italian people elected a Constituent Assembly to draft a new constitution. Before the election, two Italian government commissions had conducted investigations that cast a good deal of light on the sources of resistance against the establishment of self-governing regions. These hostile elements included many members of the central bureaucracy in Rome and of the staffs of central government field agencies. They also included numerous prefects and provincial officials who feared that the region would actually replace the province. However, all of these groups were internally divided in their attitudes toward regionalism (Rotelli 1967, pp. 195-215).

During the debates in the Constituent Assembly, the various political parties had to stand up and be counted with regard to their attitudes on regional autonomy. The parties of the Right--the moderate Liberals, the Monarchists, and the rather demagogic Uomo Qualunque (Any Man) party-- were the weakest bloc in the Constituent Assembly with about 80 seats. Their position was one of hostility toward regional autonomy and of support for continued centralization. Southern resentment against the regionalist claims of the northern CLNs may have played a role in shaping the stand of the Monarchists and the Uomo Qualunque. As for the majority of the Liberals, they were simply following the traditional centralizing course steered by Cavour and other Liberal politicians in the nineteenth century.

The Christian Democrats and the splinter parties of the Center and moderate Left (the Republican and Action parties) commanded about 280 seats, 207 of which were Christian Democratic. They were all committed to some form of regionalism (Rotelli 1967, pp. 225-42, 261-75, 284-91) In the case of the laic Center and moderate Left (the Republicans, the Action party, and a minority of the Liberal party), this posture was based in part on the ideas of such nineteenth-century federalists as Carlo Cattaneo. As for the Christian Democrats, they were somewhat inspired by the neo-Guelph tradition of Gioberti and by the regionalist stance adopted by the Popular party of Don Sturzo after World War 1. Other Christian Democratic rationales for backing regional autonomy included the desire to protect individual freedom against a central government that seemed to be in imminent danger of coming under leftist control; the hope of promoting greater popular participation in politics; and the natural tendency of Italian opposition parties to support decentralization (Rotelli 1967, pp. 275-84; Bartole 1984, p. 412; Gourevitch 1978, p. 34).

The regionalist Center and Left-Center clearly predominated over the antiregionalist Right and Right-Center. However, they lacked an absolute majority in the Constituent

Assembly, and the Left (the Communists and the Socialists) with about 230 seats held the balance of power. In 1946 and early 1947, the Communists and their allies in the Socialist party were somewhat skeptical as to the desirability of regional autonomy. They believed that they were on the point of taking power in Rome, and they expected to use their control over the central government to renovate the socioeconomic structure of Italy. They also feared that the traditional ruling classes would be able to use self-governing regions as centers of resistance against reform. Consequently, the Communists supported regional autonomy only in the special cases of Sicily and Sardinia. Roughly the same position was taken by the Socialist party, but with many more dissenting voices (Bartole 1984, p. 412; Gourevitch 1978, p. 34; Rotelli 1967, pp. 251-61).

We must stress the fact that all parties, with the exception of the Communists, were somewhat divided on the issue of regionalism. In the Constituent Assembly as a whole, the regionalists were in the majority, but their ranks were divided on questions having to do with the scope of regional power and the degree of regional autonomy (Rotelli 1967, p. 298).

The Communists and Socialists were instrumental in defeating an initial draft of Title V of the constitution--a draft that would have given the regions some exclusive powers and would have thus provided for a virtual federal system (D'Amico 1982, p. 18). They also were able to turn back Christian Democratic requests that the regions be given concurrent powers in such significant areas as industry and commerce (Leonardi, Nanetti, and Putnam 1981, p. 99). With both the moderate Right and the Left hostile, the fate of regional autonomy seemed to be in considerable doubt in the spring of 1947.

The Enactment of Constitutional Provisions for the "Ordinary Regions." What made the advent of autonomous regions finally possible was a sudden reversal of roles resulting from the cabinet crisis of May-June 1947. The upshot of this crisis was the ouster of the Communists and Socialists from the Italian cabinet. In response to their expulsion, the parties of the Left took a fresh, new look at the regional issue and modified their views to fit their new status as opposition parties. They consequently abandoned their coalition with the Right and joined forces with the moderate Left and Center (D'Amico 1982, pp. 18-19;

Rotelli 1967, pp. 323-31). The new coalition approved a new compromise proposal for Title V--a proposal to give the regions a number of concurrent powers, most of them clearly regarded as secondary in nature (e.g., hunting and fishing, local museums and libraries), but some of them (e.g., agriculture and town planning) possessing great potential importance (Leonardi, Nanetti, and Putnam 1981, p. 99). In later years, the leftist commitment to regional autonomy was to grow ever firmer. When the new constitution went into effect on January 1, 1948, having been ratified by the Constituent Assembly, Title V, providing for 14 ordinary regions and five special regions, became part of the law of the land.

Regionalism Delayed, 1948-1970

The Operation of the Special Regions. The special regions possess certain peculiar characteristics of their own and represent a somewhat different type of institutional experiment (Ballero 1983; Barbagallo 1983; Bartole 1983; Corso 1983; Immordino 1982; Onida 1983; Rolla 1982a). First of all, they all have been granted some exclusive powers, whereas the ordinary regions are confined to concurrent powers (Allum 1973, pp. 228-30). Second, their powers are defined, respectively, by special Regional Statutes (constitutions), ratified by the Constituent Assembly or by the Italian parliament (in the case of Friuli-Venezia Giulia) (Balboni and Pastori 1984, p. 668; Fried 1963, p. 229). Third, their powers and privileges appear to be far more extensive than those accorded to the ordinary regions (Allum 1973, p. 229; Aniasi 1982, p. 62; Barbagallo 1983, pp. 53-54, 62-63; Bartole 1983, pp. 1562-63; Corso 1983, p. 1589; Immordino 1982, p. 44). These powers and privileges include the right to introduce bills in the Italian parliament, or to have the president of the regional executive junta sit in on meetings of the Italian cabinet when matters affecting the region are being discussed, or to ask the Italian government to suspend the operation of laws that are clearly damaging to the region's interests (Rolla 1982a, pp. 916-17).

In reality, however, the special regions have not really been able to take advantage of the privileged position they enjoy on paper. The special statutes remain dead letters until appropriate legislation is enacted to transfer powers to the special regions. This principle, proclaimed by the Italian Constitutional Court, has in effect placed the exclusive and concurrent powers of the special regions at the mercy of the Italian government. In the case of most special regions, enacting legislation is proposed by a joint state-regional commission and then issued in the form of a presidential decree-law after ratification by the cabinet. It goes without saying that the cabinet has been very slow to act and that consequently many of the alleged powers of the special regions remain empty statements of principle (Balboni and Pastori 1984, pp. 671-72, 686; D'Amico 1982, p. 15; Onida 1983, pp. 1491, 1501; Rolla 1982a, pp. 906-8; Sorrentino 1984, p. 176).

Other negative factors have also served to restrict the powers of the special regions. As a result of the uncooperative attitude of the Italian government, many of the privileges of the special regions have been devalued, because the central government dragged its feet in extending them to the regions. For example, the Sardinian junta president has only rarely been allowed to attend an Italian cabinet meeting; and Sardinian requests to the Italian government for the suspension of Italian legislation injurious to Sardinian interests have gone unanswered (Ballero 1983, pp. 1640-42). A second restraint on the special regions is represented by their lack of clout, in both a political and an economic sense. As isolated fringe areas, they can command little outside support in trying to capture the attention of the Italian government (D'Amico 1982, p. 14). From an economic point of view, their peripheral location and the increasingly complex and interdependent character of the Italian economy make it virtually impossible for the special regions to exercise exclusive powers over some economic sphere of jurisdiction (Corso 1983, pp. 1592-93).

Today the problem of the special regions is that, in some ways, they exercise less actual power than the ordinary regions. This is because Presidential Decree-Law 616, issued in 1977, made fairly sweeping delegations of power to the ordinary regions, while the special regions were still waiting for a much greater backlog of enactment legislation to be dealt with by the Italian government. Given the requirement of governmental enactment, the special statutes of the special regions constitute a dubious privilege indeed (Aniasi 1982, p. 61; Balboni and Pastori 1984, p. 673; Rolla 1982a, p. 904). On the other hand, the special regions do enjoy some fiscal advantages over the ordinary regions, plus greater financial autonomy and fewer restrictions on the annual growth of regional revenues (Aniasi 1982, pp. 141-42; Buglione 1984, p. 294).

The Delay in Establishing the Ordinary Regions--Underlying Causes and Contending Political Forces. Before the ordinary regions could actually be set up as functioning institutions, it was necessary for parliament to pass the necessary enabling legislation providing for regional elections, the transfer of central functions and personnel to the regions, and the definition of the central-regional relationship (Bartole 1984, p. 412). This requirement proved to be a legal stumbling block, permitting the government and parliament to abort the regions by failing to act. A transitional provision of the constitution had set a one-year deadline for holding regional elections. For a few years after 1948, the deadline was periodically extended by parliament. Later, it was simply ignored (D'Amico 1982, pp. 8-9).

For many years after 1948, a succession of Italian cabinets showed a marked reluctance to push the necessary enabling legislation through parliament. The reasons for this inordinate delay in bringing the ordinary regions into being are not difficult to discern. On April 18, 1948, the Christian Democrats had won an overwhelming victory at the polls and an absolute majority in the Chamber of Deputies. Now firmly ensconced in power, the Christian Democrats began to look more kindly on the idea of a strong central government and to repudiate their earlier commitment to regional and local autonomy. They were also motivated by the fear that regional autonomy would result in the creation of a Communist-dominated Red Belt (Emilia, Tuscany, and Umbria) stretching across north-central Italy and cutting the country in two (Fried 1963, pp. 238-39; Kemeny 1981, pp. 348-50; Leonardi, Nanetti, and Putnam 1981, p. 100; Rotelli 1978, pp. 267-68). In addition to the Christian Democrats, other forces that resisted regional autonomy after 1948 included large segments of the central bureaucracy (Fried 1963, p. 239); southern politicians who feared that regional autonomy would reduce the amount of central government aid available for the depressed areas of the south (Fried 1963, p. 240); and supporters of a tight, cautious fiscal policy, who dreaded the heavy spending that the establishment of regional autonomy might entail (Leonardi, Nanetti, and Putnam 1981, p. 101).

On the other side of the ledger, the Communists and Socialists became converts to the cause of regional autonomy after being ousted from the cabinet in 1947 (Rotelli 1978, p. 263). The long years in opposition made the desirability of alternative power centers appear very enticing for parties that seemed to have no hope of coming to power in Rome.

The Establishment of the Ordinary Regions: A Consequence of the "Opening to the Left." By the early 1960s, a number of major changes in Italian political life had revived the issue of regional autonomy. The Socialist party had drifted away from its close alliance with the Communists and was no longer regarded as a potential threat to the survival of democracy. As a result, the ruling Christian Democratic party had decided to allow the Socialists to enter, or at least support, a Christian Democratic-led coalition cabinet: the so-called "opening to the Left" (Gourevitch 1978, p. 46). One of the principal demands made by the Socialists was that the ordinary regions be installed. In response to this demand, and to the new democratic credentials of the Socialist party, a sizable progressive faction among the Christian Democrats began to take a stand on behalf of regional autonomy (Gourevitch 1978, p. 46).

Thus, by the early 1960s, the cause of regional autonomy was championed by the Communists, the Socialists, some minor parties and factions of the moderate Left and Center, and powerful progressive elements in the Christian Democratic party. Also, some of Italy's most prestigious independent newspapers and some major corporations began to underwrite the drive for regional devolution (D'Amico 1982, pp. 23-24; Rotelli 1981, p. 51). The regionalist position seemed to be gaining ground both numerically and in terms of respectability and efficiency.

A number of motives seemed to underlie this renewed willingness to take the path of decentralization (Bartole 1984, p. 414; Cammelli 1980, p. 167; Caperdoni, Lassini, and Negri 1980, pp. 12-14; D'Amico 1982, p. 22; Gourevitch 1978, p. 47; Leonardi, Nanetti, and Putnam, 1981, p. 102; Putnam, Leonardi, and Nanetti 1982, pp. 1080, 1082; Putnam, Leonardi, and Nanetti 1980, p. 219; Rotelli 1981, pp. 50-51; Tarrow 1979, p. 238). Many hoped that the creation of the autonomous regions would increase citizen participation in public affairs and thus renovate Italian public life.

Others saw regionally administered programs as a way to avoid the inefficiency and bureaucratic delays that seemed to characterize the work of the central government. Still others viewed the regions as a means of relieving the central government from the plethora of pressures to which it was subjected, of providing additional outlets for the rising social tensions of the 1960s and 1970s. These arguments seem to dovetail with the arguments for decentralization discussed in Chapter 1, with one major exception: By the 1960s, there seemed to be little concern with the need to impose restraints on the power of the central government. The idea was to give the regions the power to take action rather than to give them absolute protection against any and all encroachments from the Center.

Some additional considerations were related to economic planning and to party and territorial strategies (Bartole 1984, pp. 413-15; Cammelli 1980, p. 166; Caperdoni, Lassini, and Negri 1980, p. 13; D'Amico 1982, p. 22; Gourevitch 1978, p. 47; Kemeny 1981, pp. 376-78; Leonardi, Nanetti, and Putnam 1981, p. 102; Putnam, Leonardi, and Nanetti 1982, pp. 1080-81; Rotelli 1967, p. 411; Rotelli 1978, p. 270; Tarrow 1979, pp. 236-37, 245). First of all, there was the strongly felt need to obtain information and cooperation from the grass roots in the process of drawing up economic development plans. Second, both the Christian Democrats and the Socialists regarded the regional reform as a way of redeeming the rather disappointing performance of the Left-Center governments that had governed Italy under the auspices of the "opening to the Left." For their part, the Communists saw the regions as a means of contracting new alliances and forming a new majority from which the Communist party would no longer be excluded. Finally, grass-roots territorial interests, especially in the less developed parts of Italy and at the purely local level, supported regional autonomy in the hope that it would make it easier for needy local governments and underdeveloped regions to obtain economic assistance from the central authorities.

By the late 1960s and early 1970s, this cumulation of pressures finally broke the logjam that had so long characterized the status of regional reform. Legislation providing for regional elections was passed in 1968 and 1969, and the ordinary regions finally elected their regional councils on June 7, 1970. The regional councils proceeded to draw up the regional constitutions (Statutes), which were ratified by parliament in 1971. In 1972, with the issuance of a number of decrees turning state functions and personnel over to the ordinary regions, the regions actually began to function, albeit on a very limited basis, pending the passage of more flexible enabling legislation.

THE ORDINARY REGIONS IN OPERATION, 1970-1985

The Structures and Basic Processes of Regional Government

The newly created ordinary regions drew up basic Statutes in 1970, which were ratified in 1971 by the Italian parliament. However, the regions had to act within certain previously defined structural guidelines. The constitution of 1948 and an election law passed in 1968 had prescribed the principal organs of regional government, as well as the rules for the election and composition of the regional councils (legislatures) (Balboni and Pastori 1984, pp. 675-76).

Each region was to have a regional council, an executive junta (cabinet), and a junta president (Balboni and Pastori 1984, p. 678; Evans 1979, p. 219). The regional council was to be elected by popular vote for a term of five years, on the basis of proportional representation from multimember districts. Since the electoral law prescribed that the province was to be the unit of representation in regional elections, this electoral system, with its very large constituencies, tended to favor the existing well-organized, widely based national parties, as opposed to purely local lists or new grass-roots movements (Balboni and Pastori 1984, p. 676; Bartole 1984, p. 419). The regions thus tended to adapt to the party system rather than challenge it.

The constitution also provided for the regional council to elect from its membership an executive junta and a junta president, both of whom were to be responsible to the council. The council could dismiss the junta and its president by a vote of no confidence (Angiolini 1983, pp. 456-59; Balboni and Pastori 1984, p. 678; Bartole 1984, p. 420; Evans 1979, p. 219). What was laid down for the regions, then, was a parliamentary model, not too dissimilar at first glance from the Italian parliamentary system. When scrutinized more closely, however, the regional institutional structure reveals some interesting features that seem to differentiate it from its national counterpart. First of all, the president of the regional junta is both ceremonial chief executive (corresponding to the president of Italy) and head of government (corresponding to the prime minister) (Angiolini 1983, pp. 462-67). He seems to embody both presidential and parliamentary characteristics. Yet despite this remarkable concentration of symbolic and executive functions, he is not allowed to choose the members of his own junta; they are elected by the regional council after negotiations between the parties in the majority coalition (Angiolini 1983, pp. 456-59).

The regional constitutions have designated the junta as a truly collegial body, unlike the Italian cabinet. Most executive decisions would be issued by the junta; and assessors (department heads who, collectively, compose the junta) would be allowed to take official action only for the purpose of carrying out such junta decisions (Angiolini 1983, p. 449). While the junta's control over ministerial action was thus considerably inflated, the regional council was seemingly given a more significant role to play within its limited sphere than was the Italian parliament. The basic Regional Statutes gave each regional council both legislative and rule-making functions, thus appearing to place it at least on a par with the junta, which seemed to be relegated to purely executive duties (Angiolini 1983, pp. 431-33; Balboni and Pastori 1984, pp. 678-79; Bartole 1984, p. 421). Also as noted, the regional council possessed the sole official responsibility for electing the junta and its president; and the president, unlike the Italian prime minister, played no significant role in preparing a list of nominees. Finally, the regional council was relatively protected against dissolution, which could only be invoked by a centrally appointed regional commissioner and then only in the case of a breakdown of the legal or constitutional order of such a magnitude as to pose a threat to national security (Angiolini 1983, pp. 458-59).

Regional Statutes also provided for a somewhat greater measure of participatory democracy than did the Italian constitutional system, although the difference should not be unduly stressed. There were provisions for the initiative and the referendum (both of which exist at the national level as well), and these also included purely consultative referenda having no legal effect (Angiolini 1983, pp. 444-46). More significant were the requirements for public hearings to be held by standing committees of the regional council and by numerous other public decision-making bodies. While Italian parliamentary standing committees at the national level have the power to hold hearings and call for the opinions of interested parties, standing committees of a regional council are required to do so (Angiolini 1983, pp. 481-83).

In practice, regional institutions have not turned out to be so different from the Italian model after all. The seemingly more impressive multipurpose chief executive has been at the mercy of the party and factional struggle in his bailiwick (Nanetti, Leonardi, and Putnam 1987, pp. 103-18). In some regions, where a cohesive majority party has been in power, presidents have enjoyed security of tenure and considerable political clout. (This has held true particularly in the Communist-dominated regions of north-central Italy.) In other regions, presidents have frequently had a relatively brief tenure of office before being compelled to step down.

The collegiality of the junta has been honored in the breach. Instead of taking decisions collectively, it has increasingly delegated responsibility to individual assessors, or simply allowed each assessor to march to his or her own drummer (Cammelli 1980, pp. 179-81; Caperdoni, Lassini, and Negri 1980, pp. 28-29). Also, many regional and state laws have provided for granting extensive powers of administrative initiative directly to assessorates (regional executive departments). As a result, assessors have not confined themselves to carrying out junta directives. Moreover, they have begun to build up external bureaucracies and field offices, to deal directly with the standing committees of the regional council, to consult with ministers in Rome, and even to hold interregional meetings to hammer out common policy positions to be sponsored, in as many regions as possible, by assessorates representing a given functional specialty (Angiolini 1983, pp. 449-50; Balboni and Pastori 1984, pp. 680-82). The demise of collegiality might be attributed once again to the unwieldy coalition politics imposed by the party system and by factional conflict. Some blame might also attach to intervention by the regional council and by the Italian parliament. However, when one observes the inner workings of executive branches all over the world, it would appear that collegiality was always an impossible dream.

The same might be said of the concept that the regional council could play the decisive part in the rule-making function, relegating the junta to purely executive duties. This is not the sort of thing legislatures are equipped to do in modern times, and Italian regional councils proved to be no exceptions to this rule. Once again, it was national and regional legislation that contributed to the inevitable expansion of the junta's power (Angiolini 1983, pp. 434-40). But that power was bound to expand at the expense of the council, just as the junta could hardly be expected to retain the collegiality envisioned by the drafters of the regional Statutes.

Finally, the hopes for participatory democracy have been fulfilled only in part. The legal provisions adopted by most regions to deal with the initiative and the referendum are so weak and so riddled with exceptions as to make those tools of direct democracy very difficult to utilize. The rules for electing representatives to the regional councils favor the national parties with widely distributed voting support (Angiolini 1983, pp. 444-47). There is, on the other hand, a greater tendency for regional public organs to consult members of the public--including not only technical specialists but also representatives of a variety of interest groups, ad hoc associations, and even concerned individual citizens--before reaching a decision. Also, the motives behind the decision are frequently publicized so that the citizens affected by the decision have some idea of the underlying rationale (Angiolini 1983, pp. 481-88). Participatory democracy is, in all likelihood, an unattainable ideal in a complex modern society. It is somewhat easier to approximate at the grass roots, however, and the regional capital is less remote than Rome from the point of view of the average Italian.

Relations with the Center

When examining regional relations with the Center, one must bear in mind that the ordinary regions possess no exclusive powers of their own. Their powers, defined by Article 117 of the Italian constitution, are concurrent, but in a limited sense: They can only complement and integrate the powers exercised by the central government.[2]

---

[2]Good (1978, p. 8) defines complementary legislative power as "the power to legislate in certain policy areas

To be sure, the powers conferred by Article 117 are quite broad in their potential scope. After enumerating a number of areas in which the regions may legislate, the article concludes the list with "(s) other matters eventually decentralized in constitutional laws" (Fried 1963, p. 230).

Unlike the states in a federal system, the regions cannot proceed to exercise their concurrent powers until the national government has first passed the necessary enabling legislation. It was not enough for parliament to ratify the Regional Statutes in 1971. Parliamentary action was needed to authorize the actual transfer of powers to the regions; and no major progress was achieved in this direction until the passage of Law 382 in 1975 (instructing the government to complete the transfer of functions authorized under Article 117 as suitable for performance by the regional governments) and the issuance in 1977 of Presidential Decree-Law 616 (providing for large-scale transfers of functions to the regions) (Capodieci 1983, pp. 18-28).

However, even this legislation fell far short of satisfying regional aspirations. The regions wanted "framework laws" (leggi-cornice) passed, each of which would furnish an overall survey of the distribution of power and responsibility in a given field of public policy like agriculture or public health. Without such laws, regional powers would be subject to perpetual redefinition and constant encroachment at the hands of a great number of uncoordinated central laws and decrees. This has, in fact, turned out to be the case in those areas of public policy in which the Italian parliament has as yet failed to pass the necessary framework laws (Aniasi 1982, pp. 27-30, 38, 55-56; Bartole 1984, pp. 416-17; D'Amico 1982, pp. 12-13; Paladin 1985, pp. 9-10). As of 1984, many of the great reform laws indicated in Decree 616 itself as necessary complements to the process of delegating central functions to the regions had still not been enacted by parliament. Some of the promised framework laws had finally been enacted but with the paradoxical effect of restricting regional freedom of action to a

---

within the confines of principles established either explicitly by national framework laws or implicitly in the existing body of relevant national laws." She defines integrative power as the power "to adapt details of certain national laws to the specific needs and conditions of the regions."

greater degree than the regions had anticipated (Paladin 1985, pp. 9-11).

It is evident that the concurrent powers of the regions are defined, not only by the constitution (Article 117) but also by central government laws and decrees. To be sure, occupancy-of-the-field legislation is also used in federal systems as a means of expanding federal power at the expense of states or provinces in areas of concurrent jurisdiction. The difference lies in the fact that, in a federal system, a state or privincial government may proceed to legislate until the federal government has occupied the field. In Italy, the regions had to wait for the field to be defined, partitioned, and partially allocated by the central government before they could exercise the powers assigned them by Article 117.

Another nonfederal aspect of the Italian system of regional autonomy is the centrally appointed regional commissioner, who is supposed to act as a connecting link between the region and the central government. He is named by the president of Italy on the recommendation of the prime minister and of the minister of the interior. In addition to serving as liaison between the central government and the region, the regional commissioner was supposed to fulfill a number of additional functions. He was expected to supervise and coordinate the activities of the field agencies of the central government and the relationships between central field agencies and regional agencies (Aniasi 1982, pp. 89-90; Grassi 1984, p. 177). He was also to preside over the Regional Control Commission, a body that had the responsibility of checking the legality of regional administrative acts (Grassi 1984, p. 179; Travi 1983, pp. 327-28).

In general, the regional commissioner has failed to live up to his intended role. For one thing, parliament neglected to pass the necessary enabling legislation. Also, the commissioner's administrative functions have been hampered by bureaucratic resistance at both the central and provincial levels; for both the central and the provincial bureaucracies viewed this new official as a potential cat's-paw of the region against the other levels of government (Aniasi 1982, pp. 89-90; Grassi 1984, p. 177; Travi 1983, pp. 335-36). Regardless of where responsibility may lie, the fact remains that the regional commissioner now functions mainly as head of the Regional Control Commission and as an information link with Rome. The tasks of coordinating central field offices and central-regional relations are still not subject to any clear overall direction (Travi 1983, pp. 327-28).

The regional commissioner does have a part to play in the process by which regional legislation is reviewed by the central authorities. If the commissioner believes that a bill passed by a regional council violates the constitution or is not "in the national interest," he may return it to the regional council without his signature. This veto is called a <u>rinvio</u>. If it is overridden by an absolute majority of the regional council and the commissioner still refuses to ratify the bill, the issue is decided by the Constitutional Court, which rules on the bill's constitutionality and conformance with national law, or by the parliament, which decides whether the bill threatens to damage the national interest (Good 1978, p. 11; Grassi 1984, p. 173).

This is the constitutional procedure. In actual practice there have been some changes in this series of steps. First of all, a number of framework laws have yet to be passed; and this legal gap has been filled by an assortment of fragmented, ill-coordinated national laws. This has led to much uncertainty as to the jurisdictional rights of the regions and has greatly multiplied the caseload of the Constitutional Court (Aniasi 1982, pp. 38-39). Second, in the absence of framework laws, the Constitutional Court has decided <u>all</u> cases in which it is alleged that a regional law is endangering the national interest (Aniasi 1982, pp. 38-39, 101). No such cases have been heard by parliament. A number of authorities believe that, by deciding cases in which the national interest is the issue, the Constitutional Court is injecting itself into a basically political question and is encouraging parliament to predefine the national interest and to preempt large areas of the regions' concurrent powers (Pedetta 1982, pp. 78-85, 95-96).

During the early phases of the regional experiment, before the passage of Presidential Decree 616 in 1977, the Constitutional Court tended to rule fairly consistently against the regions in jurisdictional disputes over the legitimacy of regional legislation (Good 1978, p. 15; Kogan 1975, p. 403). This has not necessarily been the product of any commitment to an antiregionalist philosophy. Rather, the Court appears to have assumed a posture of cautious judicial self-restraint, recognizing that central-peripheral relationships are going to be determined mainly by acts of parliament and by bureaucratic practices. With regard to the powers of the regions, it has deferred to the clearly rather restrictive language of the constitution and to legislation passed by parliament. The Court has shown that it is capable of judicial activism, but clearly regards this problem area as an unfavorable battleground (Rolla 1982b, pp. 100-22).

Given the fact that parliament actually has the constitutional authority to define the extent of regional powers, what, then, can the Court do? As one analyst sees it, it can rule on the coherence and rationality of state actions, thus protecting the regions from casual, unmotivated, uncoordinated expropriations of power at the hands of state agencies. It can, in other words, insist that the state legal structure defining regional rights be a rational, orderly structure (Bartole 1984, p. 416).

The Court is beginning to levy precisely this demand on the central government. In a number of recent cases, it has upheld the regional claim at the expense of the central government. Thus, the attitude of the regions toward the Court is changing. In the 1970s, regional officials often preferred to negotiate with the central government in Rome about removing or modifying objectionable provisions in a vetoed bill, rather than face almost certain defeat in the Constitutional Court (Good 1978, pp. 11-12, 15-16). This was the so-called "flight from the Court." In recent years, the regions have displayed a greater willingness to seek Court protection, and the Court--trying to restore a modicum of order in a chaotic field--seems more willing to provide it (Paladin 1985, pp. 14-16).

The relationship between the regions and the Italian parliament is another important aspect of the central-regional linkage. The parliament's failure to complete the enactment of the framework laws and of other major reform measures envisioned in Presidential Decree 616 has served to reduce the effectiveness of regional devolution. Moreover, parliament has been responsible for the passage of a great number of minor pieces of legislation that have invaded and further reduced the areas of jurisdiction allocated to the ordinary regions (Aniasi 1982, p. 10). Individual members of parliament, even leftists and progressive Christian Democrats, have frequently viewed regional officials as dangerous competitors in the struggle to control and manipulate local clienteles. Consequently, they have maneuvered behind the scenes to limit the scope and thrust of regional power, while still paying lip service to the cause of regional autonomy (Putnam, Leonardi, and Nanetti 1982, p. 1094).

Confronting a parliament with so much power to advance or damage their interests, the regions have used a variety of approaches to the problem of influencing the national legislative body. Least successful have been the formal approaches by regional councils acting as units. Regional councils have the right to introduce legislative proposals in the Italian parliament and to transmit resolutions for the purpose of directing parliament's attention to some problem or grievance. The power of legislative initiative has been used sparingly, and very few of the bills introduced have been enacted into law. As for the resolutions, they appear to have had minimal impact (Aniasi 1982, pp. 13, 93-94; Capodieci 1983, pp. 90-96, 101-2; Caretti and Cheli 1983, pp. 29-30; Spaziante 1978, pp. 25-31).

Other, less formal activities have been more successful in gaining allies in parliament. For example, members of regional councils and regional juntas have appeared before parliamentary standing committees and testified with regard to legislation affecting regional interests (Aniasi 1982, pp. 94-95; Capodieci 1983, p. 96; Caretti and Cheli 1983, pp. 31-32). Regional politicians have also acted as lobbyists in Rome, cultivating a network of formal and informal contacts among legislators and among the subcommittees and working parties that handle the less publicized work of the standing committees (Aniasi 1982, pp. 94-95; Capodieci 1983, pp. 95-96; Caretti and Cheli 1983, pp. 31-32; Spaziante 1978, pp. 53-56). Finally, the recently formed Conference of Junta Presidents has held joint meetings with some key parliamentary committees, such as the Committee on Regional Issues, the Committees on Constitutional Affairs, and the Finance Committees (Rendina 1982, pp. 96-97).

Parliament itself has developed certain mechanisms for taking regional interests into account. The Chamber of Deputies has a Regional Relations Service that acts as a clearinghouse for information, documentation, and research on regional affairs. A joint Parliamentary Committee on Regional Issues, provided for in the text of the constitution of 1948, has been entrusted with a varied assortment of advisory functions over the years. A number of laws contain provisions requiring the cabinet to seek the Committee's advice before introducing bills or issuing decrees in certain specified areas of public policy (Aniasi 1982, pp. 80–81, 96; Capodieci 1983, pp. 60–63, 87–88; Grassi 1984, pp. 173–74).

It is evident from the above discussion that regional influence on parliament is fragmented rather than unified. There is no single dominant channel of access. Some have suggested that the Regional Issues Committee, always sympathetic to regional needs, serves as such a channel, but its status as a joint committee leaves it outside the formal power structure of the two chambers. Another suggestion has been to rely on the Conference of Junta Presidents, but that body's dealings with the Italian executive branch leave little time for other endeavors. An interesting proposal has been to transform the Italian upper house (the Senate) into a regional chamber, an Italian version of the West German Bundesrat. This might entail a sharp turn in the direction of a truly federal system on the West German model. Is Italy prepared or equipped for such a step?

Actually, if the regional approach to parliament flows through a multiplicity of channels, this seems to reflect regional preferences and the reality of the parliamentary power structure. The regions have preferred to do business with parliament through committee testimony and through formal and informal lobbying. This pattern of behavior may simply represent a realistic recognition of the facts that (1) the parliamentary power structure is itself highly fragmented and (2) the real payoff lies with the executive (Spaziante 1978, pp. 6–9). After all, the executive is actually the prime mover affecting central-regional relations and is usually responsible for the delays, omissions, and encroachments that have characterized parliamentary policy toward the regions. If the regions focus their efforts on the national executive, this is simply a realistic response to the configuration of forces in the national government.

The regions have employed several different avenues of access in attempting to influence the policies and programs of the Italian national government. First of all, the presidents of regional juntas have acted as virtual regional ambassadors, cultivating many contacts with cabinet ministers and heads of agencies, as well as with key legislators, and serving as ex officio members of some cabinet committees (Angiolini 1983, p. 467). In 1981, the regional presidents began to hold regular meetings that eventually developed into a permanent Conference of Regional Presidents (Rendina 1982, pp. 95–97). The Conference has held periodic meetings for the purpose of discussing national policies affecting the regions. It has met, not only with standing committees and key legislators, but also with the prime minister and with individual ministers. On October 13, 1983, an executive decree gave institutional status to the State-Region Conference, consisting of the junta presidents, the prime minister, the minister for regional affairs, and any ministers interested in the agenda under discussion (Paladin 1985, p. 24). Thus, the mechanism is now in place for periodic summit meetings between the junta presidents and the Italian government.

Regional representatives serve on approximately 100 state organs at the national level. Some are mixed state-regional bodies; some are interregional (like the Inter-Regional Commission for Agriculture and Food Planning, attached to the Ministry of Agriculture, or the Committee of Representatives of the Southern Regions, attached to the Ministry for the South). One of the most prestigious of these organs is composed of the junta presidents--the Inter-Regional Commission, attached to the Budget and Planning Ministry and consulted by the Inter-Ministerial Committee on Economic Planning (Aniasi 1982, pp. 83-85; Mossetto 1980, pp. 39-40; Rendina 1982, p. 93). The multiplicity of these organs gives the impression that state-regional co-operation is alive and well. However, there is a grave lack of coordination, of central direction. Certainly, the job is not being done, and probably cannot be done, by the Inter-Regional Commission, whose members are very busy and overburdened.

The type of regional influence we have described thus far is often bypassed or undercut by direct agreements between national ministers and regional assessors in a given sector. We have already referred to the independent behavior of regional assessors, who have been seizing the initiative without awaiting guidance from their juntas. This pattern of behavior is only a counterpart of the national pattern. At both the national and regional levels, the functions of planning and of laying down general guidelines are not being handled adequately (Pastori 1980, pp. 214-15). As a result, ministers and assessors are relatively free to plan for their own respective economic or social sectors (Pastori 1980; see also Aniasi 1982, pp. 84-85; D'Amico 1982, pp. 103-4; Rendina 1982, p. 93).

In dealing with the regions and in maintaining surveillance over their activities, the prime minister is aided by a Regional Office and a Department of Regional Affairs. Both are part of the Office of the Prime Minister; the latter is headed by a minister for regional affairs. The Regional Office appears to be more involved with processing the regional bills sent to Rome by the several regional commissioners for approval. This procedure involves consultation with a number of ministries and with the prime minister (Marpillero 1983, pp. 187-97). The minister for regional affairs serves on several interregional commissions at the national level, gathers and disseminates information about regional policies, coordinates state activities affecting the regions, and is generally responsible for state-region relations (Aniasi 1982, pp. 82-83; Marpillero 1983, p. 212). The establishment of the State-Region Conference as an integral part of the Office of the Prime Minister further complicates the picture. There should be a great deal of interagency jockeying for position to determine who is really to have the deciding voice in regional policy in the years to come. For now, there are three contenders for the prime minister's support.

From our account of central-regional relations, it would appear that defending the regions against central government invasions of their rights is something of a lost cause. A growing number of Italian observers are becoming aware of this fact, and are more concerned with ensuring that the regions have a chance to share in the exercise of power. These analysts regard cooperative management and concertation of effort to be far more important—and attainable—than guaranteed rights (Aniasi 1982, pp. 85-89; Baldassarre 1983, pp. 44-45). The concept of cooperative federalism seems to be gaining a growing measure of acceptance from Italian regionalists.

However, in order for a reginalist version of cooperative federalism to become a reality, the regions need some limited degree of financial autonomy. This is precisely what they seem to lack. Article 119 of the Italian constitution provides that the regions are to have tax revenues sufficient to meet their normal operating needs. However, without the necessary legislative action by parliament, this constitutional provision has remained a statement of principle. By 1979, regional taxes provided only 1.6 percent of regional revenues, and the regional quota derived from state tax revenues was also very low (Aniasi 1982, pp. 18, 133; Brancasi 1984, pp. 148-52; Fraschini 1983a, pp. 951, 953-55, 967).

Approximately ninety-three percent of the financial resources of the ordinary regions are derived from state transfers, whereas only six percent come from regional taxes and regional shares of national revenues (Galeotti 1983, p. 108). Most of the money transferred by the central government to the regions is in the form of conditional grants, earmarked for specific purposes. The regions are thus transformed into virtual disbursing agencies for the Italian state (Aniasi 1982, pp. 18, 133, 141; Brancasi 1984, pp. 157, 163; Fraschini 1983a, pp. 951-53, 992; Galeotti 1983, pp. 106, 108-9). Paladin (1985, p. 12) claims that the regions have discretionary control over less than twenty percent of the money they spend.

The regional dependence on state transfers makes for long bureaucratic delays in obtaining the funds allocated under conditional grants. As a result, the regions have great difficulty in spending appropriated funds, often because those funds have not yet been made available by Rome. The phenomenon of the residui passivi, the billions of lire in unspent appropriations, cannot be attributed entirely, or perhaps even primarily, to regional inefficiency (D'Amico 1982, p. 104; Fraschini 1983a, pp. 952, 994, 996).

Finally, the fact that so often regional assessorates receive funds directly from ministries in Rome contributes to undermining the regional junta's control over regional spending policy and to weakening the principle of collegiality (Aniasi 1982, p. 134). To the extent that functional needs are placed ahead of territorial solidarity, regional autonomy is bound to suffer.

Relations with Local Governments

The establishment of the ordinary regions has had a significant impact on the system of local government. First of all, the centrally appointed prefect, who dominated each province on behalf of the minister of the interior, has been relieved of the responsibility for reviewing the legality and merits of provincial and communal acts. Instead, he has been largely relegated to the role of maintaining public order and enforcing the laws. The function of exercising surveillance over the decisions of provincial and communal governments has been assigned, in each region, to a Regional Control Committee (RCC), with several Provincial Control Committees under its supervision. This body consists of five members: one nominated by the regional commissioner, three "administrative experts" elected by the regional Council, and one judge from the Regional Administrative Tribunal (TAR) (Balboni and Pastori 1984, p. 715; De Siervo 1984, pp. 209-13).

The RCC does not seem to have been a very effective tool for maintaining regional oversight over local and provincial governments. It can rule only on the legality of communal and provincial acts; it can no longer decide the validity of such acts on their "merits" (i.e., on their advisability in terms of broader considerations of national policy). Thus, the RCC is denied precisely that function of general policy guidance that the regions were originally intended to perform (Dente 1985, p. 136; De Siervo 1984, pp. 209, 213). On the other hand, even without the power to decide cases on their "merits," the RCC has a virtually unmanageable caseload and is often compelled to postpone decisions by the expedient of asking local authorities to provide additional evidence (Aniasi 1982, pp. 120-21; De Siervo 1984, p. 216).

A second consequence of regional devolution for local and provincial governments has been an extensive delegation of functions to the local authorities. It was originally anticipated that the regions would act as sources of policy-planning and coordinating, but not administering directly (Barbera and Bassanini 1978, pp. 52-53; Evans 1981, p. 125). Under the terms of Law 382 (1975) and Presidential Decree-Law 616 (1977), numerous central functions were transferred directly to the provinces and communes by the central government (Barbera and Bassanini 1978, passim). After 1977, there was also an increase in the amount of regional delegation of power to local government units (Cammelli 1980, pp. 171-72).

Observers seem to agree, however, that the regions have shown considerable reluctance to delegate power to the local level, and that they have often preferred to set up their own machinery for handling certain functions that are indubitably of an administrative nature. When they have delegated, moreover, they have either shown a distressing propensity for prescribing very detailed procedures for carrying out the delegated tasks or have chosen to delegate merely minor nondiscretionary functions. In short, they have behaved toward the local authorities in much the same way that the central authorities behave toward the regions (D'Amico 1982, p. 102; Merloni 1983, p. 788; Rotelli 1981, pp. 56-57).

The lag in regional delegation is closely linked with a trend toward intraregional centralization. Local authorities are not kept adequately informed about regional decisions affecting their interests, nor do they have adequate input into those decisions. Some regions have held assemblies of local officials to gather advice and dispense information on impending policies. However, these gatherings were too large and formalized, and most local officials lacked the advance knowledge and expertise to challenge or even question the projects presented by regional policy makers. A number of regions have abandoned these exercises in participatory democracy as futile and embarrassing, given the low attendance rate, and now rely on circular letters to keep the provinces and communes informed (Moschini and Salvadorini 1979, pp. 55-57, 61, 63-64).

The reasons underlying regional unwillingness to delegate functions to local authorities show considerable overlap with the motives that animated Italian politicians and bureaucrats who resisted regional devolution. There is the same lack of confidence in the adequacy of the material and human resources at the periphery that centralizers always express when rationalizing their refusal to share power (Aniasi 1982, pp. 124-25; Evans 1981, p. 128). There is the same desire by the party in power not to yield a piece of the action to an opposition party strongly entrenched in the periphery: A Christian Democratic assessor can hardly desire to delegate functions to a Socialist mayor (Rotelli 1981, p. 123). There is the same self-interest of an entrenched bureaucracy that sees delegation of functions to lower levels of government as entailing loss of career opportunities and power bases (Barbera and Bassanini 1978, p. 56). On the other hand, there are motives of a purely regional nature. For example, it has been suggested that the regions have reacted to the growing ties between local governments and the central government by coming to view delegation as an indirect means of helping an antiregion coalition (D'Amico 1982, p. 102). Also, the regions can claim, with some justification, that they cannot delegate on a significant scale until parliament, by passing a new law for the organization of local government, makes it unmistakably clear what local organs are to be the long-term beneficiaries of these delegated powers (Rotelli 1981, pp. 128-29).

The same sense of restraint, engendered by the expectation that the central government must soon occupy the field, has held the regions back from legislating too boldly on questions of local and provincial organization. However, there have been some ventures into institutional repair pending definitive action by the central government—some efforts to "anticipate" central policy, as it were (Cammelli 1980, p. 169; D'Amico 1982, p. 111). They have included policies designed to favor supracommunal structures, both intercommunal associations (ranging from functional consortiums to intercommunal mountain communities) and second-tier units of government, namely, the provinces (Aniasi 1982, pp. 128-29; Merloni 1982, pp. 73-74; Vandelli 1984b, pp. 16-17).

These efforts have also included the apparently short-lived institution of the comprensorio, a territorial unit designed to replace or at least supplement the province. The comprensorio was smaller than the province and its boundaries were delineated with a view to establishing a suitable territorial entity for economic planning purposes (Evans 1979, pp. 227-28; Merloni 1983, p. 789; Rotelli 1981, p. 63). It seemed, however, to differ in size and rationale from region to region; its status vis-à-vis the province was notably ambiguous and only aroused provincial hostility; and some regions (notably Lombardy) have parted company with this seemingly abortive institutional experiment (Aniasi 1982, pp. 128-29; Rotelli 1981, p. 63). The obsession with the comprensorio seems to have distracted many regional leaders from the problem of delegating functions to real rather than hypothetical political organisms (Zariski 1985b, pp. 282-83).

Another regional policy with an indirect but very profound impact on local governments has been the decision to organize regional government along sectoral lines. Each region has set up a number of functional assessorates, corresponding to the ministries in Rome. Each assessorate has its own network of field agencies—local health districts (USLs), traffic districts, agricultural committees, and so on. Each assessorate also decides on the appropriate boundaries for its own field agency districts. In doing so, it apparently takes little account of the boundaries established by other assessorates for their field agency districts and of the wishes of local governments. The result is a jungle of regional field offices, with territorially overlapping jurisdictions, a jungle in which local authorities are hard-put not to lose their bearings (Caperdoni, Lassini, and Negri 1980, pp. 9, 19-20, 26-27, 33-34; Moschin and Salvadorini 1979, pp. 58-59; Pastori 1980, p. 214; Rotelli 1981, pp. 56, 61-62, 78, 87, 124-26). What seems to be at work here is an important underlying attitude in Italian political culture: corporatism, marked in this case by a preference for dealing with organized functional groups rather than territorial entities (Rotelli 1981, p. 32). Also to be stressed is the importance of functional fragmentation in the Italian administrative tradition (D'Amico 1982, p. 102).

The reaction of provincial and local governments to these effects of regional devolution on their spheres of interest has been a growing antiregion resistance movement. This has, in part, been provoked by the centralizing tendencies the regions have displayed. The provinces, in particular, have resented the efforts of some regions to build up the <u>comprensorio</u> as a possible future alternative to the province. Many communes apparently have felt unduly pressured by the regional favoritism shown toward supracommunal bodies and intercommunal associations. The regional policy of "anticipating" national action by experimenting with new subregional governmental units has been viewed with much suspicion (Cammelli 1980, p. 170). Moreover, regional attempts to modernize the relationship between regional and local governments have been stigmatized as unwarranted interference in local affairs (Dente 1985, p. 138). As a result, local officials have frequently sought central government support against alleged regional encroachments (Barbera 1980, p. 192; Fichera 1982, p. 99).

Another factor animating local resistance against the regions has been the entrenched self-interest, combined with municipal pride, of the large and medium-sized cities that do not need an intermediary in dealing with Rome. These larger communes have established networks of influence in the party organizations and in the national government field agencies. They command enough socioeconomic strength and bureaucratic expertise to be able to receive a respectful hearing from national leaders in the capital and from top bureaucrats. Also, they have a great deal of influence in the ANCI (National Association of Italian Communes) (Zariski 1985a, p. 76). Thus, there is no simple center-periphery conflict in Italy. A substantial number (not all, by any means) of Italian communes and provinces appear to regard the regions as representing a serious threat to their autonomy--more serious, for the time being, than the threat posed by Rome. As a result, there are frequently central-local alliances against the regions.

Interaction with Parties and Interest Groups

As we have noted, Italian political parties have tended to approach the regional question in terms of their respective national interests and aspirations. Parties entrenched in positions of national power in Rome have tended to resist regionalist pressures. On the other hand, parties that seemed to face the prospect of permanent exclusion from the cabinet have been fervent advocates of regional rights.

This situation continued to prevail after the regions became an accomplished fact. In 1977, when the Communist party was hoping to gain admittance to a Christian Democratic-led grand coalition cabinet, it agreed to a considerable reduction in the powers and functions to be delegated to the regional governments. However, after 1979, when the "historic compromise" with Christian Democracy had clearly failed to be consummated, and when the Communist party had adopted an unequivocal posture of opposition against the national government, the Communists began to appeal once again for greater local and regional autonomy (Mossetto 1980, p. 36; Tarrow 1979, pp. 254-58).

Since Italian political parties are highly centralized in structure and organization, this tendency to view regional issues from the standpoint of national partisan advantage has had a chilling effect on regional autonomy. The existing national parties were responsible for the regional election law of 1970, which uses the province as the election district and thus reinforces the existing structure of the national parties, which rely heavily on their provincial party organizations. They were also responsible for the party finance law of 1974, which funds regional parties on the basis of their strength in the Italian parliament, thus discriminating against new and strictly regional lists (Pasquino 1983, pp. 805-8). They have also encroached on regional autonomy by intervening in the negotiations for the formation of regional cabinets (juntas) and insisting on a solution worked out by central party headquarters in Rome (Bartole 1984, pp. 424-25; Graziano, Girotti, and Bonet 1984a, pp. 429-41; Putnam, Leonardi, and Nanetti 1982, p. 1092). While there have been some cases of successful regional resistance against this kind of pressure (Graziano, Girotti, and Bonet 1984a, pp. 438-41; Kogan 1975, p. 391), the national will has usually prevailed.

Still, there is some evidence that the regions are not only encountering some measure of success in withstanding the centralizing undertow activated by the Italian party system but are also beginning to have some impact on the parties themselves. The parties have created a network of regional organizations and have endowed those organizations with varying degrees of power and responsibility (Kogan 1975, pp. 397-402; Pasquino 1983, pp. 795-802). Regional legislators have become much less closely linked to local and provincial party organizations and seem to have shifted most of their political contacts from the local to the regional level (Putnam, Leonardi, and Nanetti 1982, pp. 1092-93). Since 1975, the personal qualifications of the candidate have come to be regarded by qualified observers as playing the decisive role in affecting the results of elections to the regional council--a more important role than the national party platform (Putnam, Leonardi, and Nanetti 1982, pp. 1093-94). Moreover, while power is admittedly hard to measure, regional councillors and panels of regional political observers appear to agree that the relative influence of regional political leaders on regional politics has expanded, while that of national and local leaders has diminished (Putnam, Leonardi, and Nanetti 1982, pp. 1088-93).

Thus, the verdict is not yet in with regard to the relationship between the regions and the Italian party system. On the one hand, highly centralized parties are attempting to manipulate regional politics to serve their own nationally defined purposes. The central party organizations also have allies at the local level, in the form of provincial and local public officials and party bureaucrats, who want to preserve their influence on local patronage and on the nomination of candidates for parliament (Dente 1985, pp. 141-42; Rotelli 1981, pp. 32-33). At the same time, the institutionalization of the regions creates a countervailing tendency on behalf of regionally based forces within the parties. As Dente points out (1985, pp. 141-42), the trend is in the direction of strengthening the region as a level of government; and if this trend continues, the regional party organizations should enhance their power, central and local resistance notwithstanding.

The relationship between the regions and Italian pressure groups is much less ambiguous. It is clearly evident that interest groups are paying more and more attention to the decisions of regional policy makers. While it has been pointed out that the regions act primarily as spending and regulatory agencies for national programs, the fact remains that regional authorities have a great deal of money to spend, even if most of it has been transferred to them by the state. Consequently, they must make many choices with regard to the granting of permits and licenses, the allocation of subsidies, and the approval of plans for industrial and commercial construction in urban areas (Kogan 1975, pp. 395-96; Putnam, Leonardi, and Nanetti 1982, pp. 1083-84). It is hardly surprising, therefore, that Italian interest groups have adopted a regional level of organization to supplement the already existing national and provincial levels (Guala 1983, pp. 921-22).

The importance of the regional level varies from group to group and even from region to region. For example, in Lombardy, the regional federation of industrialists is well organized and powerful and negotiates with regional authorities. In Liguria, on the other hand, the regional federation of industrialists is less influential than its provincial counterparts; and in Campania, the regional level is relatively ineffectual and has no institutionalized ties with the government of the region (Guala 1983, pp. 880-85, 891-97).

Thus, the creation of the ordinary regions has not had a uniform impact on the structure and operation of Italian pressure groups. By the same token, the political parties have not all acted simultaneously in adapting their organizational frameworks to the new phenomenon of regional devolution. The fact remains that regional devolution is making its mark on the Italian party and pressure group systems. Not only has intraparty conflict acquired a new dimension, but also the regional governments have displayed clear corporative tendencies, preferring as they do to rely for advice on functional advisory committees dominated by interest group representatives, rather than on consultative bodies representing local governments (Pinna 1982, p. 214). In their dealings with parties and pressure groups alike, the regions seem to be coming into conflict with the interests of provincial and local government and party officials, thus assuming the proverbial guise of the center that encroaches on peripheral rights.

Regional Elites: A Comparison with National Elites

Has the regional experiment given birth to a new type of governing class, less tradition-bound, more vigorous,

more closely attuned to the body politic it is meant to
serve? It is still early in the game to venture upon a
confident evaluation of the composition and caliber of the
regional elites. Some tentative conclusions can be reached,
however, and they indicate a certain degree of forward
progress, whose extent and significance must not be exaggerated.

Apart from becoming more regionally oriented (Putnam,
Leonardi, and Nanetti 1982, pp. 1090-93), members of regional councils as a whole do not seem to differ very significantly from members of parliament in their backgrounds
and career patterns (Pasquino 1983, p. 794). They seem
to reflect the peculiarities of their region of origin, as
one might expect; for example, Lombard regional councillors
tend to be younger and better educated on the average than
those from other regions (Santi 1983, p. 613). One difference between national and regional legislative elites has
been cited by Italian observers: A much smaller percentage of regional legislators possess university degrees as
compared to national legislators (Santi 1983, pp. 549, 619-20).

As a result of the initial system of recruitment (i.e.,
by transfer from the central bureaucracy and its field
agencies) and of the archaic recruitment procedures that
still hold sway in many regions, the regional bureaucracy
appears to have acquired a reputation for some of the same
maladies that afflict its Roman negative role model--inefficiency, low motivation, cumbersome administrative procedures,
and poorly trained personnel (Putnam, Leonardi, and
Nanetti 1982, p. 1097). However, there are some promising
developments in the composition and behavior of the regional bureaucracy. For one thing, the regions are increasingly able to recruit an administrative class that is
largely of intraregional origin, thus alleviating the heavily
traditionalistic and legalistic orientation that upper-level
bureaucrats of southern origin have impressed on the
Roman bureaucracy (Spalla 1983, pp. 715-26). Second, regional bureaucrats are regarded by qualified observers as
being more accessible to the public than are national bureaucrats (Putnam, Leonardi, and Nanetti 1982). And
finally, regional administrators have revealed themselves,
in a series of interviews, to have much more faith in popular control of the government and freedom of expression
than do national administrators (Putnam, Leonardi, and
Nanetti 1982, pp. 1097-1100). In short, the regional bureaucracy

may resemble the Italian national bureaucracy in socioeconomic origins and administrative shortcomings, but is far more modern and democratic in its attitudinal and behavioral patterns.

Economic Planning and the Regions

National economic planning did not become a significant item on the Italian political agenda until the 1960s (Zariski 1972, pp. 260-64). During this same decade, the cause of regional autonomy was revived and found new and potent sources of support. The two sets of goals became part of the reformist program associated with the "opening to the Left." When parliament established the authority and planning machinery for formulating a national economic plan, it also made provision for setting up a Regional Economic Planning Committee in each region. These committees (CRPEs) were to provide the central planning organs with regional projections based on the national economic plan. They proved to be too slow and too politicized to make much of a contribution to the national planning process. They did, however, play a valuable educational role in publicizing regional problems and aspirations. Furthermore, they helped to stimulate debate about regional development, created a sense of administrative and structural commitment to regional planning, and served as forerunners of the political regions (Amati 1981, pp. 70-71; Selan and Donnini 1975, pp. 272-79).

With the establishment of the ordinary regions in 1970, the regions provided for their own planning agencies in place of the CRPEs. It was generally anticipated that the regions would participate in planning at three levels. First of all, they would take an active part in the process of formulating and enacting national economic plans and programs. Second, they would prepare their respective regional development plans. And finally, they would handle the function of coordinating the planning activities and programs of local governments in each region (Simonelli 1981, p. 46). It was also expected by many ardent supporters of local autonomy that the regions would concentrate largely on planning, leaving day-to-day administrative activities to the provinces and communes (Rotelli 1981, p. 118).

Less than a decade after the passage of Decree-Law 616, it is now evident that regional economic planning has failed to live up to the expectations of its supporters. First of all, the state itself has abdicated its assigned function of national economic planning: The political crisis of the 1970s and the unexpected impact of the oil crisis of 1973 combined to induce the national government to abandon the objectives set forth in the First National Economic Plan (Amati 1981, pp. 97-98) and to eschew further efforts in the direction of comprehensive economic planning. Instead of providing the overall guidance of a national economic program, the Italian government has issued a number of sectoral plans dealing with such discrete areas as industrial reconversion, food and agriculture, and the employment of young people. These sectoral plans provide for a variety of time spans and procedures, and lack any kind of reciprocal coordination (Aniasi 1982, pp. 74-76, 97-98). They consequently have a fragmenting and disorganizing effect on regional planning. In addition to its reliance on the sectoral programs, the national government also dominates and disrupts regional planning operations by making the regions the recipients of a great number of conditional grants and by permitting parliament to enact a host of _leggine_ (minor legislation of a strictly distributive pork barrel nature). Both the grants and the _leggine_ serve to impose extra spending on the regions and to channel and limit regional discretion (Barbera 1980, pp. 189-91).

The regions have also been unable to act as effective coordinators of local government plans and operations. In part, they have been hampered by lack of sufficient authority: They are denied the power to discuss local investment plans and are only permitted to exercise control over the actual spending decisions of local governments (Barbera 1980, pp. 191-92). A second explanation for regional failure in the task of coordinating local-level planning has been the tendency for the regions to reenact the administrative sins committed by the central government: They have tended to envelop the communes and provinces in a mesh of restrictive procedures and requirements, while putting off as long as possible the actual delegation of administrative functions to local authorities (Barbera 1979, p. 739). This has helped to build up a third and very formidable barrier to regional coordination of local planning activities: the resistance of the local governments themselves. The provinces and the communes have tended to react against regional attempts to impose guidelines and restrictions on their economic goals. When discouraged or blocked at the regional level, they have frequently bypassed the region and dealt directly with the relevant ministries in Rome, from which grants and credits may be obtained (Barbera 1979; Barbera 1980, pp. 191-92; Paladin 1985, p. 21).

Finally, the regions have not been entirely successful in devising their own regional development plans, and this, too, has contributed to their inability to coordinate local planning. To some degree, as we have noted, regional planning has been hampered by the absence of a comprehensive national plan. We have also noted the fragmenting effects of the national sectoral plans, the conditional grants, and the leggine. Since the regions themselves lacked adequate sources of revenue, these outside forces tended to transform the regions into disbursing agencies, spending national appropriations for national programs in accordance with national priorities (Amati 1981, pp. 115-16; Aniasi 1982, pp. 74-75; Fichera 1982, pp. 95-96; Mossetto 1980, pp. 47-49).

Part of the responsibility for the inadequacy of the regional plans must be laid at the door of the regions themselves. Instead of concentrating their efforts on the functions of overall planning and coordination, the regions soon began to give overriding attention to their administrative chores and equipped themselves with a network of assessorates and other administrative agencies, staffed by a growing bureaucracy (Rotelli 1981, p. 118). The quality and level of commitment of the regional bureaucracies and of the regional political elites varied from region to region. This may help to account for the fact that, by the early 1980s, some regions "had approved programmatic budgets that linked regional outlays to specified regional economic priorities, whereas in Lazio and Puglia the giuntas [juntas] had merely prepared generic statements of intent, without legislative endorsement and without any practical implementation" (Putnam, Leonardi, Nanetti, and Pavoncello 1983, p. 60).

The regions have followed a great variety of approaches to economic planning: "total planning," with a wide range of goals and no clear set of priorities; reliance on econometric models; and politically inspired plans based on consultation with local governments. The plans emerging from the potpourri of approaches have been harshly criticized for lacking any agreed-upon methodology, for neglecting any adequate provision for verification or updating, and for being based on imprecise data (Amati 1981, pp. 119-20; Aniasi 1982, pp. 73-74; Caperdoni, Lassini, and Negri 1980, pp. 173-75; Paladin 1985, p. 20).

In sum, the regional record in economic planning does not seem to have been terribly inspiring. Perhaps, however, too much was expected from the regions in terms of planning performance. How, indeed, could subnational units plan with any degree of realism and assurance in the absence of a national plan and in the midst of an unstable and crisis-ridden world economy?

It was suggested in the first chapter of this book that economic planning has been partly responsible for regional decentralization. It was also noted in this chapter that many Italian advocates of regional devolution relied partly on the argument that the regions would help to improve the process of economic planning and foster economic growth. Yet it must be borne in mind that planning was only one of the motifs in the regionalist appeal. Since Italian regionalism had largely partisan and grassroots support, the technocratic appeal of regional planning could hardly have played a decisive role in putting the regions in the statute book.

The Protection of Ethnic Minorities
in the Regions

Italy has a great variety of regional traditions and regional dialects, but most of these traditions and dialects have not generated demands for state-sponsored bilingualism or threats of possible separatism. The ethnic minority problem has been almost entirely confined to the islands of Sicily and Sardinia, to the partly French-speaking region of Val d'Aosta on the French border, to predominantly German-speaking Bolzano Province on the Austrian border, and to the northeastern frontier region of Friuli-Venezia Giulia, where less than five percent of the population speak Slovenian and close to a majority speak a Friulan dialect.

In most of these regions, the ethnic-linguistic issue has not yet posed overly severe problems for the Italian government. The Sicilian regional council has passed legislation providing that steps be taken to support the study of Sicilian dialect in the public schools (Carrozza 1982, pp. 396-97). In Sardinia, the regional council has recently passed legislation, approved in principle by the Italian parliament, proclaiming eventual bilingualism for Sardinia (Carrozza 1982, p. 396; Ballero 1983, p. 1618; Melis 1979, pp. 425-35). In the case of both Sicily and Sardinia, however, these are only preliminary steps in a long process that will require regional and national approval of procedural legislation and review by the Constitutional Court. In Val d'Aosta, bilingualism is now strictly observed in the schools and in government offices after an initial period of dereliction by the Italian government in failing to pass the necessary enactment legislation, designed to fulfill the promises of 1948 (Gras and Gras 1982, p. 194; Onida 1983, pp. 1496-97, 1517-18, 1544; Stephens 1976, pp. 311-16). As for Friuli-Venezia Giulia, the relatively small Slovenian minority has been able to score some minor gains under the Regional Statute, but the Slovenian language has no official status in provincial or regional governing bodies (Bartole 1983; Carrozza 1984; Gras and Gras 1982, p. 192; Stephens 1976, pp. 536-39).

The principal ethnic bone of contention with which Italian regional devolution has had to cope has involved the dominant German-speaking element in Bolzano Province, which constitutes more than sixty percent of the provincial population (Pristinger 1980, p. 167). When Bolzano was granted autonomy after World War II, it was coupled with the much more populous Italian-speaking province of Trento to form the Region of Trentino-Alto Adige. Thus, the German-speaking majority of Bolzano became the German-speaking minority of Trentino-Alto Adige. Most of the powers devolved by the Italian national government went to the region, not the province.

To be sure, a set of bilingualist policies were adopted: a parallel system of German-speaking schools, legal parification of German and Italian in public offices and official documents, and bilingual recruitment for the public service. However, the Italian government and the government of the region soon proceeded to interpret these policies in a rather restrictive manner in order to protect the privileged position of the Italian minority (Alcock 1970, chs. 6, 7; Stephens 1976, pp. 523-26). The resulting disillusionment of the German-speaking population was manifested, at first, in the form of massive electoral majorities polled by the Südtyroler Volkspartei (SVP), and later in a series of terrorist acts committed by extremist gangs. Eventually, the advent of a Left-Center government in Rome led to the hammering out of an agreement between the Austrian and Italian foreign ministers in 1969 and the passage of a new Autonomy Statute in Rome in 1972 (Alcock 1970, chs. 10-14; Katzenstein 1977, pp. 291-92, 297-323; Pristinger 1980, pp. 162-65; Stephens 1976, pp. 526-29).

Under the terms of the new Statute, Bolzano Province has had its powers greatly extended, especially in cultural matters, so that it is no longer subject to regional domination. A quota system has been introduced for the employment of German speakers in the public service and for the allotment of public housing to German speakers, in proportion to their preponderant share of the provincial population (Carrozza 1982, pp. 397-98, 400-401; Pristinger 1980, p. 165). Moreover, German has been accorded full parity with Italian, and all documents and signs must be in both languages. In fact, German has become the dominant language in Bolzano; and in some sectors of the economy, even Italians feel obliged to express themselves in German (Pristinger 1980, pp. 179-80).

The outcome in Bolzano illustrates the danger posed by both federalism and regional devolution that a given ethnic group, having been granted control over a given region, may proceed to dominate ethnic minorities within that region. There are some faint indications that this may be happening in Bolzano, where the high quotas set aside for German speakers with regard to the allocation of public housing, public employment, and other benefits are apparently tempting some Italians to adhere to the German ethnic group. In 1981, a special ethnic census revealed a ten percent decline in the Italian ethnic group over the decade 1971-1981 and a seven percent increase in the German ethnic group. At least part of this is attributed to the assimilative capacity of a privileged linguistic majority. There is considerable apprehension that the SVP may use the device of the ethnic census to extend the quota system to other social and economic areas, thus creating a society based on communal representation and rigidifying the cleavage that divides the German and Italian communities (Carrozza 1984, pp. 400-403).

What may we conclude about the role of the regions in defending the cultural and economic rights of ethnic minorities? It is evident from our survey that the regional role is a highly restricted one. The Constitutional Court and other review organs have tended to limit the authority of the regions while assigning primary responsibility to the national government. Second, it should be noted that the Italian national government has been slow and grudging in meeting the demands of ethnic minorities. By failing for many years to adopt the necessary legislation to translate into actual performance the promises made by the Regional Statutes, the Italian government has played a very obstructive role. And its insistence on forcing the Bolzano Germans into an Italian-dominated region all but made a mockery of regional devolution. Central government obstructionism could not have been so successful under a truly federal system.

Another point--particularly applicable to Spain but nevertheless germane to the Italian case--is the importance of interregional migration in undermining the positive and conflict-reducing goals of regional devolution. In both Aosta and Bolzano, the immigration of Italian speakers has created a good deal of anxiety among the members of non-Italian ethnic groups, making them feel that their language and culture are in danger of being extinguished (Gras and Gras 1982, pp. 190-91).

Regional Policies, Performance, and Impact:
A Preliminary Balance Sheet

Until the mid-1970s, the regions were hamstrung by lack of authority and paucity of funds. The money they did receive from the state was largely doled out for purely distributive purposes. It was only in the late 1970s that some of the regions began to experiment with reform legislation in such areas as urban planning, environmental protection, and public health. Some of the regional laws adopted during this second phase were to serve as models for subsequent national legislation (Putnam et al. 1983, p. 58; Putnam, Leonardi, and Nanetti 1982, pp. 1082-84). Nevertheless, these reforms did not substantially alter the predominantly distributive bias of regional policy. Most regional legislation continued to consist of diffuse allocations of aid funds in response to local pressures (Cerea and Zorzi 1984, pp. 1138-39; Mossetto 1980, pp. 200, 211).

In other respects, too, regional performance has left a good deal to be desired. Regional administrators have apparently inherited the national bureaucracy's penchant for excessively time-consuming legalistic delays and do not seem to have really come to grips with the problem of expediting their administrative procedures (Putnam, Leonardi, and Nanetti 1982, pp. 1097-98). Regional budgets are often passed well behind schedule, sometimes as much as four to six months. This seems to be particularly true of the southern regions (Putnam, Leonardi, and Nanetti 1980, pp. 225-26). A large percentage of regional appropriations--the <u>residui passivi</u>--remains unspent at the end of each fiscal year because of a variety of factors, involving both regional and national bureaucratic red tape (Putnam, Leonardi, and Nanetti 1980, pp. 224-25; Colombini 1979). Lest one be tempted to lay the blame for this situation on nationally imposed restrictions, it should be pointed out that local administrators have complained that regional governments are much slower in handling the transfer of <u>their own</u> investment funds to local authorities than in acting as middlemen for the transfer of state funds under state guidelines (Dalla Longa 1984, pp. 1377-92). Moreover, this sluggish behavior seems to occur not only in the much-maligned south but in model regions like Lombardy as well.

Regional planning appears to have been more of a symbolic exercise than a serious effort to oversee the economic activities of local governments. One recent study found that some regions (such as the Veneto), when supervising the operations of local governments in a given policy area like pollution, fail to maintain an adequate network of communications channels and of shared responsibilities with the local governments. Administering the program in a centralized fashion, they inevitably incur lengthy delays in obtaining and processing the information they need to perform their supervisory functions (Bissoli and Lewanski 1984, pp. 1759-61). For a number of reasons--lack of leadership by the national government, regional tendencies to concentrate on functional sectors and to get bogged down in day-to-day administration, resistance by local governments--the regions have failed to live up to their anticipated role as planners and overseers for Italian provincial and local governments (Paladin 1985, pp. 19-21).

It would be highly misleading to overlook the fact that the regions vary considerably in their policies and level of performance. A number of southern observers have pointed out significant differences between Northern and Southern regional institutions and administrative practices. A region like Campania has an abnormally high proportion of its laws vetoed by the regional commissioner (often because they are poorly drafted) and distributes large sums of money to local clienteles on the basis of political considerations (Imbriaco 1983, pp. 39-43; Sales 1983, pp. 21-25).

A recent U.S. study develops a number of indicators of regional performance and derives a set of comparative scores for six Italian regions on such measures as budget promptness, spending capacity, the rate at which bills are approved, legislative innovation, reform legislation enacted, and executive stability. Almost invariably, two northern and north-central regions (Lombardy and Emilia-Romagna) rank at the top; two southern regions (Puglia and Basilicata) trail at the rear; and a northeastern and a south-central region (Veneto and Lazio, including the city of Rome) occupy the third and fourth positions (Putnam et al. 1983, pp. 58-62; Putnam, Leonardi, and Nanetti 1980, pp. 225-41). The high-performance regions are characterized by a high level of socioeconomic development, a participant and secular civic culture, and a greater degree of social stability involving the absence of massive demographic change (Putnam et al. 1983, pp. 63-72). Regional performance also seems to vary inversely with such endogenous variables as interparty conflict, intraparty conflict, and intrafactional conflict (Nanetti, Leonardi, and Putnam 1987, pp. 103-18).

How may we judge the impact of the regions on the Italian polity thus far? As we have seen, the regions have had their shortcomings with regard to performance. Above all, they have failed to fulfill the impossible mission of meeting the exaggerated expectations of their supporters. They were expected by some to lay the foundations for the reform of the Italian state; others hoped that the regions would pave the way for a thoroughgoing reform of local government; a third body of advocates viewed them as the fulcrum of the planning process; southern reformers saw the regions as the best hope for overcoming the serious lack of equilibrium between a prosperous North and a backward South; and finally, advocates of participatory democracy hoped that the regions would increase direct popular participation in political decision making. None of these hopes has come to fruition (Paladin 1985, pp. 17-23).

Still, the regions have done much to help preserve Italian democracy and to improve the quality of Italian political life. They have headed off the potential spread and radicalization of autonomist and separatist movements in Sicily, Sardinia, and the frontier zones. They have helped to arouse new energies at the grass roots and to give local elites a less parochial outlook and a greater feeling of political efficacy. And they have placed some restraints on the hegemony of the great urban centers over their surrounding metropolitan areas (Barbera 1979, pp. 727-29).

Their greatest contributions, however, have been their value in bringing government somewhat closer to the people and their very constructive influence on Italian political culture. With regard to popular support, the regions have succeeded in eliciting an increasingly pro-regionalist attitude among the public at large and among members of the "attentive" public, such as labor leaders, journalists, and businessmen (Leonardi, Nanetti, and Putnam 1981, pp. 113-15). As for Italian political culture, recent studies reveal a process of ideological depolarization in Italy. Politicians appear to have become more pragmatic and conciliatory in outlook and behavior. There seems to be less concern with basic structural reforms of a radical nature and more interest in good government and sound administration as desirable goals, per se (Putnam, Leonardi, and Nanetti 1982, pp. 1086-90). If Italian elites and the Italian mass public have come closer to acquiring the set of attitudes commonly ascribed to the civic culture model, the regions may claim part of the credit.

CONCLUSION

In our examination of regional devolution in Italy, we began by tracing the process of national unification. We saw how the difficulties involved in unifying a multi-centered territory required heavy reliance on military conquest. We saw that the supporters of unification had their strongholds in the urban areas of northern Italy and had to overcome resistance on the part of large segments of the clergy and the peasantry, plus at least a sizable minority of the landed aristocracy. The reaction of the centralizers to peripheral resistance was to impose a rigidly centralized unitary system on the newly unified kingdom.

We also followed the resurgence of decentralizing tendencies. These tendencies reached their peak shortly after World War II. They were aided by a strong backlash against the overcentralization of the Italian state (especially under fascism) and against the Fascist attempt to repress ethnic minorities. They were also strengthened by the Resistance experience.

We traced the tortuous process by which regional devolution was enacted as part of the new republican constitution of 1948, and the long delays and frustrations accompanying the actual establishment of the ordinary regions. It was all too evident, during this uncertain pilgrimage, that empirical considerations of partisan advantage had much to do with the attitudes adopted by political parties toward the decentralization of power. Those who held sway in Rome veered toward centralization, whereas the opposition parties would discover or rediscover the virtues of grass-roots autonomy.

When the regions were finally created, it was partly the result of a shift in national party alliances and in partisan and interest group strategies. Also instrumental in hastening this outcome was a rising tide of demands for political, administrative, and socioeconomic change.

We have observed the structural and operational characteristics of the regional governments. It has become evident that regional powers are severely restrained by the central government in a number of ways and that regional influence over the national government is fragmented, often along sectoral lines. Above all, the regions lack even a limited degree of financial autonomy and are therefore incapable of sharing power effectively with the central government (the "cooperative federalism" option), let alone defending their own autonomous sphere of influence. Moreover, functional relationships between regional assessorates and central government ministries have undermined the territorial solidarity of the regions—and of the center, too, for that matter. Thus, while the regions lack a truly autonomous sphere of influence to call their very own, their relationship with the center can hardly be described as a simple case of monolithic central hegemony over a hapless periphery.

In their relations with local authorities, the regions seem to be repeating the same syndrome of somewhat overbearing behavior displayed by the central authorities in Rome. This pattern of behavior has provoked an attitude of local resistance, particularly in the case of large and medium-sized cities, which prefer to do their business directly with Rome. Thus, there are frequent central-local alliances against the regions.

Thus far, the regions have had only a limited impact on the party system and the interest group system, although the effects of regional autonomy are beginning to make themselves felt. The parties are still centralized, but have created a regional level of organization that is gradually expanding its area of power and responsibility within each party. Interest groups, too, have created regional organizations, whose importance varies from region to region. In short, regional devolution is helping to bring about some changes in the Italian party and pressure group systems—changes that could once again jeopardize the interests of provincial and local governments.

Regional bureaucrats are obviously more likely to reflect the characteristics of the region they are helping to govern, whereas employees of national field agencies in that region are usually drawn from all over Italy. Also, they tend to be more accessible to the public and more modern and democratic in their attitudes than was the case with their national counterparts. Thus, the regions seem to be having a democratizing influence on elite behavior in Italy.

As we have seen, the regional record in the field of economic planning has been disappointing. The case for regional devolution must rest—as, indeed, it does—on other, more convincing rationales.

With regard to the protection of ethnic minorities, we have noted that the national government has largely occupied the field: The Italian regions cannot really extend adequate support to minority languages unless the national government agrees. And the national government has been slow and grudging in meeting minority demands. However, the very existence of autonomous regions has made for a new self-assertiveness on the part of ethnic and linguistic minorities. The regional role in this policy area may be described as restricted but significant.

Finally, regional policies have been mainly distributive, and regional administration has been cumbersome and often inefficient. Some regions like Emilia and Lombardy have maintained a much higher level of efficiency and productivity; others, particularly in the south, have lagged behind the pack. The average performance is somewhat disappointing when compared to the rather unrealistic expectations of the late 1960s.

However, the regions have some solid and worthwhile accomplishments to their credit. They have provided a safety valve for autonomist yearnings; they have aroused greater feelings of political efficacy at the grass roots; and they have brought government closer to the people. By virtue of these accomplishments, they have helped to foster a new spirit of pragmatism and compromise among Italian elites and among Italian voters. Italian democracy has not been rendered immaculate, but it has been strongly reenforced.

REFERENCES

Alcock, Antony E. 1970. The History of the South Tyrol Question. London: Michael Joseph.

Allum, P. A. 1973. Italy--Republic Without Government? New York: Norton.

Amati, Aldo Piero. 1981. Programmazione economica nazionale e regionale: Diade o dualismo. Naples: Editoriale Scientifica.

Angiolini, Vittorio. 1983. "Organizzazione di Governo." In La regionalizzazione, edited by ISAP (Istituto per la Scienza dell' Amministrazione Pubblica), vol. 1, pp. 423-531. Milan: Giuffré.

Angiolini, Vittorio, and Silvia Frego. 1984. "La provincia nella legislazione regionale: Le deleghe in Lombardia, Emilia-Romagna, Basilicata." In Le relazioni centro-periferia, edited by ISAP (Istituto per la Scienza dell' Amministrazione Pubblica), vol. 1, pp. 707-77. Milan: Giuffré.

Aniasi, Aldo. 1982. Rapporto 1982 sullo stato delle autonomie del Ministro per gli Affari regionali. Rome: Istituto Poligrafico e Zecca dello Stato.

Balboni, Enzo, and Giorgio Pastori. 1984. "Il governo regionale e locale." In Manuale di diritto pubblico, edited by Giuliano Amato and Augusto Barbera, pp. 661-720. Bologna: Il Mulino.

Baldassarre, Antonio. 1983. "Rapporti tra Regioni e Governo: i dilemmi del regionalismo." Le Regioni XI (January-April): 43-76.

Ballero, Benedetto. 1983. "Sardegna." In La regionalizzazione, edited by ISAP (Istituto per la Scienza dell' Amministrazione Pubblica), vol. II, pp. 1617-59. Milan: Giuffré.

Barbagallo, Renato. 1983. "Le peculiarità dei singoli statuti speciali con particolare riferimento alla tutela delle communità alloglota." Il Comune Democratico XXXVIII (July-August): 47-70.

Barbera, Augusto. 1980. "Regioni e sviluppo economico: La nuova frontiera." Il Mulino XXIX (March-April): 183-203.

_____. 1979. "Le Regioni dieci anni dopo." Democrazia e Diritto XIX (November-December): 725-44.

Barbera, Augusto, and Franco Bassanini. 1978. "Introduzione." In I nuovi poteri delle regioni e degli enti locali, edited by Augusto Barbera and Franco Bassanini, pp. 19-77. Bologna: Il Mulino.

Bartole, Sergio. 1984. "Il caso italiano." Le Regioni XII (May-June): 411-29.

_____. 1983. "Friuli-Venezia Giulia." In La regionalizzazione, edited by ISAP (Istituto per la Scienza dell' Amministrazione Pubblica), vol. II, pp. 1553-88. Milan: Giuffré.

Berti, Giorgio. 1984. "Il 'politico' in periferia." In Le relazioni centro-periferia, edited by ISAP (Istituto per la Scienza dell' Amministrazione Pubblica), vol. II, pp. 2079-2100. Milan: Giuffré.

Bissoli, Luisa, and Rodolfo Lewanski. 1984. "Il controllo dell' inquinamento: L'applicazione della legislazione in Veneto ed Emilia-Romagna." In Le relazioni centro-periferia, edited by ISAP (Istituto per la Scienza dell' Amministrazione Pubblica), vol. II, pp. 1679-774. Milan: Giuffré.

Brancasi, Antonio. 1984. "Finanza e bilancio." In <u>La Regione in Toscana</u>, edited by Paolo Caretti and Roberto Zaccaria, pp. 147-71. Milan: Giuffré.

Buglione, Enrico. 1984. "Entrate regionali." In <u>Annuario 1984 delle autonomie locali</u>, edited by Sabino Cassese, pp. 293-305. Rome: Edizioni delle Autonomie.

Cammelli, Marco. 1984. "Funzioni." In <u>Le relazioni centro-periferia</u>, edited by ISAP (Istituto per la Scienza dell' Amministrazione Pubblica), vol. I, pp. 57-87. Milan: Giuffré.

──────. 1980. "Cent' anni di regionalismo e dieci di regioni." <u>Il Mulino</u> XXIX (March-April): 166-82.

Caperdoni, Enrico, Angelo Lassini, and Giorgio G. Negri. 1980. <u>Governo locale: Quale potere?</u> Milan: Mazzotta.

Capodieci, Francesco. 1983. "Parlamento." In <u>La regionalizzazione</u>, edited by ISAP (Istituto per la Scienza dell' Amministrazione Pubblica), vol. I, pp. 5-131. Milan: Giuffré.

Caretti, Paolo, and Enzo Cheli. 1983. "I rapporti tra Regioni e Parlamento: Esperienza attuale e prospettive." <u>Le Regioni</u> XI (January-April): 24-42.

Carrozza, Paolo. 1984. "Minoranze linguistiche." In <u>Annuario 1984 delle autonomie locali</u>, edited by Sabino Cassese, pp. 396-406. Rome: Edizioni delle Autonomie.

──────. 1982. "Minoranze linguistiche." In <u>Annuario 1982 delle autonomie locali</u>, edited by Sabino Cassese, pp. 391-401. Rome: Edizioni delle Autonomie.

Cassese, Sabino. 1984. "La regionalizzazione economica in Italia: Un sistema alla ricerca di un equilibrio." <u>Le Regioni</u> XII (January-April): 9-17.

Cerea, Gianfranco, and Maria G. Zorzi. 1984. "I trasferimenti regionali agli enti locali: La legislazione di Lombardia, Toscana, Campania, Basilicata." In <u>Le relazioni centro-periferia</u>, edited by ISAP (Istituto per la Scienza dell' Amministrazione Pubblica), vol. II, pp. 1137-239. Milan: Giuffré.

Colombini, Lauro. 1979. Le Regioni non spendono? Indagine comparata su alcuni aspetti della gestione finanziaria delle Regioni a statuto ordinario. Bologna: Il Mulino.

Compagna, Francesco, and Calogero Muscarà. 1980. "Regionalism and Social Change in Italy." In Center and Periphery: Spatial Variation in Politics, edited by Jean Gottmann, pp. 101-9. Beverly Hills, Calif.: Sage.

Corso, Guido. 1983. "Sicilia." In La regionalizzazione, edited by ISAP (Istituto per la Scienza dell' Amministrazione Pubblica), vol. II, pp. 1589-615. Milan: Giuffré.

Crisafulli, Vezio. 1982. "Vicende della 'questione regionale.'" Le Regioni X (July-August): 495-512.

Dalla Longa, Remo. 1984. "I vincoli alle preferenze locali: I piani di investimento delle città lombarde, venete, e emiliano-romagnole." In Le relazioni centro-periferia, edited by ISAP (Istituto per la Scienza dell' Amministrazione Pubblica), vol. II, pp. 1365-437. Milan: Giuffré.

D'Amico, Renato. 1982. Regionalizzazione e sistema amministrativo: Su alcuni problemi del decentramento in Italia. Catania: Cooperativa Universitaria Libraria Catanese.

Dente, Bruno. 1985. "Central-Local Relations in Italy: The Impact of the Legal and Political Structures." In Centre-Periphery Relations in Western Europe, edited by Yves Mény and Vincent Wright, pp. 125-48. London: Allen & Unwin.

———. 1984. "Soggetti e poteri." In Le relazioni centro-periferia, edited by ISAP (Istituto per la Scienza dell' Amministrazione Pubblica), vol. I, pp. 19-45. Milan: Giuffré.

———. 1977. "Il governo locale in Italia." In Il governo locale in Europa, by Renate Mayntz, Laurence James Sharpe, and Bruno Dente, pp. 201-326. Milan: Comunità.

De Siervo, Ugo. 1984. "La Regione e gli enti locali: I controlli." In La Regione in Toscana, edited by Paolo Caretti and Roberto Zaccaria, pp. 209-17. Milan: Giuffré.

Evans, Robert H. 1981. "Local Government Reform in Italy, 1945-1979." In Local Government Reform and Reorganization: An International Perspective, edited by Arthur B. Gunlicks, pp. 112-30. Port Washington, N.Y.: Kennikat.

———. 1979. "Regionalism and the Italian City." In Western European Cities in Crisis, edited by Michael C. Romanos, pp. 215-31. Lexington, Mass.: Lexington Books.

Fichera, Franco. 1982. "Le regioni dalla programmazione ai governi parziali." Democrazia e Diritto XXII (January-February): 93-102.

Fraschini, Angela. 1983a. "Entrate." In La regionalizzazione, edited by ISAP (Istituto per la Scienza dell' Amministrazione Pubblica), vol. 1, pp. 951-82. Milan: Giuffré.

———. 1983b. "La spesa." In La regionalizzazione, edited by ISAP (Istituto per la Scienza dell' Amministrazione Pubblica), vol. 1, pp. 983-1013. Milan: Giuffré.

Fried, Robert C. 1963. The Italian Prefects: A Study in Administrative Politics. New Haven, Conn.: Yale University Press.

Galeotti, Menotti. 1983. "Produttività della spesa pubblica regionale." Il Comune Democratico XXXVIII (July-August): 101-18.

Good, Martha H. 1978. "The Policy-Making Autonomy of the Italian Regions: A Study of Legislation and Central Controls, 1970-1975." Planning and Administration 5 (Spring): 7-19.

Gourevitch, Peter. 1978. "Reforming the Napoleonic State: The Creation of Regional Governments in France and

Italy." In *Territorial Politics in Industrial Nations*, edited by Sidney Tarrow, Peter J. Katzenstein, and Luigi Graziano, pp. 28-63. New York: Praeger.

Gras, Solange, and Christian Gras. 1982. *La révolte des régions d'Europe occidentale de 1916 à nos jours*. Paris: Presses Universitaires de France.

Grassi, Stefano. 1984. "I controlli dello Stato sulla Regione." In *La Regione in Toscana*, edited by Paolo Caretti and Roberto Zaccaria, pp. 173-85. Milan: Giuffré.

Graziano, Luigi, Fiorenzo Girotti, and Luciano Bonet. 1984a. "Coalition Politics at the Regional Level and Center-Periphery Relationships: The Case of Italy." *International Political Science Review* 5 (no. 4): 429-41.

———. 1984b. "I partiti come strutture di controllo: Il processo di formazione delle giunte." In *Le relazioni centro-periferia*, edited by ISAP (Istituto per la Scienza dell' Amministrazione Pubblica), vol. 1, pp. 304-414. Milan: Giuffré.

Grew, Raymond. 1978. "Italy." In *Crises of Development in Europe and the United States*, edited by Raymond Grew, pp. 271-311. Princeton, N.J.: Princeton University Press.

Guala, Chito. 1983. "Gruppi di pressione." In *La regionalizzazione*, edited by ISAP (Istituto per la Scienza dell' Amministrazione Pubblica), vol. 1, pp. 865-949. Milan: Giuffré.

Imbriaco, Nicola. 1983. "Crisi del regionalismo in Campania: Ruolo e caratteri della Regione." *Il Comune Democratico* XXXVIII (March-April): 35-43.

Immordino, Maria. 1982. "Sicilia." *Il Comune Democratico* XXXVII (September-October): 43-57.

Katzenstein, Peter J. 1977. "Ethnic Political Conflict in South Tyrol." In *Ethnic Conflict in the Western World*, edited by Milton J. Esman, pp. 287-323. Ithaca, N.Y.: Cornell University Press.

Kemeny, Pietro. 1981. "La questione delle autonomie negli anni del miracolo economico." In Autonomie e pluralismo nelle posizioni dei partiti e delle parti sociali, edited by Roberto Ruffilli, pp. 343-437. Bologna: Il Mulino.

Kogan, Norman. 1975. "The Impact of the New Italian Regional Governments on the Structure of Power Within the Parties." Comparative Politics 7 (April): 383-406.

Leonardi, Robert, Raffaella Y. Nanetti, and Robert D. Putnam. 1981. "Devolution as a Political Process: The Case of Italy." Publius 11 (Winter): 95-117.

Marpillero, Marco. 1983. "Governo." In La regionalizzazione, edited by ISAP (Istituto per la Scienza dell' Amministrazione Pubblica), vol. 1, pp. 133-219. Milan: Giuffré.

Melis, Guido. 1979. "Dal sardismo al neosardismo. Crisi autonomistica e mitologia locale." Il Mulino XXVIII (May-June): 418-40.

Merlini, Stefano. 1984. "La programmazione." In La Regione in Toscana, edited by Paolo Caretti and Roberto Zaccaria, pp. 123-46. Milan: Giuffré.

Merloni, Francesco. 1983. "La riforma del governo locale e regionale nei paesi mediterranei." Rivista Trimestrale di Diritto Pubblico 3: 769-801.

_____. 1982. "Riforma del governo locale: Perché la Provincia." Il Comune Democratico XXXVII (November-December): 69-89.

Moschini, Renzo, and Giovanni Salvadorini. 1979. La ristrutturazione organizzativa degli enti locali. Rome: Edizioni delle Autonomie.

Mossetto, Gianfranco. 1980. La politica economica delle regioni italiane. Milan: Franco Angeli.

Nanetti, Raffaella Y., Robert Leonardi, and Robert D. Putnam. 1987. "The Management of Regional Policies: Endogenous Explanations of Performance." In Sub-

National Politics in the 1980's: Organization, Reorganization and Economic Development, edited by Louis A. Picard and Raphael Zariski, pp. 103-18. New York: Praeger.

Onida, Valerio. 1984. "Risorse finanziarie." In Le relazioni centro-periferia, edited by ISAP (Istituto per la Scienza dell' Amministrazione Pubblica), vol. 1, pp. 47-56. Milan: Giuffré.

──────. 1983. "Valle d'Aosta." In La regionalizzazione, edited by ISAP (Istituto per la Scienza dell' Amministrazione Pubblica), vol. 11, pp. 1489-552. Milan: Giuffré.

Paladin, Livio. 1985. "Le Regioni oggi." Le Regioni XIII (January-February): 7-28.

Panebianco, Angelo. 1984. "I partiti." In Le relazioni centro-periferia, edited by ISAP (Istituto per la Scienza dell' Amministrazione Pubblica), vol. 1, pp. 109-36. Milan: Giuffré.

Pasquino, Gianfranco. 1983. "Organizzazione dei partiti." In La regionalizzazione, edited by ISAP (Istituto per la Scienza dell' Amministrazione Pubblica), vol. 1, pp. 785-822. Milan: Giuffré.

Pastori, Giorgio. 1980. "Le regioni senza regionalismo." Il Mulino XXIX (March-April): 204-16.

Pedetta, Maurizio. 1982. "Sul rapporto tra interesse nazionale e potestà legislativa delle Regioni." Le Regioni X (January-April): 78-99.

Pinna, Pietro. 1982. "Deleghe." In Annuario 1982 delle autonomie locali, edited by Sabino Cassesse, pp. 209-15. Rome: Edizioni delle Autonomie.

Pototschnig, Umberto. 1983. "La riforma delle autonomie locali nel progetto governativo." Le Regioni XI (January-February): 135-48.

Pristinger, Flavia. 1980. "Ethnic Conflict and Modernization in the South Tyrol." In Nations Without a

State: Ethnic Minorities in Western Europe, edited by Charles R. Foster, pp. 153-88. New York: Praeger.

Putnam, Robert D., Robert Leonardi, and Raffaella Y. Nanetti. 1985. La pianta e le radici: Il radicamento delle Regioni nel sistema politico Italiano. Bologna: Il Mulino.

---. 1982. "L'Istituzionalizzazione delle Regioni in Italia." Le Regioni X (November-December): 1078-107.

---. 1980. "Le regioni 'misurate.'" Il Mulino XXIX (March-April): 217-45.

Putnam, Robert D., Robert Leonardi, Raffaella Y. Nanetti, and Franco Pavoncello. 1983. "Explaining Institutional Success: The Case of Italian Regional Government." The American Political Science Review 77 (March): 55-74.

Rendina, Michele. 1982. "Governo e Regioni: Un unica sede di incontro." Il Comune Democratico XXXVII (May-June): 93-106.

Rokkan, Stein, and Derek W. Urwin. 1983. Economy, Territory, Identity: Politics of West European Peripheries. London: Sage.

Rolla, Giancarlo. 1982a. "Rapporti tra livelli di governo e rilancio dell' autonomia speciale in Sardegna." Le Regioni X (September-October): 901-32.

---. 1982b. "La determinazione delle materie di competenza regionale nella giurisprudenza costituzionale." Le Regioni X (January-April): 100-22.

Romeo, Serenella (ed.). 1975. Gli enti locali nella prospettiva regionale. Milan: Comunità.

Rotelli, Ettore. 1984. "Introduzione." In Le relazioni centro-periferia, edited by ISAP (Istituto per la Scienza dell' Amministrazione Pubblica), vol. 1, pp. ix-lxi. Milan: Giuffré.

―――――. 1981. La non riforma: Le autonomie nell' età dei partiti. Rome: Edizioni Lavoro.

―――――. 1978. L'alternativa delle autonomie: Istituzioni locali e tendenze politiche dell' Italia moderna. Milan: Feltrinelli.

―――――. 1967. L'avvento della regione in Italia. Milan: Giuffré.

Sabetti, Filippo. 1982. "The Making of Italy as an Experiment in Constitutional Choice." Publius 12 (Summer): 65-84.

Sales, Isaia. 1983. "Crisi del regionalismo in Campania: Un approccio critico." Il Comune Democratico XXXVIII (March-April): 21-33.

Santi, Fiorenza Elisa. 1983. "Classe politica." In La regionalizzazione, edited by ISAP (Istituto per la Scienza dell' Amministrazione Pubblica), vol. 1, pp. 533-627. Milan: Giuffré.

Selan, Valerio, and Rosita Donnini. 1975. "Regional Planning in Italy." In Planning, Politics, and Public Policy: The British, French, and Italian Experience, edited by Jack Hayward and Michael Watson, pp. 264-84. London: Cambridge University Press.

Serrani, Donatello (ed). 1972. La via italiana alle regioni. Milan: Comunità.

Simonelli, Claudio. 1981. "La finanza regionale alla scadenza del regime transitorio: Soluzioni per l'emergenza e l'avvio della riforma." Il Comune Democratico XXXVI (October): 41-54.

Sorrentino, Federico. 1984. "Le fonti del diritto." In Manuale di diritto pubblico, edited by Giuliano Amato and Augusto Barbera, pp. 127-220. Bologna: Il Mulino.

Spalla, Flavio. 1983. "Burocrazia." In La regionalizzazione, edited by ISAP (Istituto per la Scienza dell' Amministrazione Pubblica), vol. 1, pp. 705-83. Milan: Giuffré.

Spaziante, Vincenzo. 1978. L'iniziativa legislativa delle regioni. Milan: Giuffré.

Stephens, Meic. 1976. Linguistic Minorities in Western Europe. Llandysul Dyfed, Wales: Gomer Press.

Strassoldo, Raimondo. 1985. "Regionalism and Ethnicity: The Case of Friuli." International Political Science Review 6 (no. 2): 197-215.

Tarrow, Sidney. 1979. "Decentramento incompiuto o centralismo restaurato? L'esperienza regionalistica in Italia e in Francia." Rivista Italiana di Scienza Politica IX (August): 229-61.

———. 1977. Between Center and Periphery: Grassroots Politicians in Italy and France. New Haven, Conn.: Yale University Press.

———. 1974. "Local Constraints on Regional Reform: A Comparison of Italy and France." Comparative Politics 7 (October): 1-36.

Travi, Aldo. 1983. "Amministrazione periferica." In La Regionalizzazione, edited by ISAP (Istituto per la Scienza dell' Amministrazione Pubblica), vol. 1, pp. 293-363. Milan: Giuffré.

Trupia, Piero. 1984. "L'organizzazione imprenditoriale." In Le relazioni centro-periferia, edited by ISAP (Istituto per la Scienza dell' Amministrazione Pubblica) vol. 1, pp. 169-93. Milan: Giuffré.

Vandelli, Luciano. 1984a. "Il controllo sugli enti locali dopo le Regioni: La Lombardia." In Le relazioni centro-periferia, edited by ISAP (Istituto per la Scienza dell' Amministrazione Pubblica), vol. 1, pp. 547-611. Milan: Giuffré.

———. 1984b. "Una provincia oggi: Scopi e contenuti di una indagine." Regione e Governo Locale V (January-April): 9-22.

Various authors. 1975. Dalla parte delle regione: Bilancio di una legislatura. Milan: Comunità.

          . 1973. Le regioni: Politica o amministrazione? Milan: Comunità.

Zariski, Raphael. 1985a. "Approaches to the Problem of Local Autonomy: The Lessons of Italian Regional Devolution." West European Politics 8 (July): 64-81.

          . 1985b. "The Impact of Regional Devolution on Local Autonomy: A New Chapter in Italian Center-Periphery Relations." In New Local Centers in Centralized States, edited by Peter H. Merkl, pp. 262-93. Lanham, Md.: University Press of America.

          . 1983. "The Establishment of the Kingdom of Italy as a Unitary State: A Case Study in Regime Formation." Publius 13 (Fall): 1-19.

          . 1972. Italy: The Politics of Uneven Development. Hinsdale, Ill.: Dryden Press.

4

France: The Bureaucratic State and Political Reforms

Mark O. Rousseau

France has been, and remains, one of the most tightly centralized unitary states in Western Europe. As Suleiman (1974, ch. 1) suggests, there is virtually no activity that the central government does not control or influence directly or indirectly. Historically, France has lagged behind other West European nations in giving local governments the power to make decisions affecting local affairs. As Badie and Birnbaum (1983, ch. 7) write, "The steady increase of centralization was never disputed from the Ancien Régime to the nineteenth century and on down to the present." In France, the central government has taken the lead in both political change and economic development.

The uniquely centralized nature of the French state derives from a particular set of historical traditions (Badie and Birnbaum 1983). Since the Revolution, the central government has been seen as the indispensable arbiter of the general interest (Suleiman 1974, ch. 1). This view holds that only the state can rise above the narrow particular interests of special interest groups. Of all organizations and institutions, only the state is thought to be above selfish interests. Thus, the proper role of the state is to arbitrate conflicts and disagreements between various organizations and groups. This uniquely French view of the state has been both a cause and a consequence of centralized state power in France. The centralizing tradition has meant that solutions to social and economic problems have largely been state imposed. Since the state functions as the referee of the national interest, political parties of both Left and Right believe that reforms should be imposed from above. With few exceptions, both national and local political elites have opposed decentralizing reforms that would alter these historic patterns of central control.

Although a trend toward the centralization and concentration of political power has long existed in France, this development has not occurred without interruption. Like other European nations during the past two centuries, France has experienced both periods of revolution and reaction. These shifts have produced strong parliaments during postrevolutionary periods, as in the Third and Fourth Republics, and strong executives during the reactionary periods, such as the Napoleonic empire, the Second Republic, and more recently the Fifth Republic. Much of the turbulence of French political history reflects the ongoing debate between the partisans of centralism and pluralism, each faction attempting to mold the state into its idealized model.

Centralization produces a concentration of decision making at the highest levels of the national state, even over matters of largely local import. Decentralization allows locally elected officials to exercise some degree of power over decisions related to local matters. Centralization is a response to the need for national unity, whereas decentralization represents a recognition of local diversity. As France has experienced technological, industrial, demographic, and urban change, varied interest groups have alternately desired local or national solutions to the economic and social problems posed by these changes, depending on the perceived interests of the group.

Centralization has been associated with the rise of the central bureaucracy, government by technocrats, and a more elitist concentration of political power. Decentralization has been associated with a dispersion of decision-making powers, a desire for self-management in political and economic affairs, and the self-determination of various ethnic and occupational communities. Liberal regimes in France have tended to increase local powers; authoritarian regimes have tended to restrict them.

While the centralization and consolidation of authority in Paris has been the dominant political trend, examination of the costs and consequences of centralization has continued to the present time. Political leaders across the spectrum have attacked the central government, but there is little agreement among them on the reforms needed to correct the abuses of centralization. Crozier (1974, 1982), a leading advocate of decentralization, argues that the hierarchical, centralized bureaucracy has stalemated progressive social reform. Decentralizers argue that more active and extensive citizen participation in government and decision making is desirable. Centralizers argue that only the central government can represent the general interest and preserve national unity. In spite of attacks on the central state, the weight of the centralizing tradition, as well as the special interests of those who benefit from it, acts as an ideological brake on decentralization.

Because France has experienced historical shifts and tensions between centralization and decentralization, we believe that pluralist, elitist, and center-periphery perspectives are all useful in interpreting this complex political phenomenon over long periods of time. Taken alone, each perspective is inadequate to encompass the historical shifts from revolution to reaction, from centralization to decentralization. As we have maintained, all three perspectives accept the view that political elites shape the state. Putnam expresses this succinctly when he writes: "Hence, the formulation of society's agenda of unresolved problems is usually a virtual monopoly of the political elite . . ." (1976, p. 90). Since the form of the state reflects the concerns of those who lead it, we must pay particular attention to historical changes in the composition of political elites and their goals. We believe our comparative theoretical perspective, which leads us to view participation in power and decision making as a continuum from more concentrated to less concentrated, best captures the political traditions of France.

We begin this chapter with an examination of France under the monarchy and its desire to unify the emerging nation through centralized administration. During the Revolution of 1789 and its aftermath, we observe how Jacobins and Girondists clashed over their opposing views of the role of the state. Jacobinism triumphed during the Napoleonic empire, which extended and consolidated political authority at the highest levels of the national state. With some significant exceptions, this trend continued during the Third Republic from the late nineteenth into the twentieth century. During the post-World War II period, the Fourth and Fifth Republics responded to increasingly complex social and economic problems by means of solutions tailored and administered by the central government and its administrative bureaucracy. The inability of the state to address adequately unique local problems and grievances led to increasing demands for enhanced regional and local powers. This growing dissatisfaction culminated in the enactment of major decentralizing reforms in 1981. While our analysis of centralization and decentralization is placed in historical perspective, we concentrate on post-World War II changes, particularly the reforms of the past five years. We conclude this chapter with a summary and interpretation of the issues and events we have analyzed.

ANCIEN RÉGIME

From the beginning, the nation-state in France was more tightly centralized under the monarchy than in other European nations. As the monarchs of the ancien régime extended their reign geographically, they attempted to centralize it politically, making Paris the seat of political power (Tocqueville 1969, 1955; Dayries and Dayries 1982). Although the monarchs concentrated rule in Paris, they permitted local variations in legal rights and privileges in order to secure the cooperation of locally and regionally powerful notables. The decisions of local elites were subservient to the intendant, the personal representative of the king in local jurisdictions. Important decisions requiring the advice of the king or his advisers were routinely sent by the intendant to Paris.

Tocqueville (1969), as noted in Chapter 2, distinguished between governmental centralization and administrative centralization. Observing the variations that occurred in local powers and privileges, Tocqueville argued that administrative centralization under the ancient monarchy was not extensively developed. This lack of development represented, not altruism on the part of the monarchy, but a pragmatic adaptation to the limits of national power in the face of influential local elites. Conversely, Tocqueville argued that governmental centralization, the concentration of interests common to all parts of the nation, steadily increased under the ancient monarchs, reaching its zenith under the reign of Louis XIV. Cobban (1963) writes that under Louis XIV Bourbon absolutism reached its apogee. Under Louis, the greater nobility were forced to depart from their local power bases in the provinces and surround the king at Versailles. Louis also extended his reign through his advisers, making Colbert the virtual economic dictator of all France (Chevallier 1982; Cobban 1963). This complex centralized government required considerable economic resources to function, resulting in a high level of taxation. This onerous tax burden and its inequitable imposition later contributed to the Revolution.

The smooth and effective functioning of this highly centralized state was due to the creation of an institution, unfamiliar to the Anglo-Saxon world, built around the work of the intendant. The office of intendant had its origins in the ancient Roman prefect, the personal representative of the emperor in the Roman provinces. In France, intendants chosen by the king served as his personal representatives and chief administrators in each province of the kingdom. Intendants exercised wide police, judicial, and financial functions, as well as extensive control over appointments to royal offices. Under Louis XIV, twenty-five intendants and their corps of assistants extended royal power throughout the kingdom. Intendants largely controlled and coordinated the activities and decisions of local authorities, diminishing, though not totally extinguishing, the discretionary powers of local elites (Bernard 1983).

While consolidation and centralization of state power was the dominant trend in the ancien régime, the monarchy was unsuccessful in totally suppressing the powers of the local nobility. The continued existence of local governance institutions resulted from the monarchy's inability to eliminate them. Local and regional policies not directly hostile to the monarchy or those unamenable to easy change were accommodated and assimilated in the central administrative structure. The monarchy's compromise with regional particularisms meant that such local institutions as courts and customs duties varied from region to region and province to province (Dayries and Dayries 1982). This concession to local institutions created a situation in which provinces and their elites exercised diverse powers and privileges and centralization remained incomplete (La Documentation Française 1982, pp. 12-14).

As Guérard (1969) observes, ancient France was a tangled mass of local privileges. Unable to destroy totally these varying local judicial and administrative privileges, Louis imposed on them the authority of his central agents, the intendants and his personal ministers. The personage of the king was the primary institution uniting the provinces and their varying customs and traditions. On the eve of the Revolution, France remained a strongly centralized state administered and run by the king and his appointees in a political system that of necessity tolerated varying degrees of local powers and privileges. Not until the Revolution were local privileges systematically attacked and successfully destroyed by the central government (Suleiman 1974).

REVOLUTION AND REACTION

The Revolution of 1789 began a cycle of alternating governments in which revolutionary and reactionary regimes successively replaced one another for nearly eighty years. As new political elites succeeded one another in rapid fashion, they attempted to rebuild and restructure the state in a form suitable for carrying out their goals and interests. With few exceptions, however, nearly all of these regimes continued or increased the concentration and centralization of power in Paris. For the revolutionary, centralization was essential to secure the Revolution and extend its principles to all areas of the nation. For the reactionary, centralization was necessary to preserve public order. Tocqueville observed that the revolutionary leaders opposed both the monarchy and the discretionary powers of local elites. He wrote that the Revolution was "both republican and centralizing" (1969, p. 97). Tocqueville believed that the revolutionary leaders went further than their predecessors in maintaining governmental centralization while extending administrative centralization. The centralization of political power in Paris was more conspicuous after the Revolution than before it, Tocqueville argued. Concentrated, centralized political power remained a guiding principle of the Revolution.

The ascendancy of Napoleon Bonaparte to the pinnacle of political power in 1799 signaled a major shift in the course of the Revolution. With Napoleon we see a clear example of the way elites reshape the state in their own interests. Suleiman argues that although the monarchy shaped the contours of the modern French state, the decisive role played by Napoleon cannot be underestimated. He writes: "The structure of the modern French State owes more to Napoleon than to any of his predecessors or successors" (1974, p. 13). Napoleon fashioned an administrative structure for France that has, in the main, lasted to the present time. He oversaw the creation of a centralized bureaucratic state in which decisions made in Paris were executed at the lowest level of local government, the commune (Cobban 1965a).

Under the Napoleonic regime the political power of local governments was vastly reduced. While the revolutionary leaders of 1790 had carved France into 83 departments for administrative purposes, it was Napoleon who made the department the pivotal structure of centralized administration. While departmental councils had been elected prior to Napoleon, this practice now ended. To impose centralized political power from above, Napoleon created the office of prefect. The centrally appointed prefect of each department received orders from Paris and in turn administered the department as if it were a miniature empire. In this way, the department became the key to the French administrative system and the location from which centralized Parisian authority exercised control over local government (Dayries and Dayries 1982). Under this system, no organized institutional means existed by which the unique and particular interests of local communities could be articulated.

While the primary efforts of the Revolution, and especially of its Napoleonic phase, were directed toward the centralization of power in Paris, decentralizing currents were not entirely absent. For a brief time before Napoleon, departmental councils were elected in a manner allowing some expression of local concerns. Two loose political groupings, Jacobins and Girondists, emerged, representing differing philosophies of state organization. The Jacobins initially favored a unitary, centralized state but one in which some decentralized decision making was left to local governments. Girondists, conversely, favored a more decentralized, federal-style form of government (La Documentation Française 1982, p. 15). Conflict between these two factions over the direction of the Revolution reached a peak in 1792 with the invasion of France by foreign armies. The Jacobin deputies prevailed and purged the Girondists from the ranks of the government (Lalumière 1982a, p. 48).

In the face of foreign invasion and internal insurrection, the triumphant Jacobin regime increasingly centralized all political power in Paris. Jacobin centralization thus set the stage for the Napoleonic centralization of state power, a trend that has continued to the present day.

Wahl writes, "The long struggle for democracy in France has, in fact, made Jacobins of everyone: for the left centralization is the condition for equality; for the right it has become the last bulwark against upheaval" (1980, p. xxx).

With the Girondist exception, unitary, centralized power was an ideal that animated the various revolutionary factions. The revolutionaries wished to make the Revolution, to extend liberty, equality, and fraternity to all France. In their view, this required unified political power and the elimination of local elites with their particularistic powers and privileges. The revolutionary governments went considerably farther than the ancient monarchy in the elimination of local and regional institutions. The revolutionaries sought unification, uniformity, abolition of local privilege and diversity, equality, national sovereignty, and a common legislative and administrative structure for all of France (La Documentation Française 1982, p. 12). Guérard (1969) concludes that Napoleon's administrative system, in which centrally directed prefects replaced the former intendants, destroyed all local autonomy. While this system provided for streamlined administration, it was, at the same time, rigid and undemocratic, preventing the growth and development of political institutions that could legitimately express the needs of local constituencies. In spite of its obvious strengths, this administrative structure seemed inflexible in responding to changing political realities and needs. Since governments could be altered only by violence, France for a time experienced a period of political instability in which revolutionary and reactionary governments succeeded one another. The final defeat of Napoleon in 1815 and the restoration of the monarchy was followed by a brief flowering of the Second Republic in 1848, only to be succeeded by Emperor Napoleon III in 1852. Not until 1875 did democratic government seem permanently ensured as peaceful changes at the ballot box began to replace violent overthrow.

THE THIRD REPUBLIC

The Third Republic, which emerged in 1875, following the Franco-Prussian War, brought France its first sustained constitutional democracy. The Republic ushered in a fundamental transformation of French politics in which changes of regime took place at the ballot box rather than at the barricade, and it endured until the Nazi invasion of 1940.

The democratically chosen elites of the Third Republic had different perceptions of the goals and needs of the nation than their predecessors, and attempted to reshape the state in a manner consistent with their democratic ideology. While republicanism had different meanings for different constituencies, certain key themes guided its political aims. Republicans emphasized equality, the defense of the individual, order, unity, and glory (Zeldin 1973).

The republican politicians of the time were also particularly desirous of secularizing the state. The completion of the Revolution required the disestablishment of the Church and the creation of secular public schools and other institutions. While secular education was a key plank of the republican regime, Zeldin (1973) observes that it is difficult to assess its practical consequences. Although the aims of the republican politicians were clearly different from those of their Napoleonic predecessors, Zeldin argues it would be erroneous to accept republican polemical rhetoric at face value. This seems particularly true as we assess the impact of republican legislation on the centralization of the state.

From 1871 to 1940 the relationships of local and regional governments to the national government represented a mixture of centralizing and decentralizing trends. While the dominant trend of the republic was toward the centralization of power, both centralizing and decentralizing tendencies coexisted in an ever-shifting equilibrium, just as they do today (Lalumière 1982b). The legislative record of the republic concerning the balance of power between local governments and the central government can be characterized as one of uncertainty and ambivalence (Virieux 1982). Nonetheless, in spite of this duality, the overall balance of political power drifted toward Paris, resulting in a continuation of the centralizing, Jacobin tendencies characteristic of preceding regimes. Although new legislation granted a modicum of authority to communes and departments, the triumph of republicanism contributed to the strong state tradition.

From the time of the 1789 Revolution, the department and the commune had been the major organizational structures of local government. During the July Monarchy, legislation passed in 1831 and 1833 provided for the popular election of the members of the communal municipal council and departmental general council (Virieux 1982; Dayries and Dayries 1982). The key legislation fixing the relationship of local government to the national state for nearly a century was laid down in the early years of the Third Republic. The law of 1871 provided for the election of a departmental commission exercising some executive powers, although of limited capacity, from among the members of the departmental council. The centrally appointed prefect remained the chief executive of the department. The communes were given greater powers of self-governance than the departments by the law of 1884. This law allowed the municipal council to elect a communal mayor from among its members (Virieux 1982; Dayries and Dayries 1982; Lalumière 1982a).

Although the extent of self-governance given to the commune and department by this legislation may seem minor, it did represent a devolution of decision making to local government, thereby beginning its emancipation from total subservience to the central government. The timid nature of this decentralization, under a liberal republican regime, can be explained in part by the dual role that the commune and department play in the unitary French political structure. As local governments, communes and departments represent the interests of their inherent constituencies; but at the same time these governments act as agents for the downward transmission of decisions made at the central government level. Because of the department's key role in the administrative structure, the centrally appointed prefect remained the chief executive of the department. The commune, a less significant portion of the administrative apparatus, was allowed to elect its own chief executive beginning in 1884.

The legislation of 1871 and 1884 is noteworthy because it represents an attempt of the republican political elite to recognize the legitimate rights of communal and departmental citizens and their local governments. Yet, in spite of this legislation, the centralization of political power at the national level continued during the Third Republic.

The increasing complexity of economic and social life during the nineteenth century presented problems that resulted in new responsibilities and expanded powers for the central government. In addition to dominance in such traditional functions as police powers, military force, and coinage, the central government developed a growing administrative apparatus that increasingly embraced areas of responsibility that had heretofore been the primary prerogative of local government, such as public education, the rights of the working person, public health, the provision of public services (electricity, gas, telecommunications, public transportation), and a host of other services. Thus, while the central government granted some increased political power to local government, this was offset by the vastly increased span of central activity in other areas. Growing social and economic complexity and the imposition of central solutions to the problems posed by this complexity meant that in practice local government exercised little real autonomy (Virieux 1982; Dayries and Dayries 1982). In addition, the Third Republic constitution concentrated power in the National Assembly, and this in itself became a force for an increasingly powerful and expansive central government. As Zeldin suggests, republican politicians "wanted to demolish the state when they were in opposition, but to strengthen it when they became ministers" (1973, p. 606). Thus was centralization maintained.

During this time, the regions in France did not exist as self-governing political entities, but began emerging as important administrative units for the delivery of central government services. The state increasingly deconcentrated its powers by moving into the regions state officials who were allowed some limited decision-making power. These regional officials were agents of the central government, however, and were not elected by or responsible to their local constituencies. The economic policies of the Third Republic were designed to protect the small businessman and the farmer, political allies of the republican politicians, and in this sense might be said to represent some degree of economic decentralization (Suleiman 1978). Following World War 1 the administrative region was increasingly used as an economic unit to carry out the economic policies of the central government (La Documentation Française 1982, p. 14). Likewise, the administrative regions were used in the late 1930s as agents of the war preparedness effort.

In spite of Third Republic political rhetoric emphasizing the rights of the individual, the Republic's record in increasing the participation of local citizens in government is at best mixed. While genuinely important political rights were granted to communal and departmental governments, these were diminished by the vastly increased expansion of the state into domains hitherto the responsibility of local government. The political rights granted to local government during the Third Republic are important because they represent the apogee of decentralization in the nineteenth century and a departure from the trend toward centralization that has continued to the present time. In spite of this, the drift toward political centralization continued during the Third Republic.

THE FOURTH REPUBLIC

The Third Republic collapsed in 1940 with the invasion of the German armies. Following World War II, a nationwide referendum officially put an end to it in 1945. General Charles de Gaulle emerged after the war as the strongman of France and the symbol of French unity. De Gaulle desired a free, united, and independent France (Cobban 1965b). He wished to write a new constitution in which the president would have considerably greater power than had been the case in the Third Republic. However, the French Left, particularly the Communist party, wanted a strong parliament as under the Third Republic. Though the party was unable to seize political power in France, it and other left-wing parties exercised a majority in the Constituent Assembly that met in 1946. This assembly drafted a new constitution for what would become the Fourth Republic, a constitution that made the government a parliamentary and not a presidential one. Seeing in advance that his views were unlikely to prevail, de Gaulle resigned from power before the meeting of the Constituent Assembly.

With minor differences, the constitution of the Fourth Republic closely resembled that of the prior Third Republic. As under the Third Republic, governments in the Fourth Republic changed quite rapidly, a factor contributing to occasional shifts in political and economic policies.

The leaders of the Fourth Republic largely shared the historic Jacobin ideology of central government solutions to social and economic problems. These included problems of employment, production, and inflation, as well as massive shifts in population movements and the increasing division of France into wealthy, urban, industrial regions and poor, rural, agricultural regions. While most political leaders believed the central government must be responsible for solving economic and social problems, they likewise realized that neither the central government nor local communities acting alone could properly address and solve all problems. The leadership increasingly recognized the need for some kind of intermediate, administrative level of government (Dayries and Dayries 1982).

The complexities and problems of successfully administering detailed economic and social planning from the central ministries in Paris became increasingly apparent with the adoption of centralized economic plans beginning with the first Five-Year Plan in 1946. While the need for an intermediate planning and executory body was apparent, considerable debate took place over its desirable form and functions. These debates underscored the two historically opposing points of view over the form of the ideal state, the Jacobin strong central government versus the Girondist pluralist division of powers. The very concept of strong regional government was seen as hostile to republican traditions of national unity and the general interest (Rangeon 1982, p. 66). The political leadership, largely Jacobin in ideology, feared that strong regional governments would lead to the dismantling of the nation, as well as creating an unnecessary additional level of bureaucracy. Thus, the political leaders of the Fourth Republic, while recognizing the need for intermediate regional planning bodies, believed such levels of government should function largely as downward transmitters of policies developed at the central government level. While the decade following World War 11 witnessed the beginnings of regional identities based on locally defined interests and aspirations, often centering around a commonly shared and strongly identified regional or ethnic background, these aspirations did not become translated into political realities at this time (Rangeon 1982; Chevallier 1982).

Succeeding governments of the Fourth Republic came to view the implementation of regional government as a way to rationalize centrally directed economic activity and to smooth the administration of central services. In the eyes of the political elites, the imperatives of industrial development mandated an intermediate level of regional government to adjust the periphery to the economic plans and choices made at the center (Chevallier 1982, pp. 112-14). Thus, the region, conceived as a conduit for the downward transmittal of central economic policies, seemed a desirable solution to the dual need for centralizing economic planning and decentralizing its administration.

The legislative record of the Fourth Republic largely reflects this ideological view of regional government. Steps toward regional government in the postwar years were taken because of the administrative needs of the central government, rather than the aspirations of regional communities. Although several precedents for administrative regions had occurred in the latter part of the Third Republic, the first major legislative initiatives were enacted in the latter years of the Fourth Republic (Dayries and Dayries 1982, pp. 20-24). In 1955, fifteen regional development associations (Sociétés de développement régionals or SDRs) were created by the government to develop a new political-economic initiative that would stimulate regional economic development. More importantly, at the initiative of the General Planning Commissariat, a government decree of 1956 divided France into twenty-two economic programming regions (Dayries and Dayries 1982, p. 27). While these administrative economic regions were created by the state for central planning purposes, local economic and political notables saw them as vehicles for their interests to be heard. Thus, the regional initiatives of the Fourth Republic planted the first tentative seeds of regional identity.

Much of the development of regional government in France is a direct result of a continuing dialectic between the administrative needs of the central government and the growing desire of local communities for a more direct say in their economic and social destinies. We see once again a continuation of the historic Jacobin-Girondist debate over the ideal form and function of the state. This debate, and the dialectic it set in motion, sharpened in succeeding decades.

In the international arena, France made important changes that portended an increasing internationalization of political and economic power and planning. In 1949, France's political and economic ties to the West were solidified with its entry into the North Atlantic Treaty Organization. In 1951, the government joined the European Coal and Steel Community (Cobban 1965b), which preceded the Treaty of Rome that the government ratified in 1957, making it a full member of the European Economic Community. Increasing international economic cooperation encouraged enhanced regional planning, but it also led to the enactment of European and French policies that were often in conflict with the economic aspirations of some regions, as well as of small employers and shopkeepers (Suleiman 1978; Cobban

1965b). Thus, Fourth Republic political and economic policies fueled the debate between the proponents of central direction of the economy and local interests desirous of more autonomy over their political and economic affairs. Although the economic policies begun in the Fourth Republic steered France in the direction of growing prosperity, it was the problems posed by the postwar dissolution of the French colonial empire that led to the decline and collapse of the Republic.

THE FIFTH REPUBLIC: GAULLISM

Although the economic and social policies set in motion during the Fourth Republic experienced some considerable successes, the Republic collapsed over the political crisis caused by the breakup of the colonial empire. The government managed to extricate itself successfully, not without turmoil, from its colonial holdings in southeast Asia, Tunisia, and Morocco, but fell over the issue of Algeria.

Unlike these other territories, Algeria had long been considered an integral part of the French homeland. A large French population in Algeria, the colons, put heavy pressure on the French government to preserve the status of Algeria as a French possession. By 1954, Algerian nationalists had begun a campaign of terrorism against the French military and civilian population in Algeria in an attempt to gain independence. To contain this rebellion, the French government poured considerable troops and material into Algeria so that by 1958 nearly half a million French military personnel were stationed there in an attempt to subdue the rebels. As the campaign of terrorism heightened on both sides, the civilian population in metropolitan France became increasingly disenchanted with the seemingly unending Algerian war. On May 13, 1958, when a new premier, deemed by the French nationalist forces in Algeria to be soft on the colonial issue, was about to take office, the extremists in Algeria rebelled. Under the leadership of French army officers and extremist colons, a mob invaded the French government offices in Algeria. The government in France seemed powerless to put down the revolt, as much of the army leadership in Algeria sided with the rebels (Cobban 1965b).

On May 15, General de Gaulle announced that he was ready to form a government if asked. When the situation rapidly grew more desperate, the president of the Republic asked de Gaulle to accept the premiership and form a new government. The National Assembly accepted the de Gaulle government, allowing the new premier decree powers for a period of six months with the expectation that he would at that time submit a new constitution to the nation for ratification. The new constitution was approved in a nationwide referendum held in September 1958, inaugurating the Fifth Republic. This Gaullist constitution transferred the seat of political authority from the National Assembly to the presidency and provided for a president who exercised great political power (Pickles 1966). From his new position as president and with a large Gaullist majority in the assembly, de Gaulle set about ending the Algerian imbroglio and shaping the future economic and social policies of France (Guérard 1969).

De Gaulle's vision for the future of France assumed a centralized, technocratic state in which social and economic problems were to be solved by plans developed by the central government in Paris. This meant that reforms were to be imposed from above, rather than emerging from the interests and desires of local communities and regions. De Gaulle, and his successor Pompidou, vigorously pursued a policy of appointing civil servants to key ministerial posts in the government (Suleiman 1974, pp. 35, 361). This tendency toward increased political control placed the administration in the service of party politics.

This technocratic, centralist ideology guided the Gaullist approach to regionalism. Local consultation and participation were not to be major components of regional reform (Suleiman 1974). In Gaullist hands, regionalism meant not a decentralization transferring authority and decision making to locally elected governments, but a deconcentration in which locally based central authorities were to be given greater latitude in formulating decisions, rather than routinely waiting for Paris to make them (Suleiman 1974; Safran 1977). As Safran (1977, p. 226) observes, not only did Gaullists on the Right fear powerful regional assemblies potentially controlled by anti-Gaullist politicians, but Communists on the Left also opposed decentralization for ideological reasons. Both Gaullists and Communists feared locally elected regional assemblies could lead to a dismantling and weakening of the unitary state (Berger 1974). With the tacit acquiescence of portions of the political Left, the Gaullists undertook regional reform grounded in an ideology extolling centrally administered solutions to social and economic problems. The Gaullist political elite restructured the French state in a manner congruent with its beliefs.

The increasingly important role of central economic planning created an ever-growing need for an intermediate body capable of integrating centrally developed policies in a way that recognized differences in local needs and problems (Dayries and Dayries 1982). Decree-laws issued in 1959 and 1960 harmonized state administration and service delivery by creating twenty-two regional administrative districts (Conscriptions d'action régionales, or CARs) under the leadership of a coordinating prefect. This preliminary attempt at regionalization resulted in a 1964 decree placing a regional prefect at the head of each administrative district. The regional prefect, in consultation with local officials, initiated and coordinated planning for public expenditures (Dayries and Dayries 1982, pp. 29-33). Powers of the regional prefect were extended by decrees issued in 1968 and 1970 that further deconcentrated authority, giving the prefect wider latitude in making decisions. Under this system the regional prefect emerged as the strongman of the region. The 1964 law also created in each regional administrative district a regional economic development commission (Commission de développement économique régional, or CODER). Composed principally of local political and professional elites, these commissions played a largely consultative role vis-à-vis the regional prefect.

The gradual evolution and development of the region as a unit of governmental administration embodied a politics of regionalization in which decisions about the form and functions of the region were made by the central government in Paris. These early attempts at regional reform were designed to facilitate rational economic planning and the delivery of state services. As the French economy modernized, the Gaullists created a governmental structure designed to adjust the periphery to political and economic decisions made at the center (Chevallier 1982, pp. 112-14).

Here regional devolution rested until the tumultuous years of 1968 and 1969. In May 1968, France was racked by discontent and rebellion. The growing technocratic and centralist character of administration had convinced many French people that they were disenfranchised and powerless. This sense of alienation and powerlessness was dramatically demonstrated by the student and worker revolt that for several days nearly paralyzed France. Economic and public services came to a halt while the government appeared to be on the verge of collapse (Singer 1970; La Documentation Française 1982, pp. 20-22). Once order was restored and the republic saved, it quickly became apparent to the Gaullist leadership that reforms were needed that would speak to the desires of French citizens for greater participation in political and economic life. It seemed as if some upper limit to the acquiescence of the citizenry in state-mandated centralized, technocratic decision making had been reached.

De Gaulle's response to the upheaval was to develop a regional reform package, unveiled to the electorate in 1969. He proclaimed that while centralization had been necessary for many centuries in order to create national unity, this was no longer the case. In the future, regional economic development would be the primary source of France's economic and political strength (Dayries and Dayries 1982, p. 33).

De Gaulle and the party leadership prepared a broad package of regional reforms that encompassed a basic change in orientation toward the region. Under the proposed reform, regions would become governments possessing locally elected officials having decision-making authority, within certain parameters, over the economic and social concerns unique to local residents. While the proposed regions were to be partially self-governing, their freedom of action would be less than had historically been the case for the commune and the department. The projected regions were to become specialized governments (collectivités specialisées) with limited decision-making powers. They would have primary responsibility for economic, social, and cultural development within the region (Dayries and Dayries 1982, p. 34). The unique character of the 1969 regional reform proposal represented a compromise between the Gaullist political elite's concern that powerful, locally elected regional governments might pose a threat to national unity and the growing sentiments of the populace for greater management in their own local affairs.

Article 72 of the Fifth Republic constitution permitted the creation of new levels of local government, but provided that all such governments must be administered by locally elected officials freely chosen in open elections. Since the projected reform proposed the creation of regions governed in part by councils composed of both elected and appointed members, an amendment to the constitution was required to bring the proposal in line with Article 72. For this reason, the Gaullist regional reform proposal had to be submitted to the entire population in a constitutional referendum. The reform proposal was linked with a project to reform the Senate, a proposal that also envisioned creating a Senate of both elected and appointed representatives. In the minds of many voters the regional reform package became linked to and confused with the Senate reform.

On April 27, 1969, a nationwide referendum was held on the proposal to amend the constitution. For the first time since 1958, the Gaullist party suffered a major political setback. The referendum proposal was defeated soundly by fifty-three percent of the voters. Several factors account for this surprising defeat (La Documentation Française 1982, pp. 20-23; Dayries and Dayries 1982; Lalumière 1982a, pp. 48-52). First and foremost, the referendum quickly became a debate on the Gaullist leadership and specifically on whether or not President de Gaulle should remain in office. De Gaulle had threatened resignation if his reform package were defeated. Coming so soon after the May 1968 rebellion, and perceived as a manifest political ploy on the part of the Gaullists to salvage their credibility, the referendum was used by many disenchanted voters to vote no on President de Gaulle's leadership. Thus, the defeat of the referendum reflected displeasure with the Gaullist leadership rather than a lack of desire for regional government. Furthermore, linking the regional and Senate reforms created a complex referendum in which many voters appeared uncertain about the consequences of the proposed changes.

Suleiman (1974, p. 33) argues that the reform proposal was hastily prepared and ill-conceived and arose from clearly political motivations. He suggests that the reform would not have altered the basic nature of the centralized state, but would have complicated the administrative system by introducing a new set of regional institutions lacking real authority. In addition, local elites, particularly elected officials of communal and departmental governments, opposed the creation of yet another layer of government perceived to be a barrier between themselves and the central government and its ministries. Finally, the opposition parties of the Left opposed the referendum not only for obvious political reasons, but also because the Left ideologically believed that local governments should be headed exclusively by publicly elected officials. In addition, many on the Left opposed the powerful role the state-appointed prefect would play as executive officer of the region. For all these reasons, the proposed regional reform of 1969 was soundly defeated.

The defeat of the referendum and the subsequent resignation of de Gaulle as promised created a problem for the Gaullist leadership. The party's political credibility had been damaged by the defeat and the resignation and it lacked any substantive response to the strong desire of the French people for greater participation in government. This state of affairs was addressed by newly ascended President Georges Pompidou in 1972. Pompidou's pragmatic approach to regionalism reflected his own ideological biases (Dayries and Dayries 1982, p. 40). In his view, the region should not infringe on the historic rights of communes and departments but should function simply as a collectivity of departments, permitting them to utilize more effectively the state-aided budget for public works. Pompidou strongly believed regionalism should reflect a deconcentrated level of state decision making and not a transfer of political authority to locally elected regional governments. At the same time, he recognized that economic modernization and industrialization required a new level of administration. For these varied reasons, Pompidou's 1972 regional reform was less ambitious and far-reaching than that presented by de Gaulle in 1969 (La Documentation Française 1982, pp. 42-45).

The reform law enacted by the Pompidou government in 1972 created twenty-two regions in the form of administrative regional bodies (Etablissements publics régionals, or EPRs) rather than territorial units of government, such as the commune and department. This approach had the advantage, from Pompidou's point of view, of creating a regional body that could meet the state's needs for regional administration, seemingly offer the citizenry greater participation in local affairs, and not reduce the historic rights of the communes and departments. Each region comprised a regional council, a regional prefect, and an economic and social advisory committee. The law provided only for the indirect election of the regional council rather than direct election. Thus, the council was composed of elected senators and deputies from within the region, representatives of local government elected by the departmental councils, and members designated by urban municipal councils. The regional councils tended to be made up largely of local notables and national politicians and were, from the beginning, highly politicized. The regional prefect, appointed by the state, acted as chief executive officer of the region, charged primarily with the preparation and expenditure of the portion of the state budget devoted to regional public works. Because of the prefect's control of central government budgets and activities within the region, the regional councils remained relatively powerless, as did the regional economic and social committees, which played a largely passive and advisory role.

The regions created in 1972 served primarily, particularly in their early years, as agencies for the downward transmission of policies and decisions made by the central government. They facilitated the economic and social development of the regions, particularly regional public works. By virtue of the statute governing their creation, the 1972 regions still lacked a popularly elected local body with authority to act in matters of purely local interest. This conception of the region was a direct result of the Gaullists ideological commitment to a Jacobin orientation emphasizing reform from above. The prevailing ideology of the governing elite determined the shape the state and its subdivisions should take.

The 1972 regions lacked any real autonomous authority to manage their own affairs. Indeed, they exercised less authority than would have been granted to them under de Gaulle's 1969 proposal. As administrative regions, they maintained the traditional dependence on the authority exercised by the central government (Dayries and Dayries 1982, pp. 50-63; Chevallier 1982, pp. 125-28). Further, because local politicians had traditionally opposed the creation of powerful subnational levels of government that might intervene between themselves and the central government and since the regional councils were largely composed of local politicians, the region was dependent on both departmental and communal governments as well as the central government (Safran 1977, pp. 226-32). Additionally, the regional councils, lacking indigenous administrative support staff, were forced to depend on the state agencies for day-to-day administration of regional policies. These 1972 regions may be characterized as a deconcentration of power in which state officials located in the regions were given more latitude in decisions concerning regional matters

The 1972 regionalization was not a decentralization of authority allowing regions to elect public bodies with responsibility for local decisions.

Between the Gaullist regionalization of 1972 and the socialist decentralization of 1982, the regions did slowly evolve in a manner that partially increased their autonomy. The political process set in motion by the Gaullist regionalization augmented the ongoing dialectic in which state-created administrative regions led to a gradual awakening of collective identity on the part of citizens residing within the regions. As Rangeon (1982, pp. 65-108) observes, the institutionalization of regions set in motion a dynamic process in which the region as an administrative entity produced a regional identity and collective conscience. The regions began slowly to emerge not only as institutional facts but as communities with a social reality. Many regions, it should be remembered, possessed a historical and cultural reality that dated from the provinces of the ancien régime. Although two centuries of centralization had largely succeeded in suppressing regional particularisms, the regions of 1972 had, as an unforeseen consequence, set in motion a process that was to lead to a stronger sense of regional community.

This process had important political consequences as Mény (1982, pp. 35-48) observes. In spite of the hierarchical, centralized character of the 1972 regional reform, the regions were not without some indigenous sources of political power. Mény argues that although the regional prefect was indeed the strongman of the region, he was far from a centralized despot. Mény speaks of an osmosis between the central government and regional institutions. In practice, the prefect needed the cooperation of local officials and was compelled to take their interests into account in order for his own functions to be smoothly accomplished. This interdependence leads Mény to suggest that the regional deconcentration of 1972, considered in light of the mutual consultation that evolved between the prefect and the regional governments, was a form of political decentralization in fact if not in law. He notes that a complicity in task accomplishment developed between state and local officials due to the reciprocal nature of their needs and responsibilities. As a result of this osmosis, and of the continuing pressure of regional officials for greater responsibility and authority, the regions slowly achieved greater direction in their affairs, even though no major new legislation was enacted until 1982. The increasing importance of the region as an administrative and economic unit and the desire of local officials for greater responsibility led to continued political debate in the 1970s over the desirable direction and nature of regional government.

THE FIFTH REPUBLIC: GISCARDISM

The presidential elections of 1974 opened a new era in the history of the Fifth Republic. For the first time, the government was headed not by a Gaullist but by a moderate centrist, Valéry Giscard d'Estaing. Giscard won the presidency by forming a coalition of centrist parties and running on a platform advocating a diminution of central state power with enhanced authority for local and regional governments (Lancel 1974). Giscard captured the French imagination with his calls for greater citizen participation in the management of civic affairs, particularly at the local level. During his election campaign and early years in office, Giscard's public rhetoric emphasized the necessity of pluralist structures of power for the evolution of French democracy (Giscard d'Estaing 1976). Giscard advocated pluralism in both state and private sectors and asserted that democratic pluralism requires the separation of political and economic power. This conceptualization was consistent with his attempt to stake out a position in the center of the political spectrum between collectivists on the Left and technocrats on the Right.

In spite of his initial public rhetoric, Giscard rather quickly moved from a pluralist, proregional perspective to a more elitist, centralist ideology emphasizing the supremacy of the central government's power (Dayries and Dayries 1982). In a speech at Dijon in 1975, he argued that the commune and department must remain as the basic units of local government (La Documentation Française 1982, pp. 44-45). Giscard maintained that the essential role of the regions should remain that of coordinating economic development and indicated his sympathy for the recently enacted Gaullist regional reform of 1972. Although he had run for office on a platform promising enhanced decentralization, Giscard's centralist ideology led him to approach it with considerable caution. At the same time, he was pressed by elements of his coalition and by his prior public pledges to make a good faith effort at a reexamination of the role of the regions.

The Giscard presidency can be characterized as one in which regional devolution received much study and discussion, but little legislative change in the status of the regions resulted. Several important studies of regionalism were undertaken and lengthy reports were published (La Documentation Française 1982, pp. 34-39). In 1977, a government commission sent a questionnaire to all mayors in France soliciting their opinions on the desirable forms and functions local government ought to embrace; the results of this questionnaire indicated hostility among some of them toward the interposition of an independent regional government between themselves and the central government (La Documentation Française 1982, p. 35). In 1978, the government introduced a lengthy legislative package on the rights and responsibilities of local governments into the Senate. This legislative proposal is noteworthy for an absence of recommendations mandating any substantive changes in the status of the regions. Giscard's ideological predilections and political prudence dictated that major modifications in the existing status of local government would be unwise. The 1978 proposals were debated in parliament for several years and eventually came to naught with the election of the Socialists in 1981. While the proposed legislation did not lead to substantive changes, it stimulated discussion resulting in the introduction of new ideas into the debate on the rights and responsibilities of local governments.

Giscard's presidency did produce some minor regional developments, but only under the terms of the 1972 law. The regions under Giscard gradually increased their political authority and budgetary freedom, but major changes in their form and functions did not occur. The contrast between Giscard's publicly stated aspirations for regional government and the very modest reforms achieved under his presidency can be accounted for by several factors (Rousseau 1981). The need to appease those special interest groups within his coalition that desired a continuation of strong central government, as well as opposition from some local elites, dictated a policy of caution toward regional reform. More fundamentally, Giscard's conservative values rested on a traditional belief in the efficacy of the central government and its technocrats as the most responsive structure for managing economic modernization. His commitment to a strong central authority as the organizing principle of French political and social life led

Giscard to emphasize regional deconcentration rather than regional decentralization. Thus, his regional policy was one of studied gradualism rather than substantive change.

During his tenure in office, Giscard was faced with the difficult task of juggling diverse and conflicting demands for continuity and change in a manner not only congruent with his own political ideology but also with an eye to his political future. Holding his alliance together and preparing for the presidential election of 1981 led Giscard to pursue a policy of pragmatism, eschewing reform measures that might create discord. As a consequence, the controversial issue of enhanced regional decentralization was discussed but never actually acted upon. Indeed, toward the end of his term, Giscard moderated even his verbal support for regional decentralization. His platform for the 1981 presidential election was notable for its blandness and the absence of any mention of such potentially controversial issues as regional decentralization (Le Monde 1980).

As a technocrat himself and a liberal centrist with a commitment to economic modernization, Giscard was committed to science, technology, and rational economic planning. He epitomized a belief in nonpartisan technical competence through which economic and social planning by the central government was the surest guardian of the national interest. In Giscard's view, industrialization and economic growth benefited all citizens and neutralized social and economic conflict (Birnbaum 1982, pp. 112-37). Economic modernization during the Giscard presidency, however, essentially benefited large economic enterprises at the expense of much of the traditional middle class and small entrepreneurs. His coalition of state technocrats and bureaucrats and private sector capitalists and industrialists united the political, economic, and administrative elites in France more effectively than had been the case in the preceding century (Birnbaum 1982; Suleiman 1978, pp. 223-75). This unified political and economic elite opposed the creation of autonomous regional centers having social and economic decision-making power. Birnbaum writes that the Giscard presidency was one that would "put an end to the privileged position of the politicians and elevate in their stead bureaucrats, industrialists, and senior management personnel. . . . The unity of the regime would embrace the political, administrative, and economic spheres" (1982, pp. 131-32). While he moved to consolidate national political and economic elites, Giscard also reestablished his historic links with local notables and pursued an aggressive policy of reconquest of the periphery (Mény 1982, pp. 35-48). Such policies were overtly hostile to the development of more autonomous regional governments.

In spite of these political and economic tendencies, modest evolution and change in the regions did occur. Most important was the gradual and historic change in the views of the political parties on the Left toward the regions. While historically the Left had pursued a Jacobin, centralist policy of reform from above, its exclusion from national office during the Fifth Republic forced a change in its political ideology and strategy. Isolated from national power, the Left turned to regional and local government as a base from which to work toward the capture of central state power (Chevallier 1982, pp. 117-20; Dayries and Dayries 1982, pp. 108-11). In their Common Program of 1972, the Socialists and Communists called for a rewriting of the 1972 regional legislation, arguing that the regions should become genuine territorial governments with popularly elected regional assemblies. The dialectical process of regional growth and change originally set in motion by the central government's creation of administrative planning regions was having a continuing effect.

Around the administratively defined regions, an indigenous cultural and political consciousness continued slowly to develop. Regional-based economic modernization, combined with the historic linguistic and ethnic particularisms of certain regions, created new demands by regional elites for increased participation in economic and social planning. Regionalist movements in certain areas of France, such as Brittany, Corsica, and Occitania, acted as pressure points in the demands for enhanced regional autonomy (Beer 1980). While the course of regional development in France lagged behind the experience of other European nations, such as Italy and Spain, it was nonetheless gradually evolving. The election of the Socialists to national office in 1981 heralded a considerable leap forward in the French regionalist movement.

THE FIFTH REPUBLIC: SOCIALISM

The stunning victory of the Socialist party in winning the presidency and an absolute majority in the National

Assembly brought the ongoing decentralization debate into a new political context. As noted, political and economic centralization had proceeded farther in France than in other democracies (Badie and Birnbaum 1983). Yet the French, like citizens of other modern democracies, have been increasingly rethinking the relationship of the citizen to the state and the balance between local and national governments. As Debbasch (1982, pp. 3-6) suggests, all modern democracies attempt to strike a balance between the need for national unity expressed in centralized political power and the recognition of local diversity expressed in decentralized political power. The attempt to resolve this complex balance between national unity and local diversity has, as we have seen, historically produced alternating tendencies toward the centralization and decentralization of political power in France (Birnbaum 1982). While the election of President François Mitterrand and the Socialists resulted in a change toward the decentralization of political power, tendencies toward both centralization and decentralization continue to exist in France (Lalumière 1982b, p. 57). Before examining the Socialist reform legislation, however, it is necessary to examine the varied reasons that led the Socialists so strongly to advocate regional devolution.

As our analysis has shown, the pervasiveness of the Jacobin ideology in France has meant that political parties of both the Left (Socialists and Communists) and the Right (Gaullists) have traditionally favored a strong centralized state in order that reforms might be imposed from above (Suleiman 1974; Safran 1977). Historically, the Right has seen central power as the guardian of the general interest and the indispensable means for ensuring public order and national unity. Likewise, the Left has viewed concentrated state power as a prerequisite for the seizure of power by the working class and the subsequent imposition of central economic and social planning.

For many years the parties of the Left were hostile to regionalism, which they viewed as a diversion from the primary goal of heightened class consciousness and conflict that could lead to a seizure of national power by the workers. During the 1970s, however, both the Communists and the Socialists moderated their views on the region as they increasingly came to believe that regional economic and social problems could not be solved in the absence of autonomous regional governments (Dayries and Dayries

1982, pp. 108-11). Since a change in the legal status of the regions required central government legislation, the Communists and the Socialists made regional reform a central plank in their 1972 Common Program. This document asserted that the regions should be changed from administrative bodies into genuine local territorial governments with popularly elected assemblies.

As Mény (1984a) observes, since World War II the Left has increasingly pressed for democratization at the local level, believing that popular elections are the ultimate source of legitimate power. The creation of locally elected regional assemblies was, therefore, necessary to legitimate genuine regional decentralization. For the Socialists, regional devolution represented a constructive democratic response to the Gaullist and centrist drift toward centralization and technocracy. Regional devolution coupled with economic nationalization offered the Socialists a political mechanism for opening up French society to greater citizen participation, a desire expressed most strongly in the student-led uprising of 1968.

Higher education in France, ostensibly open to all on the basis of objective competency testing, remained in practice strongly mediated by social class background (Bourdieu and Passeron 1979; Marceau 1977). Class inheritance and the replication of inequalities in educational opportunities from generation to generation meant that the exclusive <u>grandes écoles</u>, which train the topmost political and economic technocrats, drew their students almost exclusively from the existing dominant political and economic elites (Suleiman 1978). Although regional devolution would not directly alter the elitist structure of education, it was seen as a mechanism for opening up political participation to greater numbers of ordinary citizens.

As befits a unitary state, political power in France is constitutionally vested in the national government. Local governments exercise only those powers specifically granted them by the National Assembly. Political decentralization, as a result, is not simply a quality that is present or absent, but a quantity that varies in degree or amount. Greater or lesser amounts of power may be transferred from the central government to local communities.

Because decentralization is a political issue reflecting diverse struggles for political power, partisan political considerations influenced the evolution of regional government. The Socialists' ideological shift away from a

Jacobin view of the regional question represented not only a change in political thought but in political realities as well. During the period of Gaullist dominance in the 1960s and 1970s, the Left cultivated political power at the local level. Because of its heavily local constituency, the Socialist party became increasingly receptive to demands for decentralization and the creation of regional assemblies. As a staff member of the Socialist party delegation in the National Assembly emphasized to the author (Rousseau 1982a), because the Right monopolized power at the national level in the Fifth Republic, the Left was forced to develop its power base at the local level. Regional devolution and political decentralization would benefit primarily the mayors of larger socialist towns and cities, urban elites, big city political bosses, and local notables in the departments and regions (Mény 1984a; Rangeon 1982).

In part, then, the Socialist embrace of political decentralization represented a pragmatic political response to the demands of their partisan constituency. Gourevitch (1980) has emphasized the way political constraints, such as the needs of the Gaullist majority when it dominated the central government, have inhibited meaningful regional reform and the transfer of decision making to the regions. Once the Socialists held both national and local power, this political blockage to regional devolution was eliminated. This helps to explain why the Socialists and not the Gaullists initiated far-reaching regional decentralization.

Paradoxically, while the Left embraced regional devolution for ideological and political reasons, it reconsidered its position for these very same reasons. Since a Left majority held national office for the first time in the Fifth Republic, the Right's response was to cultivate local power more assiduously. The tilt to the right in several elections held after 1981 helps to explain the slowdown in the implementation of the decentralizing legislation. One conservative deputy in the National Assembly expounded to the author (Rousseau 1982b) his belief that if the parties of the Right continued to gain in local elections, the Mitterrand government might be forced to slow down its decentralization time table and perhaps its overall attitude toward decentralization as well. The election of regional assemblies was indeed postponed several times and finally set for March 1986 at the time of the general parliamentary elections (Le Monde 1985c, pp. 6-7).

As a result of the elections, which took place on March 16, 1986, a new conservative majority replaced the Socialist government in the National Assembly (Le Monde 1986b). The new conservative government, with Chirac as prime minister, captured approximately forty-five percent of the vote to emerge as the new parliamentary majority. In the first regional elections to be held in France, the coalition of conservative parties emerged victorious in twenty of the twenty-two regions (Le Monde 1986a). The vagaries of the Left's electoral fortunes in future years, and the position taken by the present conservative government toward the newly enfranchised regions, will shape the speed and extent of regional devolution over the long term.

While regional devolution is a complex social and political phenomenon reflecting diverse struggles for political and economic power in an ever-changing social milieu, it is also an institutional response to real structural constraints and needs. Although parties of the Left and Right differed in their methods of addressing regional economic and political development, both recognized the genuine need for regional reforms. The emergence of centralized economic planning since World War II increasingly necessitated some form of administrative devolution to plan and administer regional economic development. The increased growth and economic importance of the urban centers in France and the maladaptation of the existing administrative apparatus to meet the requirements of rapid urban growth constituted yet another force for enhanced local decision making. The Socialists' desire to decentralize was thus also a reaction to the bureaucratic congestion and excessive hierarchy that stifled local initiative (Ardagh 1983; Godt 1983; Luchaire and Luchaire 1983; Crozier 1982, 1974). Decentralizing decision-making authority to the region was viewed by the Socialists as a way of resolving economic and social problems at a level where their intricacies could be more immediately and simply apprehended.

The rediscovery and emergence of local ethnic and cultural identity following World War II constituted another force for greater regional autonomy. Although ethnic activism had never constituted a threat to the integrity of the unitary state in France, the Socialist emphases on local governance and worker self-management were congruent with the demands of ethnic activists for increased regional devolution (Laughlin 1985a, 1985b; Beer 1980). We have previously noted the dialectic sparked by the creation of administrative regions, which had the unanticipated consequence of creating a renewed sense of regional community. Political autonomy was one way in which ethnic activism manifested itself.

The progressive commitment of the Socialist party to regional devolution thus resulted from a convergence of varied political, economic, and social forces. The exclusion of the Socialists from national power, and their growing local constituency with its demands for enhanced autonomy, were major factors. These politically pragmatic reasons combined with the Socialist ideology of self-management helped bring about a reorientation of Socialist thinking on decentralization. Finally, the changing social and economic structure of France as a result of the post-World War 11 economic modernization created a widespread perception that changes in the structure of the centrally administered state were necessary. With this background, we now examine the legislative changes that have created a new structure of local and regional governance and administration.

The electoral victory of the Socialists moved the discussion of decentralization from the arena of debate into that of action and change. Eschewing the legislative approach of the preceding Giscard government, in which a single large and complex law was introduced, the Socialists opted for a continuing series of legislative bills. The government was anxious to redeem its promises for reform by speedily enacting some legislation, yet the magnitude of the task made it difficult to compress the many decisions about policy changes into one piece of legislation. A desire for expedient action led to the strategy of enacting an ongoing series of legislation and decrees. As Mitterrand remarked, political decentralization was to be the grand achievement of his seven-year term.

The initial enabling legislation was introduced in July 1981 and, after considerable parliamentary examination, debate, and amendment, passed final reading in the National Assembly in January 1982. Because of concern by parliamentary conservatives that portions of the bill contradicted the constitution, it was sent to the Constitutional Council the following day. After minor modification by the Council, the legislation became law on March 2, 1982. This initial legislation defined the new rights and freedoms of communes, departments, and regions (Direction Générale des Collectivités Locales 1982). The historic law of 1982 was the first step in an ongoing stream of legislation and decrees that created a historic departure in the relations of the central government with local governments, particularly the regions (Ministère de l'Intérieur et de la Décentralisation 1984a, 1984b).

A major consequence of the 1982 legislation was the fashioning of the twenty-two regions into full, functioning territorial units of government. For the first time, the regions are governed by popularly elected regional councils chosen through direct election.[1] In addition, the chief executive of the region is no longer the regional prefect, but rather each regional council selects a president from among its own members.

Regional governments will exercise control over some matters alone and in others share power with the central government, as well as other levels of local government. In areas of shared responsibility, the authority of the central government continues to remain supreme. In particular, regions will have enhanced responsibilities for housing, professional training, town planning, economic development and aid to industry, and public health and welfare. Areas of responsibility and cooperation shared with the central government include the development of public works, planning and economic development going beyond the region, environmental protection, and matters of national cultural, health, and social significance. The exact boundaries between central and regional responsibilities, as well as between the regions and local levels of government, are to be determined by the judicial courts, that will also have the responsibility of distinguishing between exclusive and shared regional powers. Succeeding laws of January and July 1983 transferred additional responsibilities to the regions, as well as to the departments and communes, in such areas as ports and waterways, the development of special educational organizations such as agricultural schools, and the management of local museums, libraries, and the like (Mény 1984b).

---

[1] By special statute, Corsica and the Overseas Departments held regional elections in 1982 and 1983, respectively. This was done to help diffuse Corsican nationalism (Savigear 1983) and to provide an opportunity to assess the effects of regional devolution before its introduction into metropolitan France.

The office and the functions of the prefect have been modified to increase substantially the autonomous decision making of all three levels of local government. In the past, the prefect played a double role, serving both as representative of the central government to local government and as chief executive of the department. Not surprisingly, the interests represented by these two roles occasionally came into conflict. Henceforth, the chief executive of the department will be the president of the departmental council, who will have primary responsibility for managing departmental affairs, while the president of the regional council will act in a similar capacity for the region. The prefect, now called "representative of the state" to signify changed responsibilities, becomes the sole representative of the central government to the department and region. Although the former prefect's duties as chief executive of the department and region have been eliminated, the responsibilities as central government representative have been strengthened. The representative of the state continues as the representative of each national ministry in the department and region and is charged with coordinating the local delivery of ministerial services, protecting the national interest, and enforcing the law. The representative of the department in which the regional prefecture is located will serve as representative of the state for the region.

The elimination of the tutelle, or a priori suppression of local initiatives by central government authorities, represents another important change. Prior to the new legislation, the prefect, acting as central government representative to local government, was able to suspend in advance legislative initiatives passed by local governments if the prefect thought they were contradictory to law or to the constitution. In practice, this meant that the prefect exercised virtual veto power over administrative and financial decisions taken by local governments. Not only did the tutelle involve legislative safeguards, it also represented potential political interference in local rule, particularly in those cases where the prefect represented a national government whose political affiliation differed from that of the majority in the local assembly. Under the new policies, legislative and budgetary acts of local authorities become operative immediately upon passage and so remain unless found to be judicially wanting after the fact. The representative of the state may no longer exercise a priori powers, thus giving local legislative bodies greater room to act on the basis of local interests.

Accounts vary on the extent to which the central government under the prior system exercised control over local governments through the prefect's tutelle. The typical prefect sees his role as that of an animator or coordinator, bringing together the various state ministries and local government services in an efficient and coordinated manner (Clauzel 1982a, pp. 71-78). Prefects argue that in practice the tutelle is rarely used. Speaking as a prefect, Clauzel maintains that the tutelle is infrequently needed, since consultation between the prefect and the local council occurs prior to council action. Clauzel argues that the prefect and the council president tend to work together in the pursuit of common interests (Clauzel 1982b, pp. 122-27).

On the other hand, in small communes, state officials and the prefect make virtually all the important legislative and economic decisions. Local representatives assert that, although the tutelle is used infrequently, it serves as a weapon through which the prefect can greatly influence local officials to censor themselves rather than face the political force of the central government through the prefect's veto (Laignel 1982b, pp. 127-29). Laignel argues that this process can occur in populous urban communes as well as in small rural ones; in particular, cities governed by political parties in opposition to the central government are particularly subject to the prefect's use of the tutelle as a political weapon. Laignel suggests that, while the tutelle may have been used infrequently, the threat of its use gave the prefect a virtual legislative and budgetary veto.

Since the representative of the state will no longer act as chief executive of the department or region, this problem should be alleviated. Under the new arrangements, the presidents of the regional and departmental councils, along with the departmental and regional representatives of the state, emerge as the strongmen of the region and department, respectively.

In spite of the new policies, the central government still retains considerable administrative and judicial control over local governments. Although the a priori prefectoral tutelle has been suspended, a posteriori administrative and judicial controls remain (Vergès 1982, pp. 130-31). Already-existing administrative tribunals will play an expanded role in reviewing local legislation that the representative of the state may appeal to them, while newly created regional accounting courts will adjudicate budgetary items brought for appeal. In the future, the tutelle, or central government oversight functions, will increasingly be judicial in nature and the role of the courts in regulating local affairs can be expected to grow. Because the constitution of the Fifth Republic requires it, the central government will continue to exercise a considerable role in local affairs, though in altered form. The centralized, unitary state clearly remains unitary.

The fundamental enabling legislation of 1982, along with the laws of January and July 1983 and the continuing stream of legislation, have created enhanced but still limited powers for communal and departmental governments as well. Local governments are permitted to engage in a variety of activities designed to promote communal, departmental, or regional economic development. Importantly, the taxing and spending powers of local governments have been revised, resulting in increased central financial support, along with greater discretion in its expenditure. Local governments will receive block grants from the state for public works (Dotation globale d'équipment, or DGE) and general governmental operations (Dotation globale de fonctionnement, or DGF) (Mény 1984b). At the same time, the central government is requiring local governments to raise at least one-half of their revenues through local taxation or borrowing in order to promote sound fiscal management.

One unplanned result of the transfer of powers to local government has been a refusal to decide which of them, commune, department, or region, shall dominate in local affairs. To avoid making this politically sensitive decision, the Socialist government refused to opt for either the region or the department as the principal actor in local affairs (Mény 1984a, 1984b; Kesselman 1983, pp. 232-33). This unwillingness to make a clear distinction among the exact responsibilities and privileges of each level of local government will likely contribute to an increasingly active role for the administrative courts in the adjudication of disputes over rights and responsibilities. Chevallier (1982, pp. 177-78) notes that both the department and the region have respective strengths that might allow either to emerge as the dominant local power. The failure to create a clear hierarchy among local governments, along with the state's inability to sustain politically and

financially two prominent levels of local government, leads
Chevallier to predict the eventual downgrading and perhaps
disappearance of either the department or the region in
the long term. The likelihood of such an outcome and its
impact on center-periphery power and decision making will
be determined as the process of regional devolution unfolds.

The economic crisis in France, with continued high
unemployment and slow economic growth, will likely have
an effect on the implementation of decentralization, especially the transfer of economic resources from the state to
local governments (Kesselman 1983). Scaled-down central
government expenditures will limit the amount of funds
transferred to local governments, as well as the ability of
local governments to generate their own tax revenues.
Thus, the consequences of devolution will be linked to
France's economic prosperity. The great economic differences between wealthier and poorer departments and regions
seem unlikely to be affected by decentralization.

The creation of local administrative services and the
quality of their personnel may unfold as one indicator of
the relative dominance of the department or the region, as
well as the effectiveness of administrative decentralization
overall. The central government has transferred some of
its administrative personnel to local governments to aid in
implementation of their new responsibilities and has given
them authority to create additional local services as desired. As Mény (1984a) observes, the development of
peripheral centers of expertise could lead local government
to compete with the central government in the provision of
services and increase, rather than decrease, bureaucratic
decision-making structures. Mény argues that local services might become quantitatively more important and yet
remain dependent on the state, resulting in an increasingly rigid administrative system.

While numerous laws and countless decrees have characterized the course of decentralization recently (Gontcharoff
and Milano 1984a, 1984b, 1983), legislative evolution under
the Socialists represents only a continuing chapter in the
interchange between the central government and local governments. Although France historically lagged behind
much of the rest of Europe in the creation of partially
self-governing regions (Rangeon 1982, pp. 106-7; Dayries
and Dayries 1982, pp. 119-21), it is now beginning to
catch up. The dialectic set in motion by the original administrative regions produced a developing sense of collec-

tive identity that can now manifest itself within the partially self-governing regions. As Chevallier (1982, p. 171) notes, the growing sense of collective regional identity forms a counterbalance to the decline of national community that is a result of the growth of the mass society in France. Indeed, the participation of the citizenry in the election of regional councils will likely help to affirm and enhance regional identity and promote the further development of center-periphery relations.

Although regional self-governance in France has reached a new plateau, France remains a centralized, unitary state. While the creation of self-governing regions appears to represent a genuine departure from the Jacobin tradition (Kesselman 1983; Dayries and Dayries 1982, pp. 120-21), central government power remains primary and indivisible. The state has given power to the regions only to the degree that they reproduce the logic of the state. The conception of the national interest defined by the central elite is largely what determines the character of regional powers.

As Mény (1984a) observes, the current reforms are not a revolution but a shift in the relative balance of power from the state to local authorities. The final outcome of these changes remains uncertain. Rangeon (1982), for one, argues that regional decentralization could result in little more than an enhanced centralization of power benefiting regional elites. As the new political reality of the region begins to create a new social reality, this possibility remains open. However, at the present time, the central government and the political interests it articulates determine the options for regional development. As the future composition of the central political elite changes, it could well reform the region in other directions. The election of the new conservative government is such a change, but at present it seems unlikely that the new government will make major changes in the present status of the regions, for several reasons. Although the conservatives have been historically unsympathetic to popularly elected regional governments, they have recognized the desirability of an intermediate level of government to facilitate central planning. More important, the conservatives hold power in twenty of the twenty-two regions in metropolitan France and thus have a power base in their regional constituency. The political dynamic set in motion by the current regional devolution will provoke unseen future consequences. In assessing the future of regional devolution, Rangeon (1982, p. 107) appropriately asks, "What regions? Which powers?"

The Jacobin tradition clearly remains quite powerful in France (Vié 1982; Galy 1977). Major sources of organized opposition to political decentralization endure, including the central bureaucracy and the conservative political parties on the Right (Luchaire and Luchaire 1983). The state bureaucracies fear a loss of their traditional powers and diminished freedom of action. State administrators argue that local officials lack the capability to manage public funds with the same rigor as the central ministries. On the political level, the conservative parties have historically feared that decentralization might so enhance local particularistic identities that the unity of the national state could be threatened. Gaullist politicians have argued that regionalism encourages the separatist tendencies of ethnic extremists and calls national identity into question. Since the Right now controls all but two of the elected regional assemblies, these concerns may momentarily subside. Certainly, the contending Jacobin and Girondist conceptions of the state that have historically characterized the evolution of democracy in France continue.

These conflicting forces and tendencies manifest themselves in a variety of ways. Political parties on the Right have opposed decentralization, while factions on the Left have disagreed on the extent and pace of decentralization. Local officials dispute the division of privileges and responsibilities among commune, department, and region and press for greater local authority. Ethnic activists desire more regional autonomy than the government has been willing to grant. Beer (1980) seems correct when he suggests that decentralization has many varied meanings to different constituencies, ranging from enhanced regionalism to complete separatism.

In spite of the significance of the devolutionary changes introduced by the Socialist government, French political decentralization evolves within the context of the historically strong and dominant central state. While the present trend toward decentralizing political power predominates, tendencies toward decentralization and centralization coexist in France (Lalumière 1982b, p. 57). The institutional mechanisms of political decentralization itself have created new and complex organizational structures. As a result, France possesses an entirely new set of political institutions, including regional assemblies and their powerful presidents, newly created administrative law tribunals, and a continuing powerful role for the representative of the state in local affairs. Mény (1984a) maintains that the introduction of decentralization by the Socialists has not altered the fundamentally authoritarian nature of the French politicoadministrative system. In this sense, the decentralization of power to regional governments represents a recentralization of power benefiting regional elites (Rangeon 1982, p. 87). In the developing structure of political power, the president of the regional council and the representative of the state are emerging as power brokers at the regional level (Chevallier 1982, p. 155). Beyond this, many and varied institutional forces favoring centralization continue. Public administration, political parties, trade unions, and business and industry are largely centralized (Mény 1982, p. 57). Each of these special interest groups constitutes a force for the continuation of centralized political authority.

Although the Socialist party's historical embrace of Jacobinism has been modified by a current political and ideological shift toward decentralization (Mauroy 1982; Rocard 1982), the Socialist government showed little evidence of policies that might have substantially altered the political institutions constituting a major foundation of concentrated state power, the grandes écoles and the grands corps. As Suleiman (1978) has shown, these institutions produce and maintain a unique state-created political power elite. The grandes écoles, which train the technocrats and bureaucrats who staff the high administration of the state, accord the state a monopoly over the creation, certification, and legitimation of political and economic elites. The grands corps comprise the elite administrative agencies that head the vast organizational apparatus of the central government. These twin institutions remain a foundation of personal privilege and vast political power that benefits the political and economic elite (Ardagh 1983).

In spite of their ambitious devolutionary political policies, the Socialists showed only moderate interest in addressing these institutional bases of elitism and centralization. In connection with a proposal to increase the number of secondary school graduates, the Socialist government commissioned a study of the grandes écoles that envisioned broadening their entrance requirements and increasing their enrollments (Le Monde 1985b).

Multiple officeholding by elected officials (the <u>cumul des mandats</u>) constitutes another institutional force for the centralized concentration of political power. Only late in its term did the Socialist government move to limit this source of concentrated power by passing a bill limiting the number of public offices held by one person to two (<u>Le Monde</u> 1985a). Conflicting institutional forces for centralization and decentralization, combined with Mitterrand's need to balance conflicting interests in a way that is politically palatable while allowing for change help explain the cautious and systematic approach to decentralization taken by the Socialist government. For these reasons, the degree to which the Socialist government's devolutionary policies will produce a more decentralized, less elitist political system is uncertain.

This does not mean that the field of political action for local governments will remain entirely subservient to central government direction. Regardless of the formal unitary structure of center-periphery administration in France, local governments have not been, nor do they remain, powerless in the face of the central government. The interrelationships between center and periphery have, over the centuries, developed in highly complex ways that belie the simple hierarchical model of administration from above. Although France is administered from Paris, center and periphery do not constitute two distinct and unrelated political poles. Mény (1982) observes that with 36,000 communes, ninety-five departments, and twenty-two regions, there exist nearly one-half million local officials in France who constitute a large pressure group. The successful prefect does not administer as a potentate, but must accommodate the interests of other central government agencies as well as local officials. Mény suggests that a complex osmosis of consultation and interdependence has developed within this network of central and local officials, so that the prefect is able to function most effectively when he cooperates with local interests. Tarrow (1977) likewise argues that, although France is a centralized state, local elites intervene as brokers between the central administration and the local community. Although representatives of the central administration have a high degree of cohesion, activist local officials are frequently able to expand their communities' share of state resources, particularly economic resources. In a similar vein, Dupuy (1985) underscores the informal relationships of compromise, coordination, and interdependence that develop between representatives of the central government and the local governments.

The work of Mény, Tarrow, Dupuy, and others makes it clear that state-local relations in France are less integrated and structurally more complex than the formal structure of centralized state power might suggest. Clearly, centralization has not meant the capricious and unchecked domination of the center over the periphery, but rather a moving equilibrium in which local officials have now less, now more, room to maneuver and negotiate with central government authorities. While the regional devolution of 1982 portends an extension of the field of political action for local officials, its impact appears to be evolutionary, not revolutionary. It formally gives greater explicit recognition to the informal practices that have developed between central and local officials. We expect the new formal structure of central-local relations to produce a somewhat different structure of informal relations, just as the old formal structure produced its unique form of informal relationships. While we have examined the principal changes in the formal administrative structure produced by the recent political decentralization, changes in the informal structure will become clear only in ensuing years as decentralization unfolds.

CONCLUSIONS AND IMPLICATIONS

As our analysis shows, the structural form of the state reflects the concerns of the political elites who rule it. As the ideologies and needs of elites change over time, structures of state power are changed to accommodate them. Political centralization and decentralization reflect the historic struggles for power that take place in a context of national political traditions and legal structures.

In France, the Jacobin tradition of the unitary, centralized state has been a staple feature of political life. Political elites of the Left and the Right have embraced this tradition to a greater or lesser degree. At the same time, the Girondist heritage, with its emphasis on a more pluralist, decentralized structure of political power, has served as a countervailing ideology of the state. Much of the turbulence of French political history reflects the ongoing debate between the partisans of centralism and pluralism, each faction attempting to mold the state into its idealized model. In spite of periodic alternations between the Jacobin and Girondist poles, the Jacobin ideology has remained dominant.

The Jacobin rationale rests on the uniquely French assumption that only a strong central government can safeguard the national interest and act as an impartial arbitrator among powerful and conflicting special interest groups. While French political elites have alternately embraced more centralized and less centralized approaches to political rule, the continuing centralization and consolidation of power in Paris has been the primary trend over time (Badie and Birnbaum 1983; Birnbaum 1982; Suleiman 1978). Both conservative and radical elites have shared the view that it is the state's responsibility to lead and control political and economic affairs. This ideology has been a major force behind the increasing concentration of political and economic power in the highest levels of the central government. Although the hierarchical, centralizing tradition has been dominant in France, local governments and their constituencies historically have not been totally lacking in political power and a degree of self-determination. As recent research has shown, central government representatives have, in practice, faced constraints in their relationships with local officials (Dupuy 1985; Mény 1982; Tarrow 1977; Grémion 1976). The French political reality is thus a complex one in which local interests have not remained powerless even though public functions are administered from Paris.

The recent political decentralization must be understood against this historical context. Although political and economic centralization proceeded farther in France than in other democracies, the French are not alone in rethinking the balance between center and peripheral power and decision making (Lalumière 1982a; Safran 1977). Following World War II, the increasing complexity of social and economic problems in France led to the imposition of central planning with solutions tailored and administered by the central government. At the same time, the seeming inability of the state to address uniquely local problems and grievances gave rise to increasing demands for enhanced regional decision making. The dialectic set in motion by the creation of regions designed to facilitate central administration and planning produced in turn a gradual awakening of regional identity that culminated in the enactment of the 1982 decentralizing reforms.

We view the recent decentralization as a developmental process that, in its present phase, is just beginning. As we have suggested, the future of decentralization will be influenced by a variety of unfolding factors reflecting changing social and political interests. While the Socialists' regional devolution represents a genuine attempt to create a more pluralist structure of participation and decision making at the local level, it remains to be seen in what ways this will change the participation of local officials and citizens in the governance of local affairs. The dynamic dialectic between center and periphery continues to evolve.

The historic shifts and tensions between centralization and decentralization persuade us that neither the pluralist power-dispersed nor the elitist power-concentrated model provides a fully adequate explanation of the structure of political power in France over long periods of time. While the elitist perspective seems to describe better the French context, limitations inhere in both perspectives. Shifts in the composition of the political elite have resulted in greater and lesser concentrations of political and economic power at different points in time. Thus, we argue that pluralist, elitist, and center-periphery perspectives are all useful in interpreting the French experience.

In the face of these changing empirical realities, we prefer to conceptualize state political power as a continuum varying from less concentrated to more concentrated, rather than as a simple power-dispersed, power-concentrated dichotomy. This conceptualization allows for empirical changes in structures of state power over time. The replacement of the Giscard regime by Mitterrand and the Socialists offers recent evidence of real shifts in the composition of political elites over time, as does the recent election of the conservative government. The change from Center Right to moderate Left portended a greater exclusion of economic elites from the government; the Socialists' political decentralization and economic nationalization policies are evidence of that. The Socialist ascent to power implied a shift toward greater pluralism and less concentration within the French political elite and a corresponding increase in the autonomy of local government. The election of the conservative government will doubtlessly mean a greater participation of economic elites in the government and open once again the possibility, although slight at present, of changes in the regions. To the extent that a continuing, long-term trend toward the Jacobin concentration of power in the central government is characteristic of France, our interpretation of political decentralization suggests that an elitist, strong-state model is a dominant pattern. We return to this issue in Chapter 6.

REFERENCES

Antoni, Anne-Cécile, and Dominique Antoni. 1982. "La Corse Face à Elle-Même." Etudes 357 (December): 611-27.

Ardagh, John. 1983. France in the 1980s. New York: Penguin Books.

Ashford, Douglas E. 1983. "Reconstructing the French 'Etat': Progress of the loi Defferre." West European Politics 6 (July): 263-70.

Badie, Bertrand, and Pierre Birnbaum. 1983. The Sociology of the State, trans. by Arthur Goldhammer. Chicago: University of Chicago Press.

Beer, William R. 1980. The Unexpected Rebellion: Ethnic Activism in Contemporary France. New York: New York University Press.

Bélorgey, Gérard. 1984. La France décentralisée. Paris: Berger-Levrault.

Berger, Suzanne. 1974. The French Political System. New York: Random House.

Bernard, Paul. 1983. L'Etat et la décentralisation. Paris: La Documentation Française.

Birnbaum, Pierre. 1982. The Heights of Power: An Essay on the Power Elite in France, trans. by Arthur Goldhammer. Chicago: University of Chicago Press.

Bourdieu, Pierre, and Jean-Claude Passeron. 1979. The Inheritors: French Students and Their Relation to Culture, trans. by Richard Nice. Chicago: University of Chicago Press.

Brehier, Terry. 1985. "Richesse et pauverté des élus." Le Monde Sélection Hebdomadaire 1932 (November 7-13), pp. 1, 6.

Chevallier, Jacques. 1982. "La Réforme Régionale." In Le Pouvoir Régional, edited by Jacques Chevallier, François Rangeon, and Michèle Sellier, pp. 109-85. Paris: Presses Universitaires de France.

Clauzel, Jean. 1982a. "France." Revue Française d'Administration Publique 21 (January-March): 71-78.

———. 1982b. "France." Revue Française d'Administration Publique 21 (January-March): 122-27.

Cobban, Alfred. 1963. A History of Modern France, vol. 1, 1715-1799. Baltimore: Penguin.

———. 1965a. A History of Modern France, vol. 2, 1799-1871. Baltimore: Penguin.

———. 1965b. A History of Modern France, vol. 3, 1871-1962. Baltimore: Penguin.

Crozier, Michel. 1982. Strategies for Change: The Future of French Society, trans. by William R. Beer. Cambridge, Mass.: MIT Press.

———. 1974. The Stalled Society, trans. by Rupert Swyer. New York: Viking Press.

Dayries, Jean-Jacques, and Michèle Dayries. 1982. La régionalisation. Paris: Presses Universitaires de France.

Debbasch, Charles. 1982. "Les mots." Les Cahiers Français 204 (January-February): 3-6.

Direction Générale des Collectivités Locales. 1982. "Droits et Libertés des Communes, des Départements et des Régions." Démocratie Locale 20 (April): 1-12.

La Documentation Française. 1982. "La décentralisation." Les Cahiers Français 204 (January-February).

Dupuy, François. 1985. "The Politico-Administrative System of the Département in France." In Centre-Periphery Relations in Western Europe, edited by Yves Mény and Vincent Wright, pp. 79-103. London: Allen & Unwin.

Dupuy, François, and Jean-Claude Thoenig. 1983a. Sociologie de l'Administration Française. Paris: Armand Colin.

―――. 1983b. "La Loi du 2 Mars 1982 Sur la Décentralisation." Revue Française de Science Politique 33 (December): 962-84.

Galy, Philippe. 1977. "L'illusion décentralisatrice." La Revue Administrative 30 (September-October): 469-74.

Giscard d'Estaing, Valéry. 1976. Démocratie Française. Paris: Fayard.

Godt, Paul J. 1983. "Decentralization in Socialist France: A Strategy for Change." The Tocqueville Review V (Spring-Summer): 215-30.

Gontcharoff, Georges, and Serge Milano. 1983. La décentralisation, vol. 1. Paris: Syros.

―――. 1984a. La décentralisation, vol. 2. Paris: Syros.

―――. 1984b. La décentralisation, vol. 3. Paris: Syros.

Gourevitch, Peter Alexis. 1980. Paris and the Provinces: The Politics of Local Government Reform in France. Berkeley: University of California Press.

Greffe, Xavier. 1984. Territoires en France: Les enjeux économiques de la décentralisation. Paris: Economica.

Grémion, Pierre. 1976. Le Pouvoir Périphérique. Paris: Editions du Seuil.

Guérard, Albert. 1969. France: A Modern History. Ann Arbor: University of Michigan Press.

Kesselman, Mark. 1983. "Commentary: Decentralization in Socialist France: What Strategy for What Change?" The Tocqueville Review V (Spring-Summer): 231-36.

Laignel, André. 1982a. "Débat." Revue Française d'Administration Publique 21 (January-March): 58-59.

———. 1982b. "France." Revue Française d'Administration Publique 21 (January-March): 127-29.

Lalumière, Pierre. 1982a. "La Décentralisation." Revue Française d'Administration Publique 21 (January-March): 48-52.

———. 1982b. "Débat." Revue Française d' Administration Publique 21 (January-March): 57-58.

Lancel, François. 1974. Valéry Giscard d'Estaing: De Chamalières à l'Elysée. Paris: Pierre Belfond.

Laughlin, John. 1985a. "Regionalism and Ethnic Nationalism in France." In Centre-Periphery Relations in Western Europe, edited by Yves Mény and Vincent Wright, pp. 207-35. London: Allen & Unwin.

———. 1985b. "A New Deal for France's Regions and Linguistic Minorities." West European Politics 8 (July): 102-13.

Le Monde. 1986a. Sélection Hebdomadaire 1951 (March 20-26).

———. 1986b. 12794 (March 18).

———. 1985a. "Cumul des Mandats." Sélection Hebdomadaire 1935 (November 28-December 4): 6.

———. 1985b. "Les principales dispositions." Sélection Hebdomadaire 1933 (November 14-20): 8.

———. 1985c. "Le gouvernement met en oeuvre ses reformes électorales." Sélection Hebdomadaire 1902 (April 11-17): 6-7.

———. 1980. "La campagne présidentielle." Sélection Hebdomadaire 1638 (March 20-26): 7.

Luchaire, François, and Yves Luchaire. 1983. Le Droit de la Décentralisation. Paris: Presses Universitaires de France.

Marceau, Jane. 1977. Class and Status in France. Oxford: Clarendon Press.

Mauroy, Pierre. 1982. C'Est Ici Le Chemin. Paris: Flammarion.

Mény, Yves. 1984a. "Decentralisation in Socialist France: The Politics of Pragmatism." West European Politics 7 (January): 65-79.

———. 1984b. "La Décentralisation." Administration 83. Paris: Institut International d'Administration Publique.

———. 1982. "La Décentralisation." Revue Française d'Administration Publique 21 (January-March): 35-48.

Ministère de l'Intérieur et de la Décentralisation. 1984a. Décentralisation: Communes, Départements, Régions, vols. 1-3. Paris: Journal Officiel de la République Française.

———. 1984b. Déconcentration, vol. 4. Paris: Journal Officiel de la République Française.

Mitterrand, François. 1981. Politique 2. Paris: Fayard.

———. 1980. Ici et Maintenant. Paris: Fayard.

Pickles, Dorothy. 1966. The Fifth French Republic: Institutions and Politics. New York: Praeger.

Putnam, Robert D. 1976. The Comparative Study of Political Elites. Englewood Cliffs, N.J.: Prentice-Hall.

Rangeon, François. 1982. "Le Pouvoir Régional." In Le Pouvoir Régional, edited by Jacques Chevallier, François Rangeon, and Michèle Sellier, pp. 65-107. Paris: Presses Universitaires de France.

Rocard, Michel. 1982. Plan intérimaire. Paris: Flammarion.

Rousseau, Mark O. 1981. "President Valéry Giscard d'Estaing and Decentralization." The French Review 54 (May): 827-35.

_____. 1982a. Personal interview, Socialist party staff member, National Assembly, Paris, July 6.

_____. 1982b. Personal interview, R.P.R. deputy, National Assembly, Paris, July 7.

Safran, William. 1977. The French Polity. New York: David McKay.

Savigear, Peter. 1983. "Corsica: Regional Autonomy or Violence?" Conflict Studies 149: 3-17.

Singer, Daniel. 1970. Prelude to Revolution: France in May 1968. New York: Hill & Wang.

Suleiman, Ezra N. 1978. Elites in French Society: The Politics of Survival. Princeton, N.J.: Princeton University Press.

_____. 1974. Politics, Power, and Bureaucracy in France: The Administrative Elite. Princeton, N.J.: Princeton University Press.

Tarrow, Sidney. 1977. Between Center and Periphery: Grassroots Politicians in Italy and France. New Haven, Conn.: Yale University Press.

Tocqueville, Alexis de. 1969. Democracy in America, trans. by George Lawrence. Garden City, N.Y.: Anchor Books.

_____. 1955. The Old Regime and the French Revolution, trans. by Stuart Gilbert. Garden City, N.Y.: Anchor Books.

Vergès, Jean. 1982. "France." Revue Française d'Administration Publique 21 (January-March): 130-31.

Vié, Jean-Emile. 1982. La Décentralisation Sans Illusion. Paris: Presses Universitaires de France.

Virieux, Jean-Marc. 1982. "Les tendances longues de la décentralisation." *Futuribles* 56 (June): 7-18.

Wahl, Nicholas. 1980. "Foreword." In *The Unexpected Rebellion*, by William R. Beer, pp. xxvii-xxxii.

Zeldin, Theodore. 1973. *France: 1848-1945*, vol. 1, *Ambition, Love and Politics*. Oxford: Clarendon Press.

5

Spain: The Multinational State and the Consequences of Incomplete State Building

Raphael Zariski

Regional devolution in Spain is an experiment that has barely begun. When the Italian constitution was being drawn up in 1946 and 1947, Spain was still under the firm autocratic control of the right-wing dictatorship headed by General Francisco Franco. It was not until 1978 that the death of Franco and the advent of a constitutional monarchy permitted the adoption of a democratic constitution, which was ratified by popular referendum in December 1978. The Spanish constitution of 1978 has provided for the establishment of a system of regional devolution that is much more complex and variegated than the Italian system.

Since the ratification of the Spanish constitution in 1978, Spain has been divided into nineteen "autonomous communities." It should be stressed, however, that only Catalonia, the Basque country, and Galicia have actually had their fundamental statutes approved in Madrid as early as 1980. In the case of the other autonomous communities, regional autonomy did not actually go into effect until 1982 or 1983. Consequently, Spain cannot yet furnish us with the kind of empirical evidence about the actual (as opposed to the potential) workings of regional devolution that we have been able to scrutinize in Italy.

Yet the Spanish experiment merits our attention and consideration, because the centrifugal forces confronted by the Spanish state are so much more formidable and threatening than those operating in Italy or France. Regional devolution in Spain is much more than an attempt to breathe new life into the political system by strengthening popular participation in the political process. To some extent, it is an effort to guarantee the survival of the Spanish state by appeasing the long-ignored resentments of the peripheral regions, to build a more lasting unity on a foundation of officially sponsored diversity.

HISTORICAL BACKGROUND: RECURRING CRISES OF LEGITIMACY

The Creation and Consolidation of the Spanish State

The fifteenth century witnessed the consummation of La Reconquista: the reconquest of Spain from the Moors. It was also during this century that substantial progress was made toward the unification of the Iberian Peninsula under a single crown. This process was completed in the early sixteenth century when the two realms of Castile and Aragón shared the same ruler and continued to do so thereafter. In short, by the sixteenth century, Spain appeared to have achieved a unity that was to elude Italy for almost three centuries (Linz 1973, p. 38).
However, contrary to the long-standing myth of a unitary, centralized Spain under oppressive Castilian control (see Beneyto 1980, pp. 173-200; Carretero y Jiménez 1980, part II), the Spanish monarchy in the sixteenth century ruled over a federation of regions, composed of several kingdoms, each recognizing the same king but retaining its own laws, customs, and institutions and exercising a considerable degree of autonomy. The dominant kingdom in this federation was the Kingdom of Castile, León, and Navarre. Castile was relatively centralized, with a powerful executive and weak representative organs, but some of its outlying areas--notably the Kingdom of Navarre and the Basque provinces--were allowed to keep their established rights and privileges and a substantial measure of self-government under their own foral laws (fueros) (Clark 1980, p. 79; Greenwood 1977, pp. 87-96). The Crown of Aragón comprised the Kingdoms of Aragón, Valencia, and Mallorca and the principality of Catalonia in Spain itself, plus some overseas kingdoms, such as Naples and Sicily. Its traditions involved a high degree of decentralization: Each kingdom had its own laws, customs, and usages. Moreover, the parliamentary assemblies of Catalonia,

Aragón, and Valencia were quite powerful and frequently blocked or modified the monarch's policy proposals, in sharp contrast to the ineffectual Castilian Cortes (parliament) (Linz 1973, pp. 39-40).

Despite the fact that the Kingdom of Castile and the various kingdoms under the Crown of Aragón enjoyed the legal status of equals, subject to the same sovereign, their political relationship was characterized by Castilian hegemony, for Castile had played the leading role in La Reconquista and far outstripped the other kingdoms in area, population, and commercial prosperity (Coverdale 1979, p. 25; Linz 1973, pp. 39-40; Suárez Fernández 1981, pp. 68-69; Vázquez de Prada 1981, pp. 82-84). Castilian hegemony acquired a kind of symbolic confirmation in the sixteenth century, when the king chose, after 1561, to reside in Madrid while being represented by a resident viceroy in each of the associated kingdoms.

Yet Castilian hegemony had its limits, for there was really no Spanish state in the modern sense of the word (Vázquez de Prada 1981, pp. 86-88). Each component kingdom had its own fiscal and monetary system, pursued its own economic policies, and was free to erect trade barriers against the other component kingdoms. Moreover, the viceroy was powerless to impose taxes without the consent of the regional parliament and of the executive committee emanating from that parliament (Linz 1973, pp. 44-45). So, when Spain projected its power into northern Europe and into the New World, this was really Castile acting in the name of Spain and providing far more than its share of the necessary manpower and financial resources.

Thus the Spanish monarchy represented a case of incomplete state building. Because of the decision to govern Spain through a set of federated kingdoms, sharing only a common monarch, the tasks of creating an efficient state and an integrated nation were left undone (Linz 1973, p. 33). The urgent need to unify the peninsula under a single monarch necessitated unusually generous concessions in order to secure the fealty of strategically located principalities and ethnic communities on the periphery. All this boded ill for the future: It would not be easy to reopen the question of completing the state-building process.

By the early seventeenth century, military and colonial adventures had seriously drained the financial reserves of the Spanish Crown, and Castile was in a state of economic and demographic decline. Reacting against this unbalanced situation, the Castilian prime minister, the Conde Duque de Olivares, induced King Philip IV to embark on a centralizing course and to demand that the associated kingdoms furnish more aid to the Crown. The net result of the Castilian bid for centralized control of Spain was quite negative. Confronted with widespread threats of rebellion and possible secession (including a Catalan popular uprising that led to a French invasion of Catalonia) and lacking the military and financial strength to cope with these threats, the Spanish monarchs had to settle for a continuation of the existing federated system (Beneyto 1980, pp. 238-43; Linz 1973, pp. 40-48; Smith 1965, pp. 194-99; Vázquez de Prada 1981, pp. 93-95). As Linz puts it, "the delay in building the Spanish state in the period of maximum glory [the sixteenth century], the prestige of its kings and influx of wealth from America, made the task more difficult in a period of decadence" (1973, p. 47).

By the beginning of the eighteenth century, 200 years of wars and imperialistic ventures had sapped the resources of Castile, and Spain was no longer the leading power on the European scene. Ironically enough, it was Spain's relative weakness that tempted foreign powers to intervene in Spanish affairs and actually helped to bring about that centralization of the Spanish polity that Olivares had striven vainly to achieve in the mid-seventeenth century. The War of the Spanish Succession was not only a war between two coalitions of European powers; it was also a virtual civil war between different regions of Spain. Castile supported the newly crowned Bourbon monarch, Philip V, while Aragón, Catalonia, and Valencia sided with the Austrian-backed pretender to the throne, the Archduke Charles. The final victory of Philip V and his European allies was followed by royal decrees divesting Aragón, Catalonia, Mallorca, and Valencia of their traditional institutions and privileges, the elimination of the customs barriers and discrete fiscal systems that had separated and differentiated the various Spanish kingdoms, and the extension of Castilian laws to the other parts of Spain (Beneyto 1980, pp. 244-51; Chapman 1965, pp. 368-72, 429-32; Smith 1965, pp. 202-204, 232-36; Vázquez de Prada 1981, pp. 96-99, 102-103, 108-109). The only areas to escape the process of centralization were Navarre and the Basque provinces, which had sided with Philip V in the war against the Austrian-backed pretender. These regions were allowed to regain their fueros (foral rights) well into the nineteenth century (Linz 1973, p. 49; Vázquez de Prada 1981, pp. 98-99).

Centralization had two striking consequences: It generated new economic policies that brought a growing prosperity to Catalonia and the Basque provinces while Castile remained relatively stagnant, and it gave birth to a widespread feeling of identification with a Spanish nation, particularly among the intelligentsia (Vázquez de Prada 1981, pp. 94-95, 97-107). Thus, by the end of the eighteenth century, the state-building process, so long deferred, seemed to have been finally completed, except in the Basque North. The nation-building process, for its part, seemed finally to be getting under way.

Comparing the process of unification and state building in Spain with that in Italy, we may observe some very intriguing contrasts. First of all, as we have already noted, unification was achieved in Spain at a very early date. Second, Spanish unification was engineered largely by a central core area--Castile and León--rather than by a virtual outside power like Piedmont. In this sense, it bore some resemblance to the French pattern. However, while both France and Piedmont had to conquer a number of feudal principalities and rival kingdoms in order to complete the unification process, Castilian military power was directed mainly against the Moors and against foreign powers that resisted Spanish expansion.

A third and very sharp distinction between Spain, on the one hand, and Italy and France on the other, should be noted. Spanish unification was not accompanied by the establishment of a centralized, unitary state. In fact, apart from the ill-starred attempt made by King Philip IV and Olivares in the early seventeenth century, the process of building such a state was postponed until the advent of the Spanish Bourbons in the early eighteenth century--a full two centuries after unification. During those two centuries, Spain operated as an unwieldy federation of kingdoms under a single monarch, bearing some resemblance to the Austro-Hungarian Empire of the nineteenth century (Linz 1973, pp. 97-98, 101-102).

By renouncing the path of forced centralization during the period of Spanish imperial hegemony, the Spanish monarchy managed to reduce the potential dangers of peripheral resistance (though such resistance did flare up from time to time, as in the early seventeenth century). However, by postponing the tasks of state building and nation building to a time of Spanish political and economic decline in the eighteenth and nineteenth centuries, it was storing up trouble for the future.

New Crises of Legitimacy in
the Nineteenth Century

The Napoleonic invasion of 1808-1814 ushered in a period of great political and institutional flux. From 1814 to 1875, Spain experienced coups, revolutions, and civil wars, and even experimented very briefly and unsuccessfully with republican institutions (the disastrous First Republic of 1873-1874). Not until the establishment of the Restoration Monarchy (1875-1923) was a measure of equilibrium finally attained. It was during the nineteenth century that centrifugal ethnic allegiances at the periphery--tendencies that had been seemingly forestalled by the centralizing measures of the early eighteenth century--emerged as a major political force and called into question the survival of the Spanish state in its unitary and centralized form. During this troubled century, several great crises raised severe doubts as to the legitimacy of the existing political system, and in the process of so doing undermined the legitimacy of the Spanish state itself. These crises included the Napoleonic invasion, the Liberal ascendancy and the Carlist Wars which that ascendancy provoked, and the Spanish defeat at the hands of the United States in 1898.

The War of Independence against Napoleonic France seemed at first to confirm the crystallization of national loyalty among the Spanish people, even among those living in peripheral areas like Aragón, Catalonia, and the Basque provinces (Olábarri Gortázar 1981, p. 113), and created a national patriotic myth. However, it also helped to generate some of the alarming centrifugal tendencies that were to manifest themselves later in the century. For one thing, the network of elected juntas, which filled the power vacuum created by the detention and forced abdication of King Ferdinand Vl at Bayonne, represented a departure from the principle of absolute monarchy and, therefore, posed a problem of institutional discontinuity--a problem that would become critical when Ferdinand Vll returned from his French exile and sought to restore the status quo ante (Díaz López 1985, p. 238). Second, the War of Independence revived forgotten feelings of grass-roots regional pride in regions like Galicia (Díaz López 1982, pp. 407-408).

Finally, the system of elected juntas tended to be dominated by Andalucía, the only major Spanish region that was not predominantly under French occupation. When a <u>cortes</u> (parliamentary assembly) was elected in 1810 to draft a constitution, Andalucian towns were able, through their representatives, to select deputies for those areas of Spain that were French-controlled and could not hold elections. Since Andalucía was a Liberal stronghold, the resulting <u>cortes</u> was a predominantly Liberal body. The constitution of 1812 was consequently a basically Liberal document, providing for a highly centralized system of central-local relations based on the French prefectoral model (Carr 1966, pp. 92-99; Chapman 1965, pp. 490-92). Thus, Spanish Liberals had adopted the centralizing posture of the French Jacobins and the Napoleonic Empire. Obviously, the Liberal program was bound to arouse bitter resentment in the periphery in the years to come.

When Ferdinand VII returned to the Spanish throne in 1814, after the expulsion of the French, his attempt to turn back the clock to an absolute monarchy led to decades of civil unrest, coups, and rebellions. By the 1830s, the Liberals, enjoying the support of the urban middle classes and of a reformist segment of the officer corps in the armed forces, had achieved a position of political superiority (Carr 1966, pp. 120-347). They adopted a highly centralized, unitary system of government and imposed serious restrictions on the established privileges of the Catholic Church. They also brought about a drastic revision in the system of local government. Spain was divided into forty-nine provinces, each headed by a civil governor, responsible to Madrid. The provincial deputation (<u>diputación</u>), or representative assembly of the province, was to have relatively little in the way of power or financial resources. The civil governor, whose status resembled that of the French prefect, was clearly in control of provincial affairs (Olábarri Gortázar 1981, pp. 113, 118, 120-23).

A traditionalist reaction against the anticlericalism, modernization, and centralization being promoted by the Moderate Liberals was not long in coming. The forces of traditionalism and of peripheral protest rallied around Don Carlos, the younger brother of Ferdinand VII, rebelling against the king's willingness to compromise with the Moderate Liberals. The Carlist Wars of 1833-1840 and 1870-

1875 were struggles between a centralizing monarchy, supported by urban Liberals and (on this issue) Progressives and the forces of clericalism and traditionalism based in outlying rural areas. As the wars progressed, the Carlists placed more and more stress on the theme of "foral rights," which were still retained by Navarre and by the Basque provinces. In the Basque country, where such privileges as exemption from Spanish customs duties and from state-imposed taxation were still a living reality, support for the Carlist movement was particularly widespread (Heiberg 1982, pp. 360-64; Linz 1973, pp. 49-52, 74-76). Even in the Basque country, however, the cities and the large commercial towns tended to side with the centralizers in Madrid, since foral rights deprived Basque industry of the protection of Spanish tariffs while denying it easy access to the Spanish market. It was the peasants and local notables in the rural areas and small towns who preferred to pay low prices for duty-free foreign industrial products while enjoying protection against competing agricultural goods from the rest of Spain (Heiberg 1982, pp. 363-64). As Giner (1984, p. 83) points out, Carlism was dominant in the rural hinterlands of those regions that actually spearheaded the process of industrialization and modernization. Yet, with Bilbao and Barcelona firmly in the centralist camp, Carlism could hardly be described as representing a united peripheral resistance against a centralizing state.

The victory of the central government in the Carlist Wars led to the abolition of foral rights in Navarre (1841) and in the Basque provinces (1877). Nevertheless, Carlism had a lasting impact: It helped sow the seeds for the emergence of regional nationalist movements in the late nineteenth century and it continued to serve as a myth in certain parts of northern Spain, especially in Navarre.

The Spanish-American War of 1898, which resulted in military defeat and the loss of Cuba, Puerto Rico, and the Philippines, was a third great crisis of legitimacy for the Spanish regime and the Spanish state. It was a terribly devastating blow to Spanish pride. In addition, the war provided Catalan nationalism with a base among the middle classes by depriving Catalan merchants and industrialists of a large share of their accustomed export markets in the lost colonies and by reenforcing Catalan suspicions regarding the alleged decadence and ineffectiveness of the Castilian state (Carr 1966, p. 547; Díaz López 1985, p. 239).

The Rise of Regionalist Movements in the Nineteenth Century

The latter part of the nineteenth century witnessed the appearance of strong regionalist movements--some of them committed to outright nationalism--in both Catalonia and the Basque country. Both of these regions shared a common resentment against the controls exercised by the Liberal centralizers in Madrid and by their agents in the field, and a common fear that further encroachments by Madrid would erode their established legal privileges. Both regions had experienced an upsurge of interest in the regional language and culture (a revival that was particularly vigorous among the writers of the Catalan Renaissance (Renaixença), while the greatest Basque writers, noted throughout Spain, continued to write in Castilian Spanish). Finally, both regions had to cope with the problems created by industrialization and by the influx of workers from other parts of Spain (Carr 1966, pp. 223, 278-81, 538-58; Clark 1980, pp. 86-88; Coverdale 1979, pp. 26-27, 32-33; Díaz López 1985, pp. 238-40; Giner 1984, pp. 83-84; Heiberg 1982, pp. 364-73; Linz 1973, pp. 50-83; Madariaga 1967, pp. 214-35; Olábarri Gortázar 1981, pp. 125-27, 145-49, 156-60, 173-74; Pi-Sunyer 1980, p. 107).

Economic interests played a key role in arousing regionalist feeling. The industrialization and growing prosperity of Catalonia encouraged the Catalan textile producers to insist on high tariffs and to evince great dissatisfaction with the free trade policies pursued by doctrinaire Liberals in Madrid. The iron and steel manufacturers of the Basque country, however, were less threatened by foreign imports and actually benefited from some newly erected tariff barriers against foreign competition. Since they, and other urban interests, dominated the Basque provincial assemblies, and since those assemblies were allowed--under the terms of the conciertos económicos (economic accords with the Spanish government) and of the foral laws--to negotiate the level of their provincial tax burden with Madrid and to decide for themselves how that burden was to be distributed, the rural areas and small towns were saddled with the lion's share of the tax burden. Consequently, in the Basque country, it was the merchants and professional people of the small towns and rural areas, as well as the peasants, who suffered the hardships that new industries and new taxes brought in their wake and who turned to the nationalist cause. In Catalonia, on the other hand, regionalist and nationalist forces could count on some support from big business.

There were some fundamental differences between the Basque Nationalist party (the PNV, founded in 1895) and the Catalan regionalist parties. First, the PNV, unlike the Catalan Lliga Regionalista (formed in 1901), lacked significant big business support and tended to have a more populist appeal, oriented toward those middle strata that had been most severely buffeted by industrialization. Second, when Catalan regionalism eventually spawned some Left-oriented parties, those parties had a rather radical and anticlerical posture, whereas the Basque PNV was always on friendly terms with the clergy. Finally, the forces of separatist nationalism were far stronger in the PNV than in the Catalan regionalist parties, and there were certain racialist and even segregationist overtones that were lacking in Catalonia. Perhaps this was due to the fact that the Basques--a much smaller ethnic group than the Catalans and speaking a language utterly unrelated to Castilian Spanish or to any other West European tongue--felt less confidence in their ability to assimilate the masses of Castilian immigrant workers.

Other regionalist movements elsewhere in Spain were much slower in making their presence felt in the nineteenth century (Díaz López 1985, pp. 240-42; Díaz López 1982, pp. 408-409; Linz 1973, pp. 84-92; Olábarri Gortázar 1981, pp. 160-69). Apart from some cultural initiatives and the formation of a few regionalist splinter groups, there was little to report. Only in Galicia was there a fairly important cultural revival and some significant political stirrings, which included one or two actual uprisings; but here again no regionalist party was formed until the twentieth century.

As we can see from this chronicle of growing regional and ethnic unrest, the early attainment of statehood had not been an unmixed blessing for Spain. By the late nineteenth century, at a time when the emotional fervor that accompanied the long-delayed state-building process was inspiring German and Italian nationalists to confront and overcome a multitude of difficulties, the Spanish state was no longer "a new creation arousing hopes but a discredited, inefficient machine" (Linz 1973, p. 103). Since the centralized, unitary state had presided over more than a century of national decline and humiliation, it was hardly surprising that the more dynamic regions of the periphery should express nostalgia for the looser federation of bygone days.

The Advent of the Second Republic and the Triumph of Regional Autonomy

Despite all the institutional turmoil that Spain had undergone during the nineteenth century, its structures of local government retained the fundamental characteristics imparted to them by the Liberal reforms of 1833-1835 (Díaz López and Morata 1984, p. 76; Olábarri Gortázar 1981, p. 122). The civil governor of the province continued to act as the administrative agent of the central government in Madrid in a manner comparable to that of the French and Italian prefects. However, he was chosen on the basis of his political loyalty to the government of the day and tended to play a much more interventionist role in local politics than did the French prefects of the Third Republic. This centralized control from Madrid had not gone unchallenged. There had been the Carlist rebellions of 1833-1840 and 1870-1875; the effort to establish a federal republic (the First Republic) in 1873-1874; a number of local uprisings in the name of municipal rights; and several governmental or legislative initiatives aimed at setting up a regional level of administration. All these decentralizing ventures came to naught, torpedoed by centralist resistance and by the opposition of the party or parties in power (Olábarri Gortázar 1981, pp. 172-74; Simón Tobalina 1981, pp. 41-56).

The civil governor, acting as provincial viceroy for the party in power, played a major role in manipulating elections through patronage, bribery, and favoritism, with the help of local bosses referred to in political parlance as caciques. This system of caciquismo in large parts of rural Spain had a great deal in common with the system of local clienteles that formed around members of parliament and prefects in large portions of southern Italy. It can easily be understood, then, why those Spaniards who wanted to bring about the reform of local government and the curbing of the civil governor's power were so insistent that regional jurisdictions be established and be endowed with substantial authority (Carr 1980, pp. 10-15; Carr 1966, pp. 366-79; Linz 1967, pp. 198-99, 202-208). However, apart from a royal decree, issued in 1913, which permitted contiguous provinces with common historical traditions and similar cultural characteristics to form associations (mancomunidades), the regionalists suffered defeat after defeat during the nineteenth and early twentieth centuries. The four Catalan provinces were the only ones to make use of the terms of this decree. The decree was abrogated and the Catalonian mancomunitat was abolished in 1925 under the dictatorship of Primo de Rivera (Carr 1980, pp. 65-66; Olábarri Gortázar 1981, pp. 174-76; Simón Tobalina 1981, pp. 57-74).

The dictatorship of General Primo de Rivera (1923-1931) put a stop to all concessions to the regional and local authorities and took steps to discourage Catalan cultural activities (Olábarri Gortázar 1981, pp. 186-87). Its policy of intransigent commitment to Castilian hegemony had the understandable effect of inflaming the resentments of the regionalist minorities. Consequently, the downfall of Primo de Rivera in 1929 and the advent of the Second Republic in 1931 set the stage for major progress toward regional autonomy.

The constitution of 1931 established an "integral state," a kind of middle way between a unitary and a federal system (Díaz López 1983, pp. 1875-76; Olábarri Gortázar 1981, pp. 178-82; Simón Tobalina 1981, pp. 75-101; Vandelli 1982, pp. 43-55). It did not divide Spain up into a set of specified autonomous regions. Instead, it stated that if one province--or two or more contiguous provinces with common historical, cultural, and economic characteristics--wished to form an autonomous region, a Statute of Autonomy could be drawn up by the petitioning province or provinces and could be submitted to the Cortes in Madrid for approval. As for those provinces that did not choose to group themselves into regional units and to draw up Autonomy Statutes, they would retain their preexisting unitary relationship with Madrid.

The first autonomous region to be formed under these terms was Catalonia. Here the regionalist Left (the Esquerra) won the regional elections of 1932 and thus gained control of the regional government (the Generalitat). The Generalitat drew up an Autonomy Statute that same year, and the Statute was endorsed in Catalonia by a plebiscite and was then amended and ratified by the Cortes in Madrid. Thus Catalonia obtained autonomy only a year after the overthrow of the monarchy.

The Basque provinces also pushed for autonomy under the new constitution (Carr 1966, pp. 617-18, 630-31; Díaz López 1983, pp. 1876-77; Olábarri Gortázar 1981, pp. 185-88, 193; Simón Tobalina 1981, pp. 92-97). However, they found the road to a Basque Autonomy Statute much harder going. First of all, as a result of the very heavy impact of immigration from other parts of Spain on the demographic composition of the Basque provinces, the PNV did not play as dominant a part on the regional political scene as did the Lliga and the Esquerra in Catalonia. Second, the Province of Navarre remained strongly attached to its Carlist monarchism and its religious traditions and therefore resisted overtures from a Basque Nationalist movement that seemed to be prepared to coexist with an anticlerical Spanish Republic in exchange for regional autonomy. But the most important adverse factor was the hostility of the Spanish Right, which came to power in the elections of November 1933 at precisely the time when the Basque Statute was finally ready for consideration by the Cortes in Madrid. Reacting passionately against what they regarded as the excessive regionalist pretensions of the Catalans, alienated by the Catalan and Asturian revolts of 1934, influenced somewhat by the narrow margin by which the Basque Statute had been approved in one of the three Basque provinces (Álava), the rightists began to turn against the Catholic and conservative Basque Nationalists who should have been their natural allies and placed the Basque Autonomy Statute very low on their list of priorities.

For their part, the Basque Nationalists now proceeded to forge an alliance of expediency with the parties of the Left and Left-Center, which were at least prepared to grant autonomy to the periphery. In 1936, with the victory of the leftist Popular Front, the Autonomy Statute finally began to make headway in the Cortes. As a result, the Basque Nationalists supported the Government against the Nationalist rebellion that broke out on July 18, 1936, while Navarre became a stronghold of the Insurgents. In October 1936, the Cortes approved the Basque Autonomy Statute. The Basque region, isolated from most of the rest of Republican Spain, enjoyed a short-lived autonomous status until its conquest and occupation by Insurgent Nationalist forces in 1937.

In the rest of Spain, no substantial progress was made toward regional autonomy between 1931 and 1936, except in the far northwest. Only in Galicia, after much delay, was an Autonomy Statute finally approved by popular plebiscite on June 28, 1936 and transmitted to the Cortes on July 15, three days before the outbreak of civil war. Since Galicia came under the control of the Nationalist rebels during the very first week of the Civil War, the Cortes never bothered to ratify the Statute.

Regionalism Suppressed: The Civil War and the Franco Regime

During the Civil War, Catalonia and the Basque homeland (Euzkadi) made the most of their fleeting period of self-rule. The Catalan government, dominated by the Esquerra party under the leadership of Luis Companys, was accused throughout the war of never quite shouldering its share of the common burden. As for the Basque Nationalist Government, it used its brief span of autonomous and isolated existence to conduct its own separate military campaign against the rebels and to cultivate semidiplomatic contacts with foreign governments. The Basque provinces fell in the spring and summer of 1937; Catalonia and the rest of Loyalist Spain were subdued early in 1939 (Carr 1980, pp. 141-44; Carr 1966, pp. 671-72; Olábarri Gortázar 1981, p. 194).

Under the autocratic regime established by Franco, rigorous centralization was restored and intensified (Díaz López and Morata 1984, p. 77; Olábarri Gortázar 1981, p. 194; Vandelli 1982, pp. 57-63). The Basque and Catalan Statutes of Autonomy were declared null and void. The special tax privileges granted to the Basque provinces by the <u>conciertos económicos</u> (economic accords) of 1878 were abrogated, as were the foral rights. Only Álava and Navarre Provinces, which had sided with the Nationalists during the Civil War, were allowed to retain certain traditional rights and privileges.

Moreover, a determined campaign of suppression was waged against the cultures of the outlying regions. Thousands of Basque and Catalan regionalist leaders were imprisoned. The use of the Catalan and Basque languages in the schools or in public places was prohibited; all official and commercial business was required to be conducted in Castilian Spanish. In Catalonia, many Catalan street names were abolished and replaced by Spanish names, no books were allowed to be published in the Catalan language, and all Catalan-speaking voluntary associations were banned (Pi-Sunyer 1980, pp. 108-109). In the Basque provinces, public documents (such as birth or marriage certificates) were altered to expunge Basque names, priests were forbidden to deliver their sermons in Euskera (the Basque language), and Basque folklore and regional folk costumes were barred from public display (Clark 1980, pp. 81-82; Heiberg 1982, p. 376). The harsh measures imposed by the Franco regime represented a powerful nationalist reaction against the unbridled regionalist tendencies that had manifested themselves under the Second Republic (Giner 1984, pp. 85-87).

The experience of the Second Republic seemed to have brought about a reversal of attitudes on the subject of regionalism. During the nineteenth century, the modernizing Liberals had preached the virtues of centralization, while the traditionalist and clerical Right had been more sympathetic to foral rights and regional autonomy. Under the Second Republic, however, the Right turned against the claims of the regionalists, making an eventual exception only in the case of Carlist Navarre and the Province of Álava. The Left, on the other hand, threw its support to the cause of regional autonomy.

To be sure, the nature of the Spanish Left had undergone some alteration. It was now dominated by Left Republicans and Socialists, rather than by the middle-class Liberals of the nineteenth century (Thomas 1961, pp. 21-28, 86-94). Then, too, the victory of the Esquerra in Catalonia, along with the defeat of the conservative Lliga, had made Catalan regionalism far more acceptable to the Spanish Left on ideological grounds. Finally, it should be borne in mind that the Left had been out of power for decades. As previously noted, parties that are denied a share of executive power at the national level are apt to become strong proponents of the rights of the periphery. Once they have acquired a taste for power in the national capital, they tend to be more susceptible to centralizing temptations.

As for the Right, it had reacted emotionally to the victories and the excesses of the Catalan regionalist Left. To many Spanish conservatives and moderates, the regionalist cause became identified with the Spanish Left, with regional separatism, with rampant anticlericalism (Giner 1984, p. 86). For this reason, the Nationalist Insurgents spurned the claims of the Basque Nationalists, who under normal circumstances would have been their natural allies, and forced them into an uneasy alliance with the Second Republic.

After World War II, the Franco regime continued to repress civil liberties while pursuing an autarkic policy of sheltering Spanish industry behind high tariff barriers (Carr 1980, pp. 155-56). In the 1960s, however, new economic policies and favorable conditions elsewhere in Europe led to a remarkable economic revolution in Spain (Carr 1980, pp. 156-61; Clark 1980, p. 90; Díaz López 1983, pp. 1878-79). This process of forced-draft modernization had its inevitable political spillover effect. The Franco regime was induced by the course of events to relax its autocratic controls over the political and cultural life of the country. In Catalonia, regionalist elements were able to form private clubs and associations by utilizing convenient loopholes in official regulations (Pi-Sunyer 1980, pp. 109-10). Restrictions on the publication and teaching of Catalan and Euskera also began to be loosened (Clark 1980, p. 82; Coverdale 1979, p. 28).

But these concessions by the regime failed to allay the rising tide of regional discontent. The forced assimilation policy of the Franco regime, and the threat of cultural extinction posed by the massive immigration of low-paid Castilian-speaking workers into the Basque country and Catalonia, had caused too much fear and resentment (Clark 1980, pp. 91-92; Heiberg 1982, p. 378; Pi-Sunyer 1980, pp. 112-13; Silva 1975, p. 232). Furthermore, an atmosphere of expectancy had been created, that further pressures would bring further concessions (Carr 1980, pp. 170-71).

Perhaps the most notable negative legacy of the Franco years was the radicalization of Basque nationalism. In 1959, the ETA (Euskadi ta Askatasuna, Euskadi and Liberty) was formed as an independent organization, offering an alternative to the passive posture of the PNV. It differed from the PNV in a number of ways: It was secular and leftist; it rejected autonomy as a goal and gradualism as a method; and it stressed the need for terrorism and armed struggle with a view to the eventual acquisition of Basque independence (Heiberg 1982, pp. 377-81). Its most spectacular exploit during the Franco years was the fatal bombing in 1973 of the automobile carrying Premier Admiral Luis Carrero Blanco (Clark 1980, pp. 92-94).

THE POST-FRANCO PERIOD

The Return of Democracy and the Regionalist Revival

In the 1970s, the Franco era finally came to a close. When Franco died in 1975, and was succeeded by King Juan Carlos under an institutional arrangement devised by the dictator six years previously, the time for change was at hand. Juan Carlos maintained an initial facade of institutional continuity with the Franco regime and rejected any sharp (and delegitimizing) break with the past. In July 1976, he appointed Adolfo Suárez, a former high official of the Franco regime, to the position of prime minister. It was Suárez, with the full support of the king, who presided over a rapid but orderly transition from traditionalist autocracy to constitutional democracy (Coverdale 1979, pp. 36-41; Díaz López 1985, pp. 242-44; Díaz López 1983, pp. 1882-94; Díaz López 1981, pp. 197-202; Simón Tobalina 1981, pp. 117-22; Vandelli 1982, pp. 83-85). Free elections to a new Cortes, which was to double as a constitutional convention, were held on June 15, 1977, and resulted in a victory for Suárez's Union of the Democratic Center (UCD). The new constitutional document was approved by the cortes on October 31, 1978, and ratified by popular referendum on December 6, 1978. A new democratic era had begun.

The return of democracy was accompanied by the vindication and resurgence of regionalism and regional autonomy. The fact that the most persistent and visible opposition to the Franco dictatorship had been mounted by Catalonia and the Basque country seemed to create a natural association between the cause of democratic resistance against Franco and the cause of regional autonomy. Thus, regionalism entered the consciousness of all sections of Spain, not excluding the dominant Castilian-speaking areas (Giner 1984, pp. 87-89; Vandelli 1982, pp. 89-90). In a sense, by its frenetic efforts to stamp out cultural diversity, the Franco regime had helped to discredit the unitary, centralized state.

The new respectability of the regionalist cause became evident after Franco's death. In his message to the country on November 22, 1975, Juan Carlos spoke of the need to recognize "regional peculiarities as an expression of the diversity of peoples that constitute the reality of Spain within the unity of the kingdom and the state"

(Díaz López 1981, p. 197). When Adolfo Suárez became prime minister in July 1976, he lost little time in moving toward regional devolution. On July 4, 1977, he included a minister for relations with the regions in his cabinet. Then, in 1977 and 1978, a series of royal decree-laws provided provisional governments for Catalonia, the Basque country, Galicia, the Canary Islands, the Valencian country, Aragón, Andalucía, the Balearic Islands, Extremadura, Castile-León, Castile-La Mancha, Asturias, and Murcía. In almost every instance, the region was given legal status after consultation and negotiation with the legislators who represented the region in the Cortes (Coverdale 1979, pp. 84-86; Díaz López 1983, pp. 1883-84; Díaz López 1981, pp. 199-200; Vandelli 1982, pp. 91-102).

The formula employed was that of preautonomy. It was only a temporary arrangement pending final approval of the new constitution. The regional organs were provided with very limited functions, largely of an administrative nature, which they performed under the strict supervision and control of the central government. The regional representative bodies were not popularly elected. Until 1979, they consisted of each region's representatives in the Cortes; thereafter, representatives of the provinces and of some municipalities were admitted to the regional representative organs (Díaz López 1981, pp. 199-201; Vandelli 1982, pp. 96-125).

The use of the preautonomy formula was not precedented. Similar provisional regimes had been authorized in Italy shortly after the Liberation to meet the urgent needs of such peripheral problem areas as Sicily, Sardinia, and Val d'Aosta. The situation in Spain, characterized by violent demonstrations and widespread terrorist activity, was manifestly more pressing and posed a clear and present danger to public security (Coverdale 1979, pp. 84, 86-87, 91, 99, 106-109). In this kind of situation, preautonomy was a way of buying desperately needed time (Díaz López 1983, pp. 1886-87).

The blanket application of the principle of preautonomy to all parts of Spain encountered relatively little resistance in 1977 and 1978, since regional autonomy had become so closely identified with democracy in the thinking of many Spaniards and since the major political parties were anxious to keep the regional issue out of politics until the process of drafting the constitution had been completed (Díaz López 1981, pp. 198-99). In including Castilian-speaking areas in the preautonomy scheme, the government was apparently motivated by the apprehension that granting autonomy only to Catalonia and the Basque country, two of the most economically advanced regions of Spain, would strike the more traditional parts of Spain as rank favoritism (Díaz López 1985, p. 243; Vandelli 1982, pp. 96-97). Moreover, the government was subjected to some grass-roots pressure from Castilian-speaking but economically depressed areas like Andalucía. People in those areas were beginning to look to regional autonomy as a possible alleviation of their economic plight (Coverdale 1979, p. 100).

The Constitution of 1978 and the Regions

The Constitution-Making Process: A Brief Summary. The Cortes that emerged from the elections of June 15, 1977 elected a committee of seven members to prepare a draft of the proposed constitution. This committee included three representatives of Suárez's centrist UCD, one Socialist, one Communist, one member of the right-wing Popular Alliance (AP), and one spokesman for the Catalan minority. The dominant role assigned to the UCD on the committee reflected its ascendancy in the lower house of the Cortes (Vandelli 1982, pp. 131-34).

The committee concluded its labors in April 1978 and presented a draft document to the Cortes. This document was debated and subjected to some revision by the lower house (the Congress of Deputies), by the upper house (the Senate), and by a joint conference committee. The final product was passed in October 1978, with only the rightists of the AP and the Basque Nationalists adopting an official stand of opposition or abstention. Approved by popular referendum on December 6, 1978, and signed by the king on December 27, the constitution became the law of the land on December 29, 1978 (Vandelli 1982, pp. 134-37; Simón Tobalina 1981, pp. 135-36).

The Attitudes of the Parties. On October 27, 1977, while the seven-member committee was engaged in its long and arduous task of preparing a preliminary draft, the Suárez government and the various parliamentary parties signed a series of agreements referred to as the Moncloa Pacts. These pacts ushered in a period of collaboration between the government and the opposition during the formative stages of the new democratic order. As a result, during the process of preparing the basic document that was to serve as the fundamental charter of Spanish democracy, it was necessary to devise a series of compromises between conflicting points of view whenever the facade of unity among the Moncloa signatories appeared to be endangered (Díaz López 1985, pp. 243-44; Ortega Díaz-Ambrona 1984, pp. 29-32; Simón Tobalina 1981, pp. 136-39; Vandelli 1982, pp. 134-39).

Nowhere was the need more evident than in the case of regional autonomy. On the far right, the AP expressed a clear preference for a centralized, unitary state with a limited degree of administrative deconcentration. On the other end of the political spectrum, the Socialists and the Communists advocated a federal system. The middle ground was occupied by the centrist UCD, which supported regional autonomy but within a unitary framework. Even the regional parties were by no means united on the issue of regional autonomy. The Basque Nationalists insisted on the full restoration of the ancient foral privileges of the Basque provinces, whereas the Catalan autonomists actually helped to draw up the system of regional devolution prescribed in the new constitution (Díaz López and Morata 1984, p. 78; Díaz López 1983, pp. 1889-93; Díaz López 1981, pp. 202-203; Vandelli 1982, pp. 133-39).

It was necessary for the framers of the constitution to work out a compromise scheme that would offer important concessions to the forces of regionalism while furnishing adequate reassurance to those Spaniards, in the AP and in the UCD itself, who championed a unitary state with a strong central government (Díaz López 1981, p. 202). The price of maintaining consensus was an ambiguous constitutional settlement; even the founding fathers were highly divided as to its true meaning and implications (Ariño Ortiz 1981, pp. 14-29).

Controversial Issues. The most potentially divisive issue that had to be confronted during the constitution-making process involved the legal relationship between the center and the periphery. On this issue, the UCD was able to impose its middle-of-the-road views and to persuade its Moncloa partners--the unitary Right and the federalist Left--to settle for a form of regional devolution. The resulting compromise between a unitary and a federalist solution is referred to as the Estado de Autonomías, the State of Autonomies (Ortega Díaz-Ambrona 1984, p. 31). In adopting this formula, however, the framers of the constitution were raising more questions than they were answering. For example, was Spain to be considered a nation (as the conservatives assumed), "a state but not a nation" (as the more intransigent Basque Nationalists would have it), or "a nation of nations" (the view taken by the more moderate regional autonomists)? Also, to what degree were the foral privileges of peripheral Spain to be fit into the new order (Díaz López 1985, pp. 244-45; Díaz López 1981, pp. 204-205; Vandelli 1982, pp. 134-39)?

Article 2 of the new constitution expressed some of these issues without really resolving them (López Rodó 1980, p. 151; Díaz López 1981, p. 204; Ortega Díaz-Ambrona 1984, p. 31). On the one hand, it referred to an indivisible Spanish nation. On the other hand, it contained a reference to regional autonomy and designated both regions and "nationalities" as prospective recipients of autonomy. The use of the term "nationalities" greatly alarmed some conservative political leaders, who viewed the label as a virtual incitement to separatist tendencies (Díaz López 1983, pp. 1903-907; Díaz López 1981, pp. 204-206). The cryptic language of Article 2 seemed to indicate that the concept of Spain as a "nation of nations" had won acceptance in the new constitution. This compromise seemed to mollify the Socialists, the Communists, and most of the Catalan autonomists. With their support and that of the UCD, the constitution passed both houses of the Cortes by an overwhelming margin (Simón Tobalina 1981, pp. 135-37; Vandelli 1982, pp. 134-39). Opposition or abstention came mainly from members of the right-wing AP (who believed that the constitution endangered Spanish national unity) and from the Basque Nationalists (who felt the constitution did not go far enough in protecting foral rights and privileges).

The fact remains that what was agreed upon was a document subject to many diverse interpretations. The compromise of 1978 did not really represent a clear and conclusive resolution of the issue of central-regional relations. Quite the contrary: It was so complex and hard to comprehend and interpret that it helped to create an unhealthy climate of uncertainty (Ariño Ortiz 1981, pp. 14-19, 27-29, 116-17).

The Autonomous Communities: Regions and Nationalities. Unlike the Italian constitution of 1948, the Spanish constitution of 1978 does not actually list the regions (referred to as autonomous communities) that are entitled to claim autonomy. Instead, it sets forth several alternative procedures whereby one or more provinces may attain the status of autonomous communities. All but one of these procedures leave the initiative of forming regional subunits to the provincial and local authorities, following the tradition established by the constitution of the Second Republic in 1931 (Díaz López 1985, p. 247; Díaz López 1981, pp. 208-209; Simón Tobalina 1981, pp. 142-44; Vandelli 1982, pp. 187-88).

Three privileged autonomous communities--Catalonia, the Basque country, and Galicia--had voted affirmatively in 1936 in a referendum to approve an Autonomy Statute. They were therefore covered by the Second Transitional Provision of the constitution, which permitted such regions to obtain full autonomy immediately, without the five-year waiting period required for ordinary regions. This procedure involved a very simplified and abbreviated initiating process: a resolution backed by an absolute majority of the members of the preautonomic regional assembly, composed of all the senators and deputies elected to the national Cortes from that region. Everything that took place after initiation--drafting of an Autonomy Statute by the regional assembly, approval by a popular referendum in <u>each</u> province of the region, ratification by each house of the Cortes, signature by the king--conformed to the procedure prescribed by Article 151, Section 2, for other regions that might want to attain full autonomy quickly (Clark 1985a, p. 6; López Rodó 1980, pp. 160-61, 166; Vandelli 1982, pp. 176-81).

In order to avoid the appearance of discriminating in favor of the three "historic regions," the framers of the constitution devised a procedure, embodied in Article 151, for offering accelerated access to full autonomy to other regions as well. This procedure entailed the same post-initiation steps outlined above for the historic regions (Clark 1985a, p. 6; Díaz López 1981, p. 209; López Rodó 1980, pp. 160-61; Simón Tobalina 1981, pp. 147, 150; Vandelli 1982, pp. 179, 188-90). However, the initiating process involved much more formidable barriers. Territories resorting to Article 151 had to obtain the consent of each provincial council and of three-fourths of the municipal councils <u>in each province</u> of the region. Moreover, they had to confront two referendums instead of one; and the extra referendum, which climaxed the initiating process, required approval by an absolute majority of all registered voters in each province. So rigorous were these requirements that only one region, Andalucía, has acquired the status of an autonomous community by relying on Article 151. Even in the Andalucían case, it was necessary for the Cortes to pass special legislation to deal with the problem posed by one province, Almería, which had failed to muster the requisite majority in the arduous first referendum (Clark 1985a, p. 6; Díaz López 1983, pp. 1895-96).

The autonomous communities established under Article 151 were entitled, in drawing up their Statutes, to lay claim to any power or function that was not expressly reserved to the central government by the long array of exclusive powers listed in Article 149 (López Rodó 1980, pp. 157-60; Vandelli 1982, p. 193). In addition, they were guaranteed certain common institutional structures by Article 152: an elected legislative assembly, an executive Council of Government, and a president chosen by the assembly and formally selected by the king (Clark 1985a, pp. 1-7; López Rodó 1980, p. 162; Simón Tobalina 1981, p. 151; Vandelli 1982, p. 194).

Most regions, however, have chosen the easier and more gradual path to full autonomy offered by Article 143. Under Article 143, the initiating process requires the consent of only two-thirds (not three-fourths as under Article 151) of the municipal councils in each province of the proposed autonomous community. Then, too, if a region had already been granted provisional, preautonomic status, its representative organ could vote by absolute majority to launch the process of applying to the Cortes for an Autonomy Statute. Such action could be substituted for the approval by each provincial assembly normally required by Article 143 (López Rodó 1980, p. 166; Simón Tobalina 1981, p. 146). Finally, there was no requirement for a referendum, either to initiate the process or to approve the Statute (López Rodó 1980, p. 156; Simón Tobalina 1981, pp. 150-51; Vandelli 1982, pp. 184-86).

However, a price had to be paid for these less demanding requirements. Territories that employed the Article 143 process could only obtain full autonomy five years after attaining the rank of autonomous communities. During this waiting period, they could only exercise those powers and functions expressly granted to autonomous communities by Article 148, whereas the more privileged Article

151 autonomous communities could also exercise all powers and functions not reserved exclusively to the central government by Article 149. Only after the waiting period had elapsed could they amend their Statutes, with the consent of the Cortes, and thus gain full autonomy (López Rodó 1980, pp. 155-62; Simón Tobalina 1981, p. 151; Vandelli 1982, pp. 193-94).

Twelve autonomous communities have been established under the terms of Article 143, as opposed to only one set up under Article 151--Aragón, Asturias, the Balearic Islands, the Canary Islands, Cantabria, Castile-La Mancha, Castile-León, Extremadura, Madrid, Murcía, Rioja, and Valencia. Of these twelve regions, six actually consist of only one province: Asturias (Asturias), Balearic Islands (Baleares), Cantabria (Santander), Madrid (Madrid), Murcía (Murcía), and Rioja (Logroño) (Clark 1985a, pp. 12-14).

Article 144 provided another method for creating autonomous communities, a method that left the initiative up to the Cortes if the national interest were at stake. This article was designed to fit special cases like the Moroccan cities of Ceuta and Melilla and was also employed to help resolve the problem of the Andalucían province of Almería (Simón Tobalina 1981, pp. 144-46). It could also be employed to compel a recalcitrant province (like Segovia in Castile-León) to join an autonomous community (Díaz López 1985, pp. 249 and 269, n. 8).

The constitution thus appeared to give rise to two classes of autonomous community, those created under Article 151 or the Second Transitional Provision enjoying full autonomy, and those established under Article 143 or 144 enjoying a temporarily much more restricted autonomy and lacking a clear constitutional commitment to provide them with representative institutions. However, full autonomy was eventually accessible to all territories possessing the status of autonomous communities.

As we can see, the Spanish constitution seemed to provide for a very heterogeneous and patchwork system of regional autonomy. Implicit in its flexibility and permissiveness were the possibilities that some Spanish autonomous communities might not be endowed with representative institutions and that there might be great variance in the powers and functions exercised by the respective regional governments. Finally, it seemed to encourage the fragmentation of Spain by permitting single provinces and even cities to aspire to regional status.

The Attempt to Restore Central Control: The Autonomic Pacts of 1981. By late 1979, it had become evident that the excessive leeway the constitution granted to centrifugal forces--permitting them to determine the structure and tempo of the devolutionary reform--would have to be corrected. The very real danger that the process of decentralization would get completely out of hand was being widely perceived.

A number of factors helped to build up a reaction against the headlong rush to autonomy that had characterized the 1977-1978 biennium. First, continued terrorist violence, especially in the Basque provinces, led to a certain public disillusionment with the policy of making sweeping concessions to autonomist demands (Elorriaga 1983, pp. 102-104, 208-11, 247-52). Second, it was feared that other regions might emulate Andalucía in employing the Article 151 procedure for obtaining autonomy and that the resulting spate of referendums would have ominous implications for the stability and legitimacy of Spain's fledgling democracy (Díaz López 1985, p. 248). Third, the referendums held, on October 25, 1979, in the Basque provinces and in Catalonia to approve the Autonomy Statutes for those two regions had been marked by an amazingly low turnout: less than sixty percent in each region. This seemed to indicate that grass-roots support for regionalist aspirations left much to be desired (Clark 1980, pp. 3-4; Clavero Arévalo 1983, pp. 118-19; Elorriaga 1983, pp. 70-75).

Influenced by these factors, the Suárez government and the UCD tried in vain in early 1980 to bring about the defeat of the referendum proposal to initiate movement toward Andalucian autonomy under Article 151. The reason behind this move was apparently the UCD's desire to designate Article 143 as the officially approved route to autonomy for all regions but the three "historic regions." As we have seen, the UCD's plans came to naught (Clavero Arévalo 1983, pp. 121-29, 131-33; Díaz López 1983, p. 1895; Elorriaga 1983, pp. 101-102, 108-10).

Other events in 1980 and 1981 further encouraged the UCD to approach other major parties with a view to hammering out a new approach to the autonomic process. Serious UCD defeats, accompanied by major victories for regionalist middle-class parties, in the Basque and Catalan regional elections of March 1980, seemed to indicate that the UCD's permissive attitude toward regionalism had gone entirely unrewarded (Clark 1985a, p. 4; Elorriaga 1983, pp. 125-44, 162, 245-46). However, the truly decisive shock to the UCD and to other democratic forces in Spain was administered by the attempted coup of February 23, 1981, which clearly indicated that significant elements of the Spanish Right, including sectors of the armed forces and the police, were losing confidence in the ability of Spanish democratic institutions to preserve Spanish national integrity (Clark 1985a, p. 5; Díaz López 1985, p. 248; Elorriaga 1983, pp. 252-54, 257-59; Preston 1984, pp. 161-83).

The abortive coup brought the reaction against the excesses of the autonomic process to a head and made it possible to transcend the rivalry and antagonism that divided the governing UCD from the Socialist party (PSOE), which dominated the opposition camp. In the aftermath of the failed coup, the two parties agreed to entrust a commission of experts, headed by Professor García de Enterría, with the task of investigating the problem of regional autonomy. The recommendations made by the commission in its report of May 1981 later formed the basis for the Autonomic Pacts between the government, now headed by Premier Leopoldo Calvo Sotelo of the UCD, and the Socialist party.

The Autonomic Pacts contained a number of key provisions. First of all, it was made clear that *all* of Spain was to consist of autonomous communities, and those communities were clearly identified and their component provinces listed (something the constitution had neglected to do). Second, it was specifically announced that, with the exception of Catalonia, the Basque provinces, Galicia, and Andalucía, all Spanish regions were expected to accede to autonomy by utilizing the procedures stipulated by Article 143. This meant a five-year waiting period before full autonomy could be obtained. Third, the Pacts set February 1, 1983, as a deadline for the approval of the Autonomy Statutes of all the remaining regions. Fourth, the Pacts provided that all autonomous communities were to have elected legislative assemblies, and executive organs responsible to those assemblies, and that elections in all the autonomous communities (with the possible exception of the four already established) were to take place on the same day (Acuerdos autonómicos 1981, pp. 15-26; Clavero Arévalo 1983, pp. 150-52; Díaz López 1985, pp. 248-51; Elorriaga 1983, pp. 259-61; Vandelli 1982, pp. 381-411).

In addition to these basic guidelines, the Pacts also included first drafts of a proposed Organic Law for the

Harmonization of the Autonomic Process (LOAPA) and of a proposed Law on the Interterritorial Compensation Fund (<u>Acuerdos autonómicos</u> 1981, pp. 26-32, 37-110; Vandelli 1982, pp. 381-411). LOAPA was not passed by the Cortes until 1982, and was declared in 1983 to be at least partly unconstitutional by a decision of the Constitutional Tribunal. Its ultimate effect on Spanish regional devolution is therefore still undetermined. The Autonomic Pacts, on the other hand, clearly have had a major impact on the pattern of regional development.

It has been pointed out that the Autonomic Pacts represented a sharp change of tack in the progress of decentralization and regional devolution. In effect, central control was reestablished over what had become a headlong and unrestrained rush to autonomy. The constitutional right to form or not to form an autonomous community and to select one of several alternative paths to autonomy was transformed into the political obligation to join an autonomous community designated from above and to do so in accordance with certain prescribed procedures. In sum, decentralization was being imposed by the center, whether the periphery was ready or not (Díaz López 1983, p. 1911).

While not legally binding, the Pacts are considered by some observers to have the status of conventions of constitutional significance, filling in troublesome gaps that the 1978 constitution had failed to deal with adequately (Vandelli 1982, pp. 403-11). They were signed, after all, by the two leading Spanish parties, which between them had won 289 of the 350 seats in the lower house of the Cortes in 1979 (Scammon 1985, p. 328).

Yet the fact that the Communist party, the right-wing Popular Alliance (AP), and the Catalan and Basque regional parties had either not given their approval (in the case of the Communists and the AP) or had not even been asked to take part in the discussions that preceded the Pacts (in the case of the regional parties) somewhat undermined the long-run authority of the Pacts. This became especially evident only a year later, in the 1982 elections, in which the UCD was reduced to minor party status, gaining only 11 seats in the lower house of the Cortes, as compared to 202 for the Socialists and 107 for the AP (Scammon 1985, p. 334). Thus, the Popular Alliance, which had not signed the Pacts, became the second-ranking party in the Cortes and the leading opposition force. It is not at all clear, then, how much binding or lasting force the Pacts will have in the future. Nevertheless, the fact remains that they chalked up several important and probably irreversible achievements in affecting the manner in which the regions acquired autonomous status during the 1981-1983 period.

The Creation of the Autonomous Communities. After the ratification of the Spanish constitution in December 1978, the process of setting up the autonomous communities got under way. In the case of the three "historic regions," which were entitled to use the accelerated procedure, events occurred at a fairly rapid clip. The Basque and Catalonian legislative bodies were elected in March 1980, and the regional government of the Galician Autonomous Community began functioning in the fall of 1981. In Andalucía, the rate of progress was a good deal slower, but the regional legislature was finally elected in May 1982. Meanwhile, the signing of the Autonomic Pacts in July 1981 ensured that Andalucía would be the last region to employ the Article 151 procedure.

By mid-1983, all but two of Spain's nineteen designated candidates for autonomous status had had their Statutes approved by the Cortes (the only exceptions being the North African cities of Ceuta and Melilla) and had elected their regional legislative bodies (Clark 1985a, pp. 3-4). There were seventeen autonomous communities in all, with Ceuta and Melilla soon to be added. Of the seventeen autonomous communities, ten represented regions composed of two or more provinces (Andalucía, Aragón, Canary Islands, Castile-La Mancha, Castile-León, Catalonia, Extremadura, Galicia, the Basque country, and Valencia), while seven represented single-province regions (Asturias, Balearic Islands, Cantabria, Madrid, Murcía, Navarre, and Rioja) (Clark 1985a, pp. 12-14).

This completion of the basic structure of the Spanish system of regional devolution was only a preview to the main event, however. The actual powers to be exercised by the autonomous communities will depend partly on the formal provisions of the constitution and of the basic Statutes of the autonomous communities, and partly on political decisions and judicial interpretations in the years that lie ahead.

THE REGIONS IN OPERATION, 1978-1984

Some Contrasts with the Italian Model of Regional Government

We begin by outlining some of the main similarities and differences between the Spanish and Italian models as defined by their respective constitutions. In comparing the two constitutions, it should be noted that the Spanish constitution has been considerably modified in practice by the Autonomic Pacts of 1981. It should also be borne in mind that the two constitutional systems have exercised a reciprocal influence on each other during their respective formative stages. The constitution of the Second Spanish Republic was frequently referred to in the course of the deliberations of the Italian Constituent Assembly in 1947. Conversely, the framers of the Spanish constitution regarded the Italian experience with autonomous regions as highly relevant to their own problems (Vandelli 1984, p. 450).

The Italian and Spanish models of regional government resemble each other in some important respects. First of all, the Italian regions and the Spanish autonomous communities have both been inserted as intermediate levels into what were previously highly centralized systems of local government. Second, the units of local government below the regional level display a striking affinity. Italy's approximately 8,000 communes are matched by some 8,600 municipalities in Spain; Italy has ninety-four provinces as compared to fifty in Spain, but the data on average population per province for the two countries are remarkably similar. Third, both countries have in effect fashioned the same two distinctive categories of regional government: regions that enjoy a special and therefore somewhat privileged status (the "special" regions in Italy, the "historic" communities and the Article 151 autonomous communities in Spain) and regions that must conform to a standard set of norms (the "ordinary" regions in Italy, the Article 143 autonomous communities in Spain). Finally, in both Italy and Spain, the ordinary regions have been entrusted with roughly similar powers by their respective constitutions (Merloni 1983, pp. 776-83).

As we have observed, however, the Italian constitution prescribes a single procedure for acquiring regional autonomy and names the regions that are to receive autonomous status. The Spanish constitution, on the other hand, indicates at least four alternative paths to regional autonomy, and fails to identify the regions that are entitled to attain it. It leaves the determination of the numbers and territorial extent of the autonomous communities largely to the initiative of the groups of provinces, or even single provinces, that may choose to apply for autonomous community status (Merloni 1983, p. 779; Vandelli 1984, pp. 451-53).

This distinction between the two constitutions has been largely eliminated, however, by the Autonomic Pacts of 1981, which do enumerate Spain's nineteen prospective autonomous communities, specify the procedure by which fifteen of those communities are to earn their autonomy, and have been interpreted as implying that autonomy no longer depends on grass-roots initiative (Acuerdos autonómicos 1981, pp. 15-21; Díaz López 1983, p. 1911). The only elements of grass-roots discretion that survive are a provision in the Pacts that permits the single-province regions of Cantabria and Rioja to join Castile-León if they so desire (Acuerdos autonómicos 1981, pp. 32-33) and a constitutional provision permitting Navarre to join the Basque Autonomous Community (López Rodó 1980, pp. 166-67).

Other contrasts also concern the formation and content of the basic Statutes of the regions and autonomous communities. In Italy, the Statutes of the ordinary regions are drawn up by elected regional councils. There is no provision for local government approval or popular endorsement by referendum during the process of initiating autonomy proposals or ratifying Autonomy Statutes. In Spain, on the other hand, the local authorities and--in some cases--the voters are directly involved in the process of Statute formation (López Rodó 1980, pp. 155, 160-61; Merloni 1983, p. 283).

Moreover, the Spanish constitution is much more flexible and indeterminate than the Italian with regard to regional powers. While Article 117 of the Italian constitution itemizes the concurrent powers that the regions may wield, Spanish constitutional guidelines are much less precise. Article 148 specifies a number of powers that all autonomous communities may exercise concurrently if they so desire. After five years (this waiting period does not exist for "historic" communities and Article 151 communities), an autonomous community may revise its Statute, with the consent of the Cortes, in order to expand the powers claimed in the original Statute. The sole restriction on this expansive capability is the constitutional proviso in Article 149.3 that an autonomous community may not encroach on the exclusive powers granted to the central government by Article 149.1 (Díaz López 1985, pp. 252-55; López Rodó 1980, pp. 156-60; Merloni 1983, p. 782).

One final distinction between the two constitutional frameworks that is relevant to regional devolution has to do with the composition of the Senate, the upper house of parliament. The Italian Senate and the Spanish Senate are both elected from regional constituencies. However, the Italian Senate is elected largely on the basis of the population of each region (one senator for each 200,000 inhabitants), with only a modest measure of overrepresentation afforded to regions with a population of less than 1.2 million. Then, too, Italian senators represent regional voters, not regional governments. By way of contrast, the Spanish Senate provides some representation for the <u>governments</u> of autonomous communities, while still having most of its members elected by popular vote. Most Spanish senators are elected by the voters of the respective autonomous communities, which they represent on the basis of five senators from each province--a formula that greatly overrepresents small provinces. But a sizable minority of senators are chosen by the legislative assemblies of the various autonomous communities. The formula for representation in this case is as follows: Each autonomous community is entitled to one senator, plus an additional senator for each million inhabitants. Vandelli estimates that eventually the Spanish Senate should include 200 members elected by the voters at the province level and 45 members elected by community legislatures (1984, pp. 457-60)

Thus, the Spanish Senate, while a far cry from the West German Bundesrat, provides a substantial minority voice for the representatives of regional legislatures and ensures a significant degree of overrepresentation to the smaller autonomous communities and smaller provinces. In these two ways, it comes much closer to the federal ideal than does the Italian Senate. Nevertheless, all this is offset by the fact that the Spanish Senate is much weaker than the lower house of the Cortes (the Congress of Deputies), whereas in Italy the two chambers are equal in power (Vandelli 1984, pp. 458-60).

The comparison reveals some fairly clear-cut differences between the Italian and Spanish models of regional devolution, as expressed by their respective constitutions.

It also calls our attention, however, to the fact that the Autonomic Pacts of 1981 have partially narrowed these differences. As a result of the Pacts, the centrifugal tendencies encouraged by the 1978 constitution have been subjected to a greater measure of central control. Both the Centrist cabinet of Calvo Sotelo and the Socialist cabinet under Gonzalez have imparted a centralizing tilt to their policies vis-à-vis the autonomous communities.

The Structure and Basic Processes
of Regional Government

As we have previously noted, the constitution of 1978 and the Autonomic Pacts of 1981 combined to ensure that all the autonomous communities were to be equipped with roughly the same basic policy-making structures. Within these fairly broad limits, they would be free to draw up their own fundamental Statutes; but each Statute would require the approval of the Cortes in Madrid before it could go into effect (Acuerdos autonómicos 1981, pp. 21-26; López Rodó 1980, p. 162). Moreover, in accordance with an agreement that formed part of the Autonomic Pacts, all the autonomous communities that had acceded to autonomous status after July 1981 and had utilized Article 143 in attaining that status would be required to hold their regional elections on the same day (Acuerdos autonómicos 1981, pp. 21-22; Martín Mateo 1984, p. 131). This requirement would apply to all the communities except Catalonia, the Basque provinces, Galicia, and Andalucía.

Each autonomous community was to have an elected regional assembly, a president elected by that assembly to head the executive branch, and an executive Council of Government. Also, according to the constitution, each community was to have a superior tribunal of justice to exercise judicial functions. However, as recently as 1985, Clark (1985a, p. 7) was unable to point to a single autonomous community that had actually set up such a tribunal, even though the Regional Statutes explicitly provide for it.

The regional assembly was to be elected by popular vote for a term of four years, on the basis of proportional representation, with the additional and somewhat incongruous proviso that the various zones of an autonomous community's territory would be adequately represented. Most autonomous communities (with the obvious exception of the single-province communities) have used the province as the electoral district for choosing members of the regional assembly and have tended to allot a disproportionately large share of the seats to the smaller, that is, less populous, provinces. This overrepresentation of small provinces in the regional assembly tends to replicate a similar pattern that is clearly visible in the arrangements for the election of the two houses of the national Cortes (Martín Mateo 1984, pp. 128-30; Vandelli 1982, pp. 240, 387-88). In this respect, Spain certainly deviates from Italian usage. In the elections of the Italian regional councils, population is assigned much more weight in allocating representation than is the case in Spain.

The constitution of 1978, as supplemented by the autonomic Pacts, also provided that the regional assembly was to elect a president, from among its own members, to head the executive Council of Government. While the constitution was silent on the question of how the Council of Government was to be chosen, a number of Regional Statutes have since declared that the members of the council are to be picked by the president. The president and the council over which he or she presided were to be jointly responsible to the regional assembly. The assembly could dismiss the president by a constructive vote of no confidence: a motion of censure, backed by an absolute majority of the regional assembly membership, and having the effect of simultaneously removing the president and naming the successor. Here again, as in Italy, the system of regional government was parliamentary in structure and operation (Martín Mateo 1984, pp. 132-43; Vandelli 1982, pp. 235-46, 387-89). However, it was by no means on all fours with the Italian model.

If we compare the Italian and Spanish structures of regional government, certain commonly shared features immediately become evident. The elementary structural similarities are obvious. Not only does the parliamentary form prevail, but there is also a neat equivalence among the principal institutions. Thus, the Italian regional council corresponds to the Spanish regional assembly, and the Italian regional junta is the counterpart of the Spanish council of government. In both countries, moreover, the president of the region combines the symbolic functions of a ceremonial chief executive with the political and administrative functions of a head of government (Martín Mateo

1984, pp. 136-39; Vandelli 1982, pp. 241-42). There is also a curious dualism in both regional systems: The five Italian special regions and the three Spanish historic communities plus Andalucía all enjoy a separate status, apart from that of the ordinary regions or the Article 143 communities. This status is more privileged in some cases (e.g., the Basque country and Catalonia), somewhat less privileged in others (some of the Italian special regions), but it is definitely of different orders of magnitude and quality. One illustration of this special status is the fact that, in both Italy and Spain, ordinary regions hold their legislative elections on the same day, whereas special regions in Italy and historic communities plus Andalucía in Spain march to their individual drummers in setting the date for regional elections.

Yet, behind the surface likeness, there is considerable divergence between the two systems of regional government. First of all, the Spanish regional president appears to be far more powerful than his Italian counterpart. The constructive vote of no confidence, a device that has bolstered executive strength and stability in the Federal Republic of Germany, protects the Spanish regional president against the frequent overthrows that have befallen presidents of Italian regional juntas. Also, the power to choose members of the council of government has been conceded to the presidents by a number of Spanish Regional Statutes, whereas in Italy the junta is elected by the regional (legislative) council after extensive negotiations between leaders of the parties forming the majority coalition (Martín Mateo 1984, pp. 138-39; Vandelli 1982, pp. 388-89). Finally, Spanish electoral laws and the Spanish party system seem to produce one-party cabinets quite frequently at both the national and regional levels. This, too, contributes to the strength of the regional president.

Another contrast between the two regional structures is the variance in the degree to which they conform to their respective national models. While the institutional framework of Italian regional government deviates from the national governmental edifice in a number of secondary but nonetheless significant respects, Spanish regional institutions are very much in line with their national counterparts, at least in the case of the ordinary autonomous communities. Thus, for example, standing committees in Italian regional councils have been denied the power (long exercised by standing committees in the Italian national parliament) to pass legislation themselves without having to submit it to the whole house. In Spain, on the other hand, standing committees in the regional assemblies have been granted this power, just like their opposite numbers in the Cortes (Vandelli 1982, pp. 240-41, 244-46). It would appear, then, that Spanish regional institutions were not visualized by their framers to be a chosen instrument for improving on defective national institutions. Quite the reverse was the case in Italy, where it was hoped that institutional innovation at the regional grass roots would be a means of regenerating the central government (Merloni 1983, p. 779).

Relations with the Center

The relationship between the Spanish autonomous communities and the central government is still in the process of being defined. Since most Spanish autonomous communities did not actually come into existence until 1982 and 1983, and since even the Basque region and Catalonia acquired their autonomy as recently as 1979, we lack the rich heritage of institutional experience and accompanying scholarly commentary that the Italian case provides.

Unlike the Italian constitution, which lists the powers of the regions and makes it clear that those powers are concurrent, the Spanish constitution fails to furnish a lucid, comprehensive description of the distribution of powers between the central government and the autonomous communities (Ariño Ortiz 1981, pp. 30-54; Díaz López 1985, pp. 253-55; Esteban and López Guerra 1983, pp. 377-98; Leguina Villa 1984, pp. 61-83; López Rodó 1984, pp. 55-78, 133-36; Martín Mateo 1984, pp. 179-200, 210-21; Simón Tobalina 1981, pp. 174-78; Vandelli 1982, pp. 247-70, 289-94). Article 148, Section 1, lists a number of subject areas over which the autonomous communities may exercise jurisdiction, but does not specify whether these powers are exclusive or concurrent. Article 149, Section 1, on the other hand, contains a long list of exclusive powers attributed to the national government. However, it also stipulates, with regard to some of these powers, that the central government is authorized to legislate on general principles and broad policy directives in these fields, while the autonomous communities are entitled to legislate on the details of policy.

Thus far, then, we have seen no mention of exclusive regional powers. This void is filled, but not very adequately, by Article 149, Section 3. This section does two things: It confers on the autonomous communities the right to exercise certain unspecified residual powers--powers not listed in Articles 148 and 149 and not yet preempted by the central government. Its second and more important contribution is a brief, rather cryptic, reference to "the exclusive jurisdiction" of the autonomous communities. Thus, the principle of exclusive regional power is introduced, without having its connotations spelled out.

The question left unanswered by Article 149, Section 3, is the obvious one: What are these exclusive powers that the autonomous communities may exercise? A broad interpretation would include all the powers listed in Article 148, Section 1. However, a number of the powers listed there are explicitly qualified as having to be shared with the central government or as having to be exercised within the broad framework established by central policy directives. Since the constitution offers no adequate guidance on this subject, the question has to be resolved by the autonomous communities themselves, when they draw up their basic Statutes, and by the Cortes, when it approves those Statutes. In fact, the Statutes of the various autonomous communities contain lists of exclusive powers to be exercised by the community organs, lists that can be surprisingly broad in scope. As Ariño Ortiz puts it, "The decisive instrument [in the distribution of power] is not the Constitution but the Statutes" (1981, p. 32).

Yet the Statutes only serve to complicate the issue further. For it turns out that, all too frequently, the basic statute of an autonomous community claims exclusive powers that coincide or overlap with exclusive powers assigned to the central government by Article 149, Section 1 (López Rodó 1984, pp. 63-67; Martín Mateo 1984, p. 188). The resulting conflicts have required resolution by the Constitutional Tribunal on a case-by-case basis. In dealing with such cases, the Constitutional Tribunal has ruled that autonomous communities may exercise their exclusive jurisdiction over those aspects of a policy area that do not affect the general interests of the nation and that (with some qualifications) do not have a direct impact on the affairs of neighboring autonomous communities. It has also attempted to define the boundary between "basic legislative powers," which some provisions of Article 149 reserve exclusively for the central government in specified policy areas, and the more detailed rule-making powers that the autonomous communities are entitled to exercise in those same policy areas (López Rodó 1984, pp. 69-78). Nevertheless, these distinctions made by the Constitutional Tribunal in individual cases do not really foreclose the need for further litigation.

There is considerable disagreement among Spanish scholars over the question of whether or not the autonomous communities really possess exclusive powers. One school of thought argues that all the powers of the autonomous communities are really concurrent and that the central government retains overriding legal control (Ariño Ortiz 1981, pp. 40-41; Díaz López 1985, pp. 252, 253, 255, 256). A second school of thought, adopting a more selective interpretation, believes that some, but not most or all, of the powers listed in Article 148, Section 1, are actually or potentially exclusive (Esteban and López Guerra 1983, pp. 386-88; Leguina Villa 1984, pp. 67-69; Martín Mateo 1984, pp. 217-21). This more selective approach fails, however, to provide a clear and unambiguous answer to our dilemma. A third group of scholars view certain sections of the constitution as opening the floodgates to a never-ending series of centrifugal pressures against the Spanish state, bringing about a disastrous erosion of the powers of the central government and the emergence of a quasi-federal system (López Rodó 1984, pp. 99-109, 133-36). Some go a step farther and claim that the constitution makes no adequate provision for central supremacy, so that Spain could easily degenerate into a kind of disorderly confederacy (Burgos 1983, pp. 55-84, passim).

On the basis of the rulings of the Constitutional Tribunal, the first of these theses appears to have achieved somewhat greater credibility. In any event, it would appear that the Spanish autonomous communities, in exercising their concurrent powers (and perhaps even in wielding their "exclusive" powers within the restrictive limits the decisions of the Constitutional Tribunal seem to be defining), have to wait for positive actions on the part of the central government. In each autonomous community, a Mixed Commission on the Transfer of Powers, representing both the central and the regional governments, has to authorize each transfer of power from Madrid to the region on a case-by-case basis.[1] After the Mixed Commission has given its approval, the proposed transfer is sent to the central government to be enacted by decree or rejected (Clark 1985a, p. 9; Estatuto de Autonomía de Valencia 1982, pp. 119-22).

There is some disagreement as to how expeditiously this Mixed Commission system is working. The minister for territorial administration declared on February 24, 1983, that the process of transferring powers had reached levels of progress toward the final goal of eighty-five percent in Catalonia, seventy-five percent in the Basque country, and twenty-five to thirty percent in Galicia (Vandelli 1984, p. 455). On the other hand, others have portrayed the transfer process as characterized by an unduly slow rate of progress and by insufficient financing, and have alleged that these malfunctions have seriously delayed the achievement of regional autonomy (Clark 1985a, p. 9; Pin Arboledas 1984, pp. 162-68).

As far as legislation is concerned, it is evident that, even after powers have been transferred, the Spanish autonomous communities, like their Italian counterparts, may feel unable or unwilling to pass laws in a given area of policy in the absence of a national framework law defining the distribution of responsibility in that policy area. The lack of such framework laws has apparently had the effect of limiting legislative output on the part of regional assemblies (Díaz López 1985, p. 252). The Constitutional Tribunal has held, in a 1981 decision, that regional assemblies may pass legislation in the absence of a national framework law covering the policy area in question, but that in so doing they must respect limits prescribed by "the principles which may be rationally deduced from existing legislation" (Vandelli 1984, p. 451). In short, central occupancy of the field need not be a physical reality

---

[1] A recent decision of the Constitutional Tribunal (April 7, 1983) holds that powers assigned to an autonomous community by its basic Statute cannot be subject to this transfer procedure. However, even if there is no need to transfer formal powers from Madrid, it is still necessary to transfer personnel and financial resources (Martín Mateo 1984, p. 273).

in order to deter penetration by the regions; the Constitutional Tribunal may infer its intangible presence.

The Spanish equivalent of the Italian regional commissioner is the government delegate, appointed by royal decree on the basis of the prime minister's recommendation. As in Italy, he or she is the liaison between the autonomous community and the central government. However, this official does not have any supervisory or quasi-judicial control over the government of the autonomous community (Martín Mateo 1984, p. 284; Vandelli 1982, pp. 313-16). Also, he or she has no power to ratify or veto (the Italian rinvio) legislation passed by the regional assemblies. The government delegate can only recommend to the central government that it should proceed to impugn the constitutionality of the offending legislation before the Constitutional Tribunal (Tolivar Alas 1981, pp. 133-36, 143-44). Vis-à-vis the autonomous communities, then, the delegate's role is considerably less active and prominent than that of the Italian regional commissioner (Vandelli 1982, pp. 315-16).

The Constitutional Tribunal in Spain performs a role very similar to that of the Italian Constitutional Court in Italy (Tolivar Alas 1981, pp. 130-31). It decides conflicts between the central government and the autonomous communities. It can pass on the constitutionality of central and regional laws, and also of regional executive rulings issued by the autonomous communities and having the force of law (Díaz López 1985, pp. 256-57). Cases may be brought before the Constitutional Tribunal by the prime minister, by the public defender, by fifty members of either house of the Cortes, or by the collective executive organs (cabinets) and regional assemblies of one or more autonomous communities (Vandelli 1982, p. 320).

It is all too evident from our earlier discussion that the Constitutional Tribunal is going to be relied on heavily as an instrument for hammering out a distribution of governmental power that is only roughly outlined in the constitution. As of early 1984, it had heard forty cases in which the constitutionality of central and regional laws and decrees was called into question (Díaz López 1985, pp. 258-59).

It would be highly premature, so soon after the establishment of the Constitutional Tribunal in 1979, to venture any firm judgments as to the Tribunal's emerging pattern of behavior. At this point, however, it can certainly be stated that the Constitutional Tribunal has already displayed a rather independent bent by declaring several portions of LOAPA (the Organic Law for the Harmonization of the Autonomic Process) unconstitutional, in a decision handed down in August 1983. In its ruling, the Constitutional Tribunal declared that parliament had no right to usurp the Tribunal's function of interpreting the constitution (Vandelli 1984, pp. 472-73). The Constitutional Tribunal was thus taking at least a temporary stand against the counteroffensive of the centralizers. It remains to be seen how long this decentralizing mood--so out of tune with the Tribunal's recent decisions on exclusive and concurrent powers--will endure.

As yet, there is little conclusive evidence regarding the relationship that is developing between the autonomous communities and the Cortes. However, the passage of LOAPA in 1982 by a Socialist-Centrist majority, over the strong opposition of the regionalist parties and the Communists (Elorriaga 1983, pp. 295-96, 326), would certainly suggest that the mainstream of the Cortes was committed to a unitary Spain and was not prepared to allow centrifugal pressures to impose an excessive degree of political heterogeneity on the Spanish polity. The Socialist victory in the parliamentary election in the fall of 1982 seems to confirm this suggestion.

In their relations with the Cortes, the autonomous communities are vouchsafed a number of rights and guarantees. Like their Italian counterparts, they have the privilege of introducing legislation in the central parliament. However, there seems to be a greater likelihood in Spain than in Italy that this kind of initiative may have a meaningful impact. First of all, the Spanish regions may introduce bills in policy areas constitutionally reserved for the central government (Díaz López 1985, p. 258). Second, a regional assembly may select three of its members to push for its legislation during sessions of the Cortes, and these delegates may actually take part in Cortes debates. Third, a regional assembly that wishes to introduce a bill in the Cortes may approach the cabinet first and try to get the bill sponsored as a government measure (Vandelli 1984, pp. 460-61).

As was previously noted, the regional assemblies of the autonomous communities are entitled to choose almost one-quarter of the members of the Senate, the rest being elected by the voters in each province. In most cases, the senators selected by the regional assemblies continue to serve simultaneously as regional legislators (Vandelli 1984, pp. 457-58). Thus, the governments of the autonomous communities have a voice--albeit, a minority one--in the upper house of the Cortes. This affords them some measure of special protection. For one thing, before the central government can take action to compel an autonomous community to fulfill its constitutional obligations, the Senate must agree by an absolute majority (Díaz López 1985, p. 257; Vandelli 1984, p. 459). Also, passage of a harmonization law, which is designed to overcome discrepancies between the legislative measures adopted by a number of autonomous communities, requires an absolute majority of both houses of the Cortes, thus giving the Senate a veto power (Esteban and López Guerra 1983, p. 399).

Apart from the provisions cited, which seem designed to give the regional assemblies a somewhat more prominent role in affecting national decision making than the Italian regional councils are able to play, the autonomous communities also are legally entitled to be consulted before the central Council of Ministers introduces a government bill affecting their rights or interests directly or involving their concurrent powers (Vandelli 1984, p. 471). They can also participate, through their designated representatives, in the work of the Senate Committee on Autonomy and on Territorial Organization and Administration (Vandelli 1984, pp. 462-63). It must be conceded, however, that the literature on Spain simply does not portray the kind of dense network of consultation and collaboration that links the Italian regions to the Italian parliament. In all likelihood, this gap may be attributed to the fact that the autonomous communities have barely come into existence.

The Spanish Cortes similarly has some power to supervise regional behavior in certain areas and has begun to develop mechanisms (like the aforementioned Senate committee) for dealing with the regions. Cooperative agreements among autonomous communities require the approval of the Cortes, and the same is true of formulas for distributing money among the autonomous communities from the Interterritorial Compensation Fund (Díaz López 1985, p. 258; Vandelli 1984, pp. 459, 462-63). And any reform of a regional basic Statute requires Cortes approval.

Central-regional relations among executive organs are still in their early formative years in Spain. Observers of the subnational political scene point to the fact that

Spain has not yet developed the highly organized system of semiinstitutionalized dialogue between the state and the regions that takes place in Italy (Wright 1984, p. 1171). There is no indication as yet that the presidents of the autonomous communities have formed anything comparable to the Italian Conference of Regional Junta Presidents, or are planning to meet collectively on a regular basis with members of the Spanish Council of Ministers in a state-region conference on the recently fashioned Italian model.

Vandelli (1984, pp. 467-71) directs our attention to the fact that certain provisions of the Spanish constitution tend to promote an arm's-length relationship between the state and the autonomous communities. For example, the Italian regional commissioner may use the period between his or her initial veto of a regional bill and the final decision to appeal to the Constitutional Court (in the event the regional council has refused to modify it) as a time for negotiating with the regional government in an effort to obtain mutually acceptable amendments. The Spanish government delegate, on the other hand, has no veto or formal negotiating power, and simply submits a recommendation to the Spanish government that the legislation should or should not be appealed to the Constitutional Tribunal. The idea underlying the Spanish system seems to be that the national executive branch should not engage in bargaining with regional executives over conflicts of powers, but should let the courts decide the outcome of any disputes.

However, there is evidence that the actual functioning of the Spanish system and the passage of time are bringing it closer to the Italian consultative style. According to recent statements by the minister for territorial administration, there has been an increasing tendency for the ministry to engage regional officials in informal "conversations," the purpose of which is to obtain modifications in objectionable regional laws in exchange for the central government's agreement not to challenge the constitutionality of said laws before the Constitutional Tribunal. As a result, the percentage of regional laws and decrees brought before the Constitutional Tribunal declined from 1.2 percent, during the period December 1981-January 1982, to 0.6 percent during a corresponding period in 1982-1983 (Vandelli 1984, pp. 469-70).

In other respects, too, central-regional contacts are becoming more numerous and fruitful. True, the mixed commissions and the mixed sectoral commissions have left much to be desired in their handling of the transfer of powers to the regional level. However, once the transfer has been consummated, a more collaborative relationship between center and periphery appears to be feasible. For example, in a number of functional fields such as agriculture and fishing—fields in which the central government and the autonomous communities share concurrent powers—sectoral conferences have been convened. Participants in these conferences include the central government minister responsible for the functional field in question and corresponding regional ministers (called councillors in Spain rather than assessors) from the autonomous communities. Their purpose is to coordinate state and regional policies in their respective functional fields (Vandelli 1984, p. 471; Martín Mateo 1984, pp. 286-87). To deal with regional financing, there is also a Council on the Fiscal and Financial Policy of the Autonomous Communities, consisting of the minister of finance and of economic affairs, the minister of territorial administration, and the treasury councillors from the autonomous communities (Martín Mateo 1984, p. 287). This council has not held many meetings or been particularly active as yet (Pin Arboledas 1984, p. 163). All this is still in its infancy, to be sure, but a beginning is being made.

In dealing with the autonomous communities and in coordinating central-regional relations, the prime minister has a few institutional aids at his or her disposal. The minister for territorial administration seems to correspond fairly closely to the Italian minister for regional affairs. The coordination of government policies with regard to regional affairs is entrusted to two bodies: the Government Commission In Charge of Autonomic Policy and the Interministerial Commission for Autonomic Development (Vandelli 1982, pp. 357-59). As may be surmised from the lower ranking status of most of its members as compared to the Government Commission, the Interministerial Commission prepares plans and policy proposals for final approval by the Government Commission. It has been alleged by Pin Arboledas (1984, pp. 163-64) that the Interministerial Commission and the Committee on Public Investments—two bodies on which the autonomous communities have no representation—have been frequently used by the central government to arrive at decisions in areas that lie within the jurisdiction of the mixed committees or of the Council on Fiscal and Financial Policy. Once again, however, it should be stressed that these rather rudimentary structures and relationships reflect the very brief time span covered by the Spanish autonomous communities as functioning institutional entities.

While the relations between the Spanish central government and the autonomous communities are still ill defined, and the Spanish regional situation is about as prefatory today as was that of Italy before the promulgation of Presidential Decree-Law 616 in 1977, some Spanish scholars (like their Italian colleagues) are already beginning to use the term "cooperative federalism" to define the intrinsic character of the central-regional linkage (Esteban and López Guerra 1983, p. 394). The financial arrangements accompanying Spanish regional devolution seem to vindicate this interpretation of reality, for they do much to placate the fears of those who see the autonomous communities as agents of the eventual disintegration of the Spanish state.

Article 156, Section 1, of the 1978 Spanish constitution recognizes the financial autonomy of the Spanish autonomous communities. Article 157, Section 1, provides that the resources of the autonomous communities are to include their own taxes, tax revenues ceded to them wholly or in part by the state, and the revenues from surtaxes imposed on existing state taxes. In addition, the autonomous communities are to receive transfer payments from the general state budget and from the Interterritorial Compensation Fund (Clark 1985a, p. 10; Ferreiro Lapatza 1981, pp. 163-66, 169-70, 180-84; López Rodó 1980, pp. 163-64; Martín Mateo 1984, pp. 253-56; Merloni 1983, p. 785).

As a number of Spanish scholars clearly demonstrate, the financial autonomy granted by the constitution to the autonomous communities is subjected to a number of very confining restraints. First of all, the taxing powers of the autonomous communities are derived, not original, and can only be exercised after prior authorization by state law. Moreover, the Cortes, in passing enabling legislation, may impose certain limits on the regional taxing powers it grants (Esteban and López Guerra 1983, p. 393; Ferreiro Lapatza 1981, pp. 164-65). Second, in providing for the financial autonomy of the autonomous communities, Article 156, Section 1, states that this autonomy can only be exercised in coordination with the state budget and in accordance with the principle of solidarity with other Spaniards (Ferreiro Lapatza 1981, p. 164; López Rodó 1980, p. 163). The solidarity principle implies that the richer regions are expected to contribute more than their share of funds to the task of correcting social and economic imbalances among the autonomous communities of Spain (Díaz López 1985, pp. 246-47). And, finally, the taxing power of the autonomous communities is restricted within very narrow confines (Ferreiro Lapatza 1981, pp. 170-73).

Transfer payments from the central government are likely to play an increasingly dominant role in filling regional coffers in Spain, as they presently do in Italy. It is not yet clear how dependent the autonomous communities are becoming with regard to conditional grants for earmarked purposes—or even whether such a trend is under way at all. In the area of unconditional grants, the autonomous communities have been obtaining most of their funds from two sources. One source is the general state budget, which includes appropriations to individual autonomous communities. These grants are intended to ensure the maintenance of a minimum level of services by each member community. The other source is the Interterritorial Compensation Fund, which is supposed to constitute at least thirty percent of the public investment money appropriated each year for the general state budget and is to be distributed among the autonomous communities on the basis of certain criteria employed to assess relative need (López Nieto and Fernández Rodrígues 1981, pp. 200-204, 207-26, 277-82, 293-391). These criteria include per capita income, net emigration, land area, and rate of unemployment.

Some of the wealthier regions (notably the Basque country) have objected to the formula used to determine how much each autonomous community should pay into, and receive from, the Interterritorial Compensation Fund. They claim that the formula is so calculated as to discriminate against the richer provinces of Spain, and that it takes little account of the recession that is hitting the old industrial areas of the north. In 1983, for example, the Basque region paid over 6 billion pesetas more into the Fund than it received, thus seriously draining its own capacity to replace or repair aging infrastructures in the Basque provinces (Clark 1985a, p. 10).

Any survey, however concise, of regional finance in Spain requires a brief reference to the Basque country (Guipuzcoa, Álava, and Vizcaya Provinces) and the single-province region of Navarre. The four provinces that make up these two autonomous communities are referred to as "historic territories" because they still claim their ancient foral privileges. While the foral privileges were abolished after the Second Carlist War, they were replaced in 1878 by <u>conciertos económicos</u> (economic accords) between Madrid and each "historic territory." Under the terms of these economic accords, each province was entitled to lay and collect its own taxes, after negotiating with Madrid, and then pay a fixed quota into the coffers of the central government (Heiberg 1982, p. 364). The accords were cancelled by the Franco regime in the case of the two provinces (Guipuzcoa and Vizcaya) that had backed the Republic during the Civil War, but are now once again in force in all four of the "historic territories."

Under the present system, the central government <u>does</u> exercise some coordinating authority: No new tax rates may be imposed or existing tax rates altered without approval by the central government and ratification by the Cortes. Also, the Basque regional government now plays a role in the system: It receives a contribution from each province to the regional budget; its representative sits on the Mixed Commission (with central and provincial representatives) to negotiate the amount each province is to remit to Madrid; and it negotiates with the Spanish Ministry of the Treasury over the annual level of central government spending in the Basque country (Martín Mateo 1984, pp. 251, 258-60, 264-66). So far, the system has worked reasonably well despite long, drawn-out negotiations (Clark 1985a, pp. 8-9), but there is a great potential for friction and possible deadlock.

Relations with Local Governments

In view of the fact that the Spanish autonomous communities have had such a brief institutional existence thus far, it is hardly surprising that the problem of regional-local relations has not yet acquired clearly discernible contours. That tension between regional centers and provincial and local peripheries which has been observed in Italy has not yet become salient in Spain, although some signs of friction have already manifested themselves.

In examining regional-local relations in Spain, we should begin by noting one significant difference between the Spanish and Italian systems. As we have seen, control over provincial and communal acts is vested, in Italy, in a largely administrative organ, the Regional Control

Committee. In Spain, on the other hand, this control function is entrusted to the ordinary judiciary and takes the form of declaring local acts legal or illegal after, not before, they have gone into effect. Only in the case of powers delegated by the autonomous communities to the provincial and/or local governments are the regional authorities entitled to maintain administrative oversight and to grant or withhold prior approval of local decisions (Esteban and López Guerra 1983, p. 327; Tolivar Alas 1981, pp. 150-55). It should be stressed, finally, that this judicial control over local and provincial acts is to be exercised in the national interest. The Constitutional Tribunal has indicated that the Superior Tribunal of Justice, which the constitution has provided for as the leading judicial organ in each autonomous community, is to be regarded as a state organ rather than a community organ (Martín Mateo 1984, p. 201).

The delegation of functions to local and provincial authorities has failed to conform to any consistent or clearly defined pattern. The constitution of 1978 had proclaimed the principle of local and provincial autonomy but neglected to spell out its implications or to specify what powers local governments were to exercise. The task of determining what functions the local and provincial governments were to perform was left to the discretion of the national Cortes and of the framers of the basic Statutes of the autonomous communities. The Autonomic Pacts of 1981 opened up further possibilities when they declared that autonomous communities could—within guidelines established by national or regional legislation—transfer or delegate some of their own functions to provincial governments, entrust the administration of their field services to local and provincial governing bodies, or simply coordinate the activities of local and provincial authorities. It was evident, by 1982, that the constitution and the Autonomic Pacts left open a variety of options for the Cortes and the regional founding fathers to consider in the years to come (Esteban and López Guerra 1983, p. 326; Martín Mateo 1984, pp. 326-28; Merloni 1983, p. 795; Vandelli 1982, pp. 306-307, 389-90).

As a result of this constitutional permissiveness, there has been a great deal of variation in the role assigned to local governments by the basic Statutes of the autonomous communities. The Catalan Statute, in line with Catalan historical tradition, has a definite antiprovincial bias and provides for the creation of regional field services at the local level (Merloni 1983, pp. 794-95; Vandelli 1982, pp. 307-308). In fact, subsequent Catalan legislation, declared unconstitutional by the Constitutional Tribunal, sought to turn all provincial functions over to specially created districts (<u>comarcas</u>), each comprising a number of municipalities (Díaz López and Morata 1984, pp. 83-84; Martín Mateo 1984, pp. 332-33; Vandelli 1982, pp. 376-79). In its antiprovincial posture, Catalonia is definitely outside the Spanish political mainstream. Most of the other regions have chosen to carry out a number of their assigned functions by utilizing the resources and personnel of the local and provincial governments (Martín Mateo 1984, p. 335; Vandelli 1982, pp. 307-308).

In the Basque country--the other great exception--a special situation prevails. Unlike the Catalan Statute, the Basque Statute assigns a very significant role to the local governments, especially to the provinces. The principle of <u>foralidad</u>, acknowledged in the Spanish constitution and bolstered by long-established historical traditions, has resulted in a privileged status for the Basque provinces of Guipuzcoa, Alava, and Vizcaya. The Basque Statute designates these provinces as "historic territories," recognizes their right to maintain their own distinctive subregional political institutions, and assigns them a number of exclusive powers not possessed by provinces elsewhere in Spain. These powers include the power to lay and collect taxes, with the sole exception of customs duties and the proceeds of state monopolies (Martín Mateo 1984, pp. 333-35).

The balance of power between the Basque autonomous community and its component "historic territories" is still in a state of transition with the ultimate outcome by no means assured. The very fact that each province, regardless of population, has the same number of representatives in the Basque parliament (Clark 1985b, p. 81) clearly indicates the strong concern for provincial rights that persists in the Basque country. In a singular effort to deal with potential regional-provincial disputes, the basic Statute of the Basque Autonomous Community provides that, whenever such a dispute arises over the question of conflicting jurisdictional claims, an arbitration commission is to be set up, with half of its members chosen by the Basque government and half by the provincial government concerned with the issue. This commission is charged with resolving the controversy with a decision binding on both parties (Martín Mateo 1984, pp. 304-305). On November 25, 1983, the Basque parliament adopted the Law on Relations Between the Common Institutions of the Autonomous Community and the Foral Organs of the Historic Territories, which will henceforth serve as a frame of reference and fundamental code for the complex problem of regional-provincial relations in the Basque country (Ministerio de Administración Territorial 1984, pp. 125-34).

The Spanish constitution permits the autonomous communities to engage in a certain amount of institutional experimentation by creating new units of subregional government, consisting of groups of municipalities consolidated into districts (comarcas). However, there are certain constraints on such experimentation; for example, the existence of the provinces is constitutionally guaranteed, and any change in the boundary of a province can be accomplished only by passing an organic law in the Cortes. With regard to municipalities, on the other hand, the autonomous communities may change the boundaries of municipalities located within their respective jurisdictions, without having to obtain the consent of the Cortes (Esteban and López Guerra 1983, pp. 323-25). All in all, the Spanish constitution appears to allow the Spanish regions a great deal of leeway in organizing and reorganizing their subregional governmental systems—far greater leeway than their Italian counterparts enjoy. As a result, most of the basic Statutes of the Spanish autonomous communities provide for the formation of comarcas (Ministerio de Administración Territorial 1984, pp. 24-25), whereas the Italian comprensorio seems to be withering on the vine.

It is still very early in the game (most of the autonomous communities are less than five years old) to speak of an antiregional resistance movement in Spain. Nevertheless, there is a strong possibility that such a movement will emerge as soon as the autonomous communities have achieved a degree of institutionalization comparable to what the Italian regions have attained. Some contemporary phenomena may well prove to be harbingers of the kind of central-local alliance against regional power that we observed in Italy. First of all, the very fact that nine of Spain's nineteen autonomous communities (seven out of seventeen if we exclude the North African city-regions of Ceuta and Melilla) are single-province regions indicates that there is still a strong and widespread sense of provincial loyalty that has had to be appeased. Also, it should be recalled that some provinces (like Segovia vis-à-vis Castile-León or Navarre vis-à-vis the Basque country) have bitterly resisted being forced into a regional context[2] (Clavero Arévalo 1983, pp. 73-83; Linz 1981a, 1981b, passim; Wright 1984, p. 1175). Then, too, some regions are characterized by only lukewarm popular support for regional political autonomy (this is especially true of Castile-León and Castile-La Mancha) or are torn by interprovincial rivalries, as in the case of Andalucía and Valencia (Martín Mateo 1984, pp. 335-36). So, as regional institutions consolidate themselves in Spain and carve out their niche in the scheme of things, we may look for these intraregional centrifugal tendencies to acquire greater prominence.

Relations with Political Parties

The role played by political parties in the Spanish process of regional devolution appears to deviate from the Italian experience in a number of significant ways. First of all, it has been noted that the pressure for regional autonomy in Spain was initiated mostly by ethnic or linguistic movements based in the regions and by regionalist parties speaking exclusively on behalf of the interests of the periphery. In Italy, on the contrary, the drive for regional devolution emanated primarily from the center and reflected the shifting strategic goals of one or the other of the two major national parties--The Christian Democrats and the Communists--as well as the reformist aspirations of some elements among the national governing elites (Wright 1984, p. 1168).

The two party systems are faithful reflections of the diversity of origins differentiating the two movements for regional autonomy. A second major difference between Spain and Italy is represented by the much greater electoral strength of Spanish regionalist parties. In Spain, regionalist parties command close to ten percent of the votes in some national elections and dominate both the Catalan and Basque governments. They are also beginning to display some moderate voting strength in regions where

---

[2]Navarre was successful in asserting its claim to autonomy and became a single-province region, but Segovia's objections went unheeded.

the national parties have been virtually unchallenged--regions like Andalucía, Aragón, the Balearic Islands, the Canary Islands, and Extremadura. Quite apart from their performance at the polls, which has not yet earned them major-party status outside the Basque country and Catalonia, they have been able--by virtue of their growing electoral presence, coupled with their militant dedication--to shape the thinking and condition the behavior of the major national parties (Díaz López 1985, pp. 263-65; Mény 1984, pp. 1146-48; Wright 1984, p. 1171). Thus, the UCD, the Socialists, and the Communists have all, at various times, felt compelled to yield to autonomist demands, in order not to surrender more votes to the vociferous regionalist parties (Mény 1984, pp. 1147-48).

By way of contrast, regionalist parties are extremely weak in Italy, except in such border areas as Trentino-Alto Adige and Val d'Aosta, and do not constitute a significant presence in most Italian regions (Wright 1984, p. 1171). Rather than seek to advance their goals by forming a regionalist party, voters in a given Italian region are more apt to establish close and enduring ties with one of the national parties, viewing that party as a kind of political patron of the region. The unswerving support given to the Christian Democrats by the Veneto, Sicily, and most of continental southern Italy is one example of this tendency; the "Red Belt" in north-central Italy is another (Mény 1984, p. 1146).

A third distinction is related to the national parties in the two countries. In Italy, they are powerful and well organized and have in effect dominated and channeled the process of regional devolution. Instead, Spanish national parties are protagonists in a fragile, recently established national party system, and they have been too weak to control the autonomic process or even to maintain hegemony over the key industrial regions of Catalonia and the Basque country, where regionalist agitation has been particularly vehement (Mény 1984, pp. 1161, 1165; Wright 1984, p. 1171). From a short-range point of view, the weakness of Spanish national parties has certainly bolstered the regionalist forces. However, there has been one highly negative by-product, which does not promise well for the future: The regionalist parties are not adequately integrated into the national party system. Consequently, their segregated political existence has prevented the kind of automatic intermingling and collaboration between central and regional elites that has characterized the Italian party system and helped to entrench and reenforce regional institutions in Italy (Díaz López 1985, p. 267).

Finally, Spanish and Italian parties have differed with respect to the style adopted in coping with the regional issue. For example, the national parties in Spain worked very hard to maintain a consensus on the question of regional autonomy and to keep said question out of the political arena, because they did not want the issue to interfere with the delicate arrangements involved in moving gradually from the autocracy of the Franco regime to a constitutional democracy. It was this universal desire to avoid destabilizing the newly fledged democratic regime that led to the ambiguous compromise that made the constitution so hard to interpret (Mény 1984, pp. 1158-60). No such constraints existed in the Italian context, where fascism had been thoroughly discredited and violently uprooted by 1946, and could no longer be regarded as a credible threat. In Italy, therefore, the parties could allow their conflicting views and interests free rein when addressing themselves to regional problems.

Thus far, we have pointed to a number of ways in which the relationship between Spanish parties and the Spanish autonomous communities could be distinguished from their Italian counterpart. Nevertheless, we must not lose sight of the fundamental points of similarity between them. In both countries, for example, centrist and leftist forces came to equate regional autonomy with the anti-Fascist resistance struggle and the eventual achievement of democratic institutions; and this was a natural reaction against the rigidly centralizing posture of the Fascists.

Above all, we should also emphasize the presence of that possibly universal tendency for political parties to change their tack on regional questions in response to their own shifting political and electoral interests. To cite one instance, the centrist UCD was so alarmed by the electoral gains chalked up by regionalist parties and so disillusioned by its own declining electoral fortunes that it switched from a policy of "regionalism à la carte" (allowing all regions to seek maximum autonomy under the Article 151 procedure) to a policy of "coffee for everybody" (insisting that most regions settle for limited autonomy under the less disruptive Article 143 procedure) (Mény 1984, p. 1162). The Socialists, too, evinced a great deal of malleability on regional questions. Although they had championed regional autonomy while in opposition, their posture became more centralist as they drew nearer to the seat of power and as the abortive military coup of 1981 revealed the festering conservative reaction against regional gains. The same Socialist party that had backed Andalucía's autonomist demands against UCD opposition was prepared, after the attempted coup, to sign the Autonomic Pacts (which prescribed "coffee for everybody") with the UCD and to support the controversial LOAPA (Mény 1984, pp. 1162-64). Moreover, after coming to power, the Socialists have continued to adopt a go-slow policy toward regional autonomy, at least according to the viewpoint of the regionalist parties (Clark 1985b, pp. 78, 86; Pin Arboledas 1984, pp. 159-68).

Regionalism and Ethnic Issues

The protection of minority languages and dialects is a major issue in Spain, and not only in the border areas and the remote periphery as in Italy. Spain's ethnic minorities are militant and demanding and play a dominant role in some of the country's most industrialized and prosperous regions (see Clark 1980, pp. 75-100; Coverdale 1979, pp. 21-35, 83-86, 90-91, 97-102, 106-10, 113-24, 128-30; Gras and Gras 1982, pp. 19-20, 29, 35-39, 49-51, 62-63, 88-91, 114-16, 120-25, 146-49, 195-207; Greenwood 1977, pp. 81-102; Linz 1973, pp. 32-116; Pi-Sunyer 1980, pp. 101-15; Shabad and Gunther 1982, pp. 443-77; Silva 1975, pp. 217-52). The regions in which other languages besides Castilian are spoken include Catalonia, with a population of over 5.6 million; Valencia, with a population of over 3.6 million; Galicia, with over 2.8 million; the three provinces of the Basque country with over 2.1 million; and the Balearic Islands with almost 700,000. The total population of these regions is over 14.8 million--about forty-one percent of Spain's total of almost 36 million (Trujillo 1979, pp. 46-47).

To be sure, these regions have large numbers of immigrants from other parts of Spain; this is particularly true of Catalonia and the Basque country. A more accurate picture of the importance of non-Castilian languages is furnished by the findings of Spanish public opinion surveys. According to these data, thirty-eight percent of a Spanish-wide sample reported that they spoke a language other than

Castilian: sixteen percent spoke Catalan; eleven percent, Valencian; nine percent, Galician; and two percent, Basque (Linz, Gómez-Reino, Orizo, and Vila 1982, p. 510).

Yet, despite the fact that linguistic minorities constitute such a large percentage of the population of Spain and despite the prosperity of some of the more ethnically conscious non-Castilian regions, the fact remains that the regionalist parties have failed to monopolize the votes of their respective ethnic groups. In fact, outside of the Basque country and Catalonia, they have not even succeeded in attaining major-party status. In the Basque country and Catalonia, they do dominate regional politics; but even in these ethnically militant regions, many voters continue to cast their ballots for national parties in national elections (Linz, Gómez-Reino, Orizo, and Vila 1982, p. 513).

In the 1986 parliamentary elections, the regionalist parties increased their representation in the Cortes from twenty-four seats to thirty-five, including eighteen in Catalonia and thirteen in the Basque country. They thus dominated the Cortes delegation from the Basque country (The Economist 1986, p. 43), while continuing to rank behind the national parties in Catalonia. Thus, the Basque country, where such intransigent parties as Herri Batasuna are beginning to outstrip the relatively moderate Basque Nationalists, represents an ever more intractable problem for the rest of Spain.

Since the adoption of the constitution, the institutional response of the Spanish and regional governments to the ethnic problem has been remarkably swift. Castilian is still the official language of Spain, and all citizens are required to be able to use it; but five regions (Catalonia, the Basque country, Galicia, Valencia, and the Balearic Islands) have established a "co-official" regional language (Clark 1985a, p. 2).

The greatest progress toward bilingualism has been made in the Basque country and Catalonia. The Basque and Catalan Autonomy Statutes guarantee all Basques and Catalans the right to know and use their regional languages, as well as Castilian. However, even before the passage of the Autonomy Statutes, the Spanish government had issued decrees providing for a gradual shift to truly bilingual education. This would necessitate setting up two separate systems of schools, one for the children of Castilian-speaking immigrants. In both school systems, however, children would be required to learn both Castilian and the regional language. In Catalonia, it was planned to implement bilingualism uniformly throughout the region; but in the Basque country, immediate implementation of bilingualism was to take place only in Basque-speaking areas, and change was to occur much less rapidly in other zones (Shabad and Gunther 1982, pp. 461-62, 464-67).

There are disturbing signs that the newly established governments and the politicians in these two key regions may not be content with these gains. This is particularly true in Catalonia, whose language (unlike Basque) can be spoken without too much difficulty by a large number of immigrants from other parts of Spain. Some Catalan politicians have spoken out in support of Catalan monolingualism in the school system and in government offices. Linguistic discrimination has allegedly taken place in the hiring policies of the Catalan government and in the professional meetings conducted by the Catalan teachers' association (Shabad and Gunther 1982, pp. 466-71). Yet, as of 1983, Giner could write that "the mass media and education [in Catalonia] were still overwhelmingly biased towards the Spanish, rather than the Catalan" (1984, p. 94).

The immigrant issue is a major factor in Basque and Catalan politics. More than one-third of the Basques and more than one-third of the people in Catalonia were born in other parts of Spain (Shabad and Gunther 1982, pp. 444-85). To expel them or somehow encourage them to return to their home provinces is next to impossible. Yet their very presence threatens the cultural integrity of the Basque country and Catalonia. So a laissez-faire policy seems to be out of the question too. That leaves the possibility of pressuring them into cultural assimilation, a course being considered in both Catalonia and the Basque country. However, such a course invites intervention from Madrid. For example, in 1982, the Spanish Ministry of Education intervened on a number of occasions on behalf of Castilian-speaking parents in the Basque country who did not want their children to be forced to learn Euskera (Clark 1985a, pp. 9-10). It is evident that neither the Basque nor the Catalan government has full, unchallenged control over the cultural life of its regional bailiwick. Intraregional ethnic minorities (Castilian-speaking in these cases) can count on some central protection against oppressive or discriminatory treatment at the hands of the regional majority.

One extreme cultural-political concession made to the Basque region by Madrid has been the establishment of a Basque autonomous police. However, the force has less than 2,000 members and is confined to such duties as traffic control and building security. The bulk of the law enforcement mission is still the function of the central government (Clark 1985a, p. 8). The failure of Madrid to hand over full law enforcement responsibility to the Basque government has been one of the main grievances voiced by disgruntled extremist elements in the Basque country.

After observing the operation of the Italian and Spanish forms of regional devolution in dealing with ethnic issues, we might tentatively conclude that the Spanish system has been much more responsive to the needs expressed by regionally based ethnic groups. However, this responsiveness may well be an artifact of the greater size, consistency, and self-assertiveness of ethnic minorities in Spain and of a situation characterized by widespread political violence.

CONCLUSION

In examining Spanish regional devolution, we delineated the process by which the Spanish political system was established and consolidated. As noted, Spain was a case of incomplete state building; and the Spanish Empire in the sixteenth and seventeenth centuries was actually a set of federated kingdoms, sharing a single monarch but possessing different laws and political traditions. Only in the eighteenth century, when Spanish imperial power and the Castilian resources on which that power was based were in a state of steady decline, was this loose federation replaced by a centralized, unitary state.

The Napoleonic wars helped to foster that sense of nationalism which is so vital to successful nation building, but they also contributed to the internal victory of a centralizing Liberal faction. A postwar centralizing campaign launched by the Liberals provoked the rise of strong regionalist movements on the periphery--a reaction that led to the Carlist Wars and to the eventual emergence of ethnically based regionalist parties. In Catalonia, ethnic regionalism has strong business support; in the Basque country, it depended on the peasantry and middle strata of the less developed hinterland.

We observed the victory of the regionalist forces during the short-lived Second Republic of 1931-1939, when both the Basque country and Catalonia were granted autonomy. With Franco's victory in the Civil War of 1936-1939, total centralization was imposed on outlying regions, and ethnic minorities suffered cultural repression. As a result of the experience of the Second Republic and of the subsequent Franco regime, the Right turned against regionalist claims, whereas the Left embraced the cause of regional autonomy--a complete reversal of the attitudes that had prevailed during the nineteenth century.

With the return of democracy in the mid-1970s, the regionalist cause, which had acquired a new respectability as a symbol of resistance against Franco, enjoyed the support of the dominant parties of the Center and Left, and of the Crown as well. However, during the process of drawing up the constitution, it was necessary to devise a series of rather ambiguous compromise formulas in order not to alienate the Rightist and Right-Center minority and to avoid a possible military reaction. The resulting constitution was a complex, confusing document, open to many interpretations, and seeming to invite a headlong "rush to autonomy." The Autonomic Pacts of 1981, signed by the UCD and by the Socialist party, represented an attempt to reestablish central control of the autonomic process, impose some uniformity and order on that process, and reassure the restive forces on the Right, including the ever-threatening military.

A preliminary survey of the structure and operation of the new Spanish regional governments revealed some significant contrasts with the Italian model. Local authorities and regional voters were much more involved in the process of forming the regional basic Statutes than was the case in Italy. The Spanish constitution is much less explicit in defining regional powers than is its Italian counterpart. And, finally, the Spanish Senate provides a considerable degree of overrepresentation for the smaller regions and smaller provinces, and represents regional governments to some extent, unlike the Italian Senate. Thus, the Spanish Senate is based, to some degree, on federal principles of representation. However, the tilt toward centralization represented by the Autonomic Pacts has somewhat narrowed the differences between the Spanish and Italian models.

We noted that the Spanish autonomous community is endowed with a more powerful president than is the Italian region. Also, the communities in Spain tend to conform much more closely to the national model in their structure and practices than do the regions in Italy. In short, they do not appear to be visualized by their framers as a chosen instrument for improving defective national institutions.

The extent of the power allocated to the autonomous communities by the constitution is still unresolved in the mid-1980s. It is clear that the central government in Spain, as in Italy, has ample power to restrain, to check, to encroach on regional terrain. Delays in the process of transferring power, the lack of framework laws to serve as guidelines for regional action, arbitration by the Constitutional Tribunal on a case-by-case basis—these all appear to represent at least a rough approximation of the Italian pattern. An interesting recent development, out of line with the trend toward some measure of recentralization, is the Constitutional Tribunal's decision in August 1983 to declare unconstitutional certain sections of the LOAPA. This willingness to provide some protection against parliamentary assaults on regional autonomy seems to be in line with a similar trend we observed in the case of the Italian Constitutional Court.

The Spanish regions seem to have somewhat more power than their Italian counterparts to affect national decision making in the Cortes and in the Council of Ministers. As yet, not enough time has elapsed for Spain to develop the kind of dense central-regional consultative-collaborative network that has been constructed in Italy. However, the actual functioning of the Spanish system seems to be bringing central-regional relations somewhat closer to the Italian style and away from the arm's-length relationship the Spanish constitution appears to promote.

In their relations with local governments, the autonomous communities have adopted a variety of postures. Some, like Catalonia, have definitely sought to restrict local or provincial powers; most have chosen to utilize the resources and personnel of local and provincial governments in carrying out their assigned functions; one region, the Basque country, has shown great respect for long-established provincial rights based on foral laws and traditions. As yet, it is too early to discern any clear signs of an antiregional movement developing at the local and provincial levels, but such a movement might well emerge in the future in view of the strong local and provincial loyalties that were clearly discernible in Spain in the early 1980s.

In Spain, as we observed, the pressure for regional autonomy came from the grass roots and was initiated by ethnic or linguistic movements for the most part, whereas in Italy the major national parties sparkplugged the drive for regional devolution in order to serve their own strategic interests. Also, regionalist parties show much greater electoral strength and political influence in Spain than they do in Italy. This, plus the weakness of national parties in Spain, has prevented the kind of collaboration and intermingling between national and regional elites that has contributed to strengthening of regional institutions in Italy. Far too often, Spanish national parties conform to, or react against, regional pressures, instead of trying to channel and redirect those pressures. One basic similarity must be stressed, however: in both countries, political parties tend to change their tack on regional questions in response to their shifting political and electoral interests.

Ethnic problems play a much more important role in Spanish central-regional relations than is the case in Italy, and linguistic minorities constitute almost forty percent of the population of Spain. Partly because of the sheer size of the problem, partly because of the intensity of regional feelings, the Spanish government has been willing to make very significant concessions, even to the extent of permitting five Spanish autonomous communities to embrace bilingualism. These concessions have been so far-reaching that the rights of the Castilian-speaking minorities in outlying regions are now in some jeopardy, and these minorities may eventually have to call in Madrid for protection. Thus, the Spanish model affords greater protection to the ethnically deviant periphery, but also permits the oppressed of yesterday to become the oppressor of tomorrow.

It is much too early to reach any firm conclusions about the success or ultimate impact of Spain's experiment with regional devolution. Even early returns are few and far between. There is a feeling among qualified observers that the central government in Madrid is trying to impose significant restraints on the scope and extent of regional autonomy. The attempt to impose LOAPA was part of this recentralizing drive, in the eyes of some authorities in the field (Clark 1985a, pp. 4-5; Díaz López 1985, pp. 259-61).

Have the autonomous communities at least alleviated regionalist tensions and mitigated grievances? Here again, it is hazardous to venture an opinion. In most regions, ethnic unrest does not appear to have escalated over the past few years. Perhaps the establishment of regional autonomy headed off such a danger in regions like Galicia and Valencia. Yet there is some negative evidence to consider as well: the continuing disaffection and violence in the Basque country (Clark 1985b, pp. 85-86, 88-89) and the recent electoral gains made in the 1986 elections by Herri Batasuna, the Basque extremist nationalists (The Economist 1986, pp. 43-44). It remains to be seen whether Spain's concessions to peripheral ambitions will have the effect of allaying internal tensions or will only serve to aggravate those tensions.

REFERENCES

Acuerdos autonómicos firmados por el Gobierno de la Nación y el Partido Socialista Obrero Español el 31 Julio de 1981. 1981. Madrid: Servicio Central de Publicaciones de la Presidencia del Gobierno.

Ariño Ortiz, Gaspar. 1981. "El Estado do las Autonomías: Realidad política, interpretación jurídica (Contribución al estudio de un enigma jurídico-estatal)." In La España de las Autonomías (pasado, presente y futuro), by Varios Autores, vol. II, pp. 9-117. Madrid: Espasa-Calpe.

Beneyto, Juan. 1980. Las Autonomías. El poder regional en España. Madrid: Siglo Veintiuno Editores.

Bonime, Andrea R. 1985. "The Spanish State Structures: Constitution Making and the Creation of the New State." In Politics and Change in Spain, edited by Thomas D. Lancaster and Gary Prevost, pp. 11-39. New York: Praeger.

Burgos, Javier de. 1983. España: Por un Estado federal. Barcelona: Argos Vergara.

Carr, Raymond. 1980. Modern Spain 1875-1980. New York: Oxford University Press.

_____. 1966. Spain 1808-1939. London: Oxford University Press.

Carretero y Jiménez, Anselmo. 1980. Los pueblos de España (introducción al estudio de la nación española). Mexico City: Escuela Nacional de Estudios Profesionales Acatlan-Universidad Nacional Autónoma de Mexico.

Chapman, Charles E. 1965. A History of Spain (originally published 1918). New York: Free Press.

Clark, Robert P. 1985a. "Spain's Autonomous Communities: A Case Study in Ethnic Power Sharing." European Studies Journal 11 (no. 1): 1-16.

_____. 1985b. "Madrid and the Ethnic Homelands: Is Consociational Democracy Possible in Post-Franco Spain?' In Politics and Change in Spain, edited by Thomas D. Lancaster and Gary Prevost, pp. 64-93. New York: Praeger.

_____. 1980. "Euzkadi: Basque Nationalism in Spain Since the Civil War." In Nations Without a State: Ethnic Minorities in Western Europe, edited by Charles R. Foster, pp. 75-100. New York: Praeger.

Clavero Arévalo, Manuel. 1983. España desde el centralismo a las autonomías. Barcelona: Planeta.

Coverdale, John F. 1979. The Political Transformation of Spain after Franco. New York: Praeger.

Díaz López, César Enrique. 1985. "Centre-Periphery Structures in Spain: From Historical Conflict to Territorial-Consociational Accommodation?" In Centre-Periphery Relations in Western Europe, edited by Yves Mény and Vincent Wright, pp. 236-72. London: Allen & Unwin.

_____. 1983. "Spagna." In La regionalizzazione, edited by ISAP (Istituto per la Scienza dell' Amministrazione Pubblica), vol. 11, pp. 1863-920. Milan: Giuffré.

―――――. 1982. "The Politicization of Galician Cleavages." In The Politics of Territorial Identity: Studies in European Regionalism, edited by Stein Rokkan and Derek W. Urwin, pp. 389-424. London: Sage.

―――――. 1981. "The State of the Autonomic Process in Spain." Publius 11 (Summer): 193-217.

Díaz López, César Enrique, and Francesc Morata. 1984. "L'Espagne." In La réforme des collectivités locales en Europe: Stratégies et résultats, edited by Yves Mény, no. 4755, pp. 73-100. Paris: La Documentation Française: Notes et Etudes Documentaires.

Elorriaga, Gabriel. 1983. La batalla de las autonomías. Madrid: Editorial Azara.

Estatuto de Autonomía de Valencia. 1982. Madrid: Instituto de Estudios de Administración Local.

Esteban, Jorge de, and Luis López Guerra, with the collaboration of Eduardo Espín and Joaquín García Morillo. 1983. El régimen constitucional español, vol. 11. Barcelona: Labor Universitaria.

Ferreiro Lapatza, José Juan. 1981. "La financiación de las Autonomías." In La España de las autonomías (pasado, presente y futuro) by Varios Autores, vol. 11, pp. 153-86. Madrid: Espasa-Calpe.

Giner, Salvador. 1984. "Ethnic Nationalism, Centre and Periphery in Spain." In Spain: Conditional Democracy, edited by Christopher Abel and Nissa Torrents, pp. 78-99. London: Croom Helm.

Gras, Solange, and Christian Gras. 1982. La Révolte des Régions d'Europe Occidentale de 1916 à Nos Jours. Paris: Presses Universitaires de France.

Greenwood, Davydd J. 1977. "Continuity in Change: Spanish Basque Ethnicity as a Historical Process." In Ethnic Conflict in the Western World, edited by Milton J. Esman, pp. 81-102. Ithaca, N.Y.: Cornell University Press.

Heiberg, Marianne. 1982. "Urban Politics and Rural Culture: Basque Nationalism." In The Politics of Territorial Identity: Studies in European Regionalism, edited by Stein Rokkan and Derek W. Urwin, pp. 355-87. London: Sage.

Leguina Villa, Jesús. 1984. Escritos sobre autonomías territoriales. Madrid: Tecnos.

Linz, Juan J. 1985. "From Primordialism to Nationalism." In New Nationalisms of the Developed West, edited by Edward A. Tiryakian and Ronald Rogowski, pp. 203-53. London: Allen & Unwin.

───. 1981a. "Peripheries Within the Periphery." In Mobilization, Center-Periphery Structures, and Nation-Building, edited by Per Torsvik, pp. 335-90. Oslo: Universitetsforlaget.

───. 1981b. "La crisis de un Estado unitario, nacionalismos periféricos y regionalismo." In La España de las Autonomías (pasado, presente y futuro) by Varios Autores, vol. II, pp. 649-752. Madrid: Espasa-Calpe.

───. 1979. "Un sociologo ante el problema: Una España multinacional y la posibilidad de una democraci consociacional." In Federalismo y regionalismo, edited by Gumersindo Trujillo, pp. 127-57. Madrid: Centro de Estudios Constitucionales.

───. 1973. "Early State-Building and Late Peripheral Nationalism Against the State: The Case of Spain." In Building States and Nations: Analyses by Region, edited by S. N. Eisenstadt and Stein Rokkan, vol. II, pp. 32-116. Beverly Hills, Calif.: Sage.

───. 1967. "The Party System of Spain: Past and Future." In Party Systems and Voter Alignments: Cross-National Perspectives, edited by Seymour M. Lipset and Stein Rokkan, pp. 197-282. New York: Free Press.

Linz, Juan J., Manuel Gómez-Reino, Francisco A. Orizo, and Dário Vila. 1982. Informe sociologico sobre el

cambio politico en España, IV Informe FOESSA, vol I.
Madrid: Editorial Euramerica.

López Nieto, Antonio, and Fernando Fernández Rodríguez.
1981. "La solidaridad y el desarrollo regional en la
Constitución y en la LOFCA." In La España de las
Autonomías (pasado, presente, y futuro) by Varios
Autores, vol. II, pp. 191-404. Madrid: Espasa-Calpe.

López Rodó, Laureano. 1984. Estado y Comunidades
Autónomas. Madrid: Publicaciones Abella.

―――. 1980. Las Autonomías, encrucijada de España.
Madrid: Aguilar.

Madariaga, Salvador de. 1967. Spain: A Modern History.
New York: Praeger.

Martín Mateo, Ramón. 1984. Manual de derecho autonómico.
Madrid: Instituto de Estudios de Administración Local.

Mény, Yves. 1984. "La posizione delle Regioni nello
sviluppo e nella trasformazione dello Stato: Un'
analisi comparata delle politiche di regionalizzazione
in Francia, Italia, e Spagna." Le Regioni XII
(November-December): 1137-65.

Merloni, Francesco. 1983. "La riforma del governo locale
e regionale nei paesi mediterranei." Rivista Trimestrale di Diritto Pubblico 3: 769-801.

Ministerio de Administración Territorial. 1984. Secretaria
General Tecnica. Regimen Local. Madrid.

Mughan, Anthony. 1979. "Modernization and Regional
Relative Deprivation: Towards a Theory of Ethnic
Conflict." In Decentralist Trends in Western Democ-
racies, edited by L. J. Sharpe, pp. 279-312. London:
Sage.

Olábarri Gortázar, Ignacio. 1981. "La cuestión regional
en España, 1808-1939." In La España de las autonomías
(pasado, presente, y futuro), by Varios Autores, vol. I,
pp. 111-99. Madrid: Espasa-Calpe.

Ortega Díaz-Ambrona, Juan Antonio. 1984. "The Transition to Democracy in Spain." In Spain: Conditional Democracy, edited by Christopher Abel and Nissa Torrents, pp. 21-39. London: Croom Helm.

Pi-Sunyer, Oriol. 1980. "Dimensions of Catalan Nationalism." In Nations Without a State: Ethnic Minorities in Western Europe, edited by Charles R. Foster, pp. 101-15. New York: Praeger.

Pin Arboledas, José Ramón. 1984. "El Gobierno socialista y el proceso autonómico." In Un año de socialismo, edited by Oscar Alzaga, pp. 157-73. Barcelona: Argos Vergara.

Preston, Paul. 1984. "Fear of Freedom: The Spanish Army After Franco." In Spain: Conditional Democracy, edited by Christopher Abel and Nissa Torrents, pp. 161-85. London: Croom Helm.

Scammon, Richard M. 1985. "A Summary of Spanish National Election Results, 1977-1982." In Spain at the Polls, 1977, 1979, and 1982, edited by Howard R. Penniman and Eusebio M. Mujal-León, pp. 319-34. Durham, N.C.: Duke University Press.

Silva, Milton M. da. 1975. "Modernization and Ethnic Conflict: The Case of the Basques." Comparative Politics 7 (January): 227-51.

Shabad, Goldie, and Richard Gunther. 1982. "Language, Nationalism, and Political Conflict in Spain." Comparative Politics 14 (July): 443-77.

Simón Tobalina, Juan Luis de. 1981. El Estado autonomico y sus matices federales. Madrid: Instituto de Estudios de Administración Local.

Smith, Rhea Marsh. 1965. Spain: A Modern History. Ann Arbor: University of Michigan Press.

Suárez Fernández, Luis. 1981. "Las raíces históricas de la pluralidad." In La España de las Autonomías (pasado, presente y futuro) by Varios Autores, vol. 1, pp. 23-73. Madrid: Espasa-Calpe.

The Economist. 1986. "More of the Same in Spain, Only Less So." (June 28): 43-44.

Thomas, Hugh. 1961. The Spanish Civil War. New York: Harper.

Tolivar Alas, Leopoldo. 1981. El Control del Estado sobre las Comunidades Autónomas. Madrid: Instituto de Estudios de Administración Local.

Trujillo, Gumersindo. 1979. "Federalismo y regionalismo en la Constitución española de 1978: El Estado 'federo-regional.'" In Federalismo y regionalismo, edited by Gumersindo Trujillo, pp. 13-48. Madrid: Centro de Estudios Constitucionales.

Vandelli, Luciano. 1984. "Regioni e regionalismo: Il caso spagnolo. Aspetti dei rapporti tra Stato e autonomie regionali." Le Regioni XII (May-June): 448-73.

_____. 1982. El ordenamiento español de las Comunidades Autónomas. Madrid: Instituto de Estudios de Administración Local (Spanish translation by Fernando López Ramón and Pablo Lucas Murillo de la Cueva). Original work was L'ordinamento regionale spagnolo (Milan: Giuffré, 1980).

Vázquez de Prada, Valentin. 1981. "La epoca moderna: Los siglos XVI a XIX." In La España de las autonomías (pasado, presente y futuro), by Varios Autores, vol. 1, pp. 77-110. Madrid: Espasa-Calpe.

Wright, Vincent. 1984. "Regioni e regionalizzazione in Francia, Italia, e Spagna." Le Regioni XII (November-December): 1166-80.

6

Conclusions and Interpretations

Mark O. Rousseau
Raphael Zariski

CENTRALIZATION AND DECENTRALIZATION:
MEANINGS AND THEORETICAL AMBIGUITIES

As our analysis suggests, positive benefits exist in both centralized and decentralized political structures. The problem is to find the desirable balance between the two. As we noted, political elites differentially weigh the ideological and pragmatic costs and benefits of centralization and decentralization. Our present concern lies not with assessing the utility of these political value judgments, but rather with interpreting centralization and decentralization theoretically.

Our analysis has examined the institutional basis of political power in modern societies. Centralization implies a highly developed central state structure in which administrative decisions having largely local consequences are made at the highest levels of the national state. Decentralization or devolution posits a political structure in which locally elected officials have greater latitude in making decisions concerning local affairs. A change from more centralized to more decentralized decision making presupposes a change in the structure of institutional arrangements. How are we to understand and interpret such changed institutional structures? Our theoretical tradition fails to provide a clear guide for understanding regional devolution as a political and social process, as our review of pluralist, elitist, and center-periphery theory made clear. Dye (1983) captures the complexity of the theoretical literature when he observes that theories of power postulate both hierarchy and polyarchy in political and economic institutions. The very concepts of centralization and decentralization result in interpretational ambiguity.

If we posit centralization and decentralization as dichotomous polar opposites, the substantive contrast between the two seems clear. Yet such a simple polarization violates the complexities observed in our empirical analysis of Italy, France, and Spain.

Our solution to these conceptual ambiguities and multiple traditions has been to develop a comparative theoretical perspective. Because political power is a complex phenomenon, and structures of central and regional power change through time, we believe no one theoretical interpretation to be entirely correct or erroneous. Perhaps we can best think of centralization and decentralization as sensitizing concepts that force us to ask what the concentration or dispersion of political power means in terms of the functioning of specific organizational structures. We, therefore, characterized political power in its centralized or decentralized form as varying along a continuum rather than as a simple dichotomy. Comprehending political power as a continuum from more concentrated to more dispersed is congruent with the changing realities of political power in these three European nations over time. This continuum conceptualization helps us perceive power as a social and political process rather than as a simple static structure. It reminds us that power structures and processes vary from nation to nation and time to time.

Interpreting political centralization and regional devolution remains a conceptual problem for continuing research and theoretical analysis. Because political power is a complex phenomenon, varied interpretations of it are inevitable, perhaps desirable. Our analysis of the changing relationships of political power in Italy, France, and Spain illustrates the empirical complexity that leads to theoretical diversity. Whether the political institutions of these three nations exhibit evidence of similar long-term trends in political power is a question to which we turn in the following discussion.

CENTRALIZATION AND DECENTRALIZATION UNDER A SYSTEM OF REGIONAL DEVOLUTION: CONTRIBUTING FACTORS AND UNDERLYING RATIONALES

Our examination of the Italian, French, and Spanish experiments with regional devolution has yielded many insights into the factors promoting centralization and decentralization in Western democracies. To be sure, these insights are still somewhat tentative, since all three experiments are still in their early stages, and two (France and Spain) are virtually in their infancy.

We have witnessed the reaffirmation of many of the factors cited in Chapter 1 as favoring centralization or decentralization. For example, it has been clear that, to some degree, regional devolution in France and Italy has been the result of pressure from a modernizing segment of the central bureaucracy seeking a more efficient form of central planning, based on a more accurate appraisal of grass-roots problems. Such an appraisal, it was believed, could be furnished by regional planning authorities (Wright 1984, p. 1172). The goals of greater administrative efficiency, more comprehensive and realistic central planning, the elimination of red tape represented by a plethora of jurisdictionally overlapping functional agencies--these were all objectives that certain forward-looking sectors of the central bureaucracy could espouse (Wright 1984, pp. 1168, 1171-72; Bognetti 1984, p. 1083; Mény 1984b, pp. 1142-43). A related motive for regional devolution was simply to relieve the central government of bureaucratic overload by handing troublesome and sometimes highly controversial distributive functions over to the regions (Leonardi 1984, p. 509). At the same time, less progressive elements of the central bureaucracy were apt to resist territorial encroachments by regional authorities on their functional turf (Bognetti 1984, pp. 1097-101).

Regional devolution was also seen as a means of dealing with the grievances of the periphery. Some regional interests (such as the Basques and the Catalans) saw devolution as a way of clearing away obstacles to the development and expansion of economic and social energies at the grass roots (Mény 1984b, pp. 1141-42). Elites in more backward regions saw devolution as holding forth hope for a greater share of centrally generated economic development aid, a kind of compensation for regional economic imbalances (Mény 1984b, pp. 1140-41). This was true of regions like Andalucía, Brittany, and Sicily. Advocates of national unity would occasionally support regional devolution as a means of forestalling regional separatism (witness the creation of the Italian special regions, the hasty grant of autonomy to the Basque country and Catalonia) (Mény 1984b, p. 1142). Finally, the survival of ethnic loyalties, and the demand by ethnic minorities

Conclusions and Interpretations / 271

that their cultural and linguistic survival be guaranteed, provided a strong and passionate current of support for regionalist tendencies (Mény 1984b, pp. 1145-46; Wright 1984, p. 1169). In Spain, where the state-building process was not actually brought to completion until the country entered a period of decline in the eighteenth century, these ethnic loyalties actually endangered the integrity of the Spanish state. Nor has that danger been entirely dispelled.

In Italy and France--unlike Spain, where parties were weak and ethnic motivations loomed large--the interests of national parties played a key role in both promoting regional devolution and resisting its progress. Here again, as in the case of the bureaucracy, the center was divided against itself, with some national parties defending central control and others championing grass-roots autonomy. Moreover, as we noted, parties would alter their stance on centralization-decentralization issues in accordance with their own shifting interests and concerns (Mény 1984b, pp. 1153-56, 1164-65; Wright 1984, p. 1168). There was very little ideological constraint or consistency in their attitudes over an extended time span (note the frequent reversals of role by Italian and Spanish parties).

Finally, there was a strong democratizing strand in the movement for regional devolution (Mény 1984b, pp. 1143-46, 1154-55). Regionalism was supposed to encourage spontaneous initiative from below, to bring government closer to the people, to give the individual a greater sense of civic competence. It was hoped that new forms of democratic participation--neighborhood councils, civic action groups, open committee hearings, and the like--would flourish under the benevolent aegis of regional government. These democratizing impulses were further stimulated by the widespread reaction against the overcentralization that had prevailed under fascism (Wright 1984, pp. 1169-70). In a sense, regional autonomy--at least in Italy and Spain--had become identified with democracy. However, it should be stressed that not all the grass-roots forces were arrayed on the side of regional devolution. As we noted, many local governments feared the region as a potential usurper of local rights and powers, and actually looked to the national capital for protection (Bognetti 1984, pp. 1097-101). This, too, is a continuing source of tension in central-regional-local relations.

Thus, in the three countries under scrutiny, we have confirmed the presence of a bewildering variety of causal factors and underlying motives that seem to underlie the centralization-decentralization controversy and that may serve to promote or obstruct regional devolution. The struggle for and against regional autonomy seems to have been, and to continue to be, a variable-sum game involving temporary and frequently changing coalitions. In this contest, today's opponent becomes next year's ally, and vice versa. The issue of centralization versus decentralization often appears to be instrumental in nature, serving the interests of those who seek to achieve other goals by tinkering with the territorial distribution of power. In effect, competing elites are prone to use this issue as a convenient weapon for attaining vital ideological, strategic, or policy objectives.

THE ROLE OF POLITICAL ELITES

As our analysis of Italy, France, and Spain has shown, the structural organization of the state reflects the concerns of the political elites who rule it. As ruling elites change, they alter state structures in ways congruent with their ideologies and goals. Centralized and decentralized state structures echo historic struggles for political power that develop in a particular national tradition. Since the historical traditions and particular problems confronted by political elites vary, it is not possible to predict with certainty the forms in which the state will be shaped. Nonetheless, some empirical regularities obtain.

Most basically, the structural organization of the state does not occur in a political vacuum. As Putnam (1976, pp. 90-91) asserts, a society's agenda of problems is formulated by its political elite who typically control the terms of debate. Similarly, Birnbaum (1982) argues that understanding the ideologies of those who occupy top positions in the state sheds considerable light on the nature of the state itself, since the state is translated into reality in the form of particular institutions controlled by the ruling elite. Our analysis has addressed ways in which state organization is related to the particular challenges perceived by its political leadership.

In France, we observed that the Jacobin centralized state has been a stable feature of state organization as elites of both Left and Right attempted to impose reform from above. The Girondist tradition, grounded in a more pluralist, decentralized state, has served as an alternative frame of reference. Although the Jacobin view has predominated, French politics reflects the continuing struggle between advocates of these two views. In Italy, a different historical situation confronted its political leadership with distinctive problems. The long delay and difficulty in completing national unification raised concerns about the fractional tendencies perceived to be inherent in regional devolution. Establishment of the Italian regions in the late 1940s and early 1970s occurred only when shifts in political party alliances and partisan strategies outweighed these traditional fears. Finally, in Spain, still different problems prompted the leadership to structure the state in ways congruent with its prescriptions for national development. The early failure to develop a centralized state in the seventeenth century, combined with the enduring grievances of peripheral regions, has caused the Spanish leadership to form regional institutions to mollify regional resentments rather than to strengthen popular participation in the political process as in Italy and France.

While political elites endeavor to mold the state in ways congruent with their interests, historical traditions and institutional structures can limit their ability to do so. As Suleiman (1974, p. 17) argues, the development of a centralized state depends on a variety of historical factors, including elites' responses to societal demands. In Spain, the relationships of peripheral regions to the central government forced the seventeenth-century monarchs to settle for a continuation of the existing federated system. Later, after a period of centralized rule, the Napoleonic intervention of 1808-1814 revived and exacerbated the centrifugal tendencies of the Spanish state. The regions' historical strengths and the tradition of foral rights prevented the national leadership from imposing a fully centralized state on the legally unified but ethnically and culturally divided nation.

In Italy, national unification preoccupied successive generations of political leaders. When the partisans of unification triumphed, they imposed a tightly centralized, unitary government on the newly unified Italian nation. This rigidly centralized system ultimately sparked a decentralizing reaction, forcing the political leadership to respond to new problems and eventuating in the development of modern Italian regionalism.

In France, historical traditions and institutional structures likewise constrained the course steered by the leaders of successive regimes and parties. The inability of the seventeenth-century monarchs to eliminate entirely provincial rights confronted the successive regimes of the revolutionary periods with the problem of forming a fully centralized national state. Napoleon gave centralization a firm structural foundation through the creation of the grandes écoles and grands corps. Once fashioned, these institutional structures limited the ability and willingness of the French elite to alter the centralized nature of the state (Suleiman 1978). In all three countries, then, while ruling elites shaped the state, historical traditions and institutional structures restrained their capacity to do so.

Additionally, these traditions and structures create continuities in the problems elites face, although they may vary in their solutions to them. In both Italy and France, central economic planning contributed to regional devolution as ruling elites perceived the need for an intermediate level of government to administer centrally derived policies. To be sure, party ideologies and interests influenced perceptions about the role of regional governments. In Italy, central economic planning became a national priority about the time the regional autonomy issue came to the fore again in the 1960s. The two questions became associated in the reformist program of the newly developing "opening to the left." While other important factors contributed to Italian regionalism, the national and regional planning goals of the political leadership played a contributing part.

In France, the perceived need for regional participation in centrally developed five-year plans played an even greater role in the emergence of the political regions than in Italy. Political leaders of both Left and Right espoused the need for an intermediate planning and executory body, although the specifics of regional organization constituted a point of vivid debate. The Pompidou government's 1972 legislation created regional bodies that largely transmitted centrally developed policies downward, reflecting conservative Jacobin fears that regional governance would lead to a weakening of the nation state. The advent of a Socialist government in 1981 granted the regions not only an increased role in planning but considerably enhanced political autonomy as well. Thus, in both Italy and France, the issue of economic planning prompted the ruling elites to reshape the state to accommodate their differing visions of center and periphery.

Conclusions and Interpretations / 275

We are not suggesting that political leaders always respond to issues as a simple function of party ideology. Political opportunism and changing party interests play a major role, as our analysis has shown. Leaders of both Left and Right have alternately supported or opposed regional devolution as it enhances or diminishes their election prospects. In Italy, we observed that parties that shared national power in Rome tended to resist regionalist pressures, whereas parties largely denied national governmental power frequently became advocates of regional rights. For example, the Communist party leadership, which had espoused regional devolution when out of power, came to reconsider its position in the 1970s, when it seemed that they might participate in national governance. In the late 1970s, when the historic compromise with the Christian Democrats failed to occur, the Communist leadership again began supporting regional autonomy.

In France, also, the vagaries of national politics influenced the views of party elites toward regional devolution. While historically the Left had supported a strong central government, its exclusion from national power during the Gaullist era led it to develop a local political base. This local constituency made Socialist leaders increasingly receptive to growing demands for enhanced regional authority. When they reached national office in 1981, the Socialists enacted their far-reaching program of regional devolution, although with somewhat diminished ardor as conservative parties had already begun to cultivate a local base with some success.

Finally, in Spain, we saw how shifting fortunes influenced party leaders' views of regionalism. For many decades, the conservative Carlists actually supported foral rights in their opposition to the Liberal centralists. Later, the conservative parties in Madrid opposed their natural allies, the Basque Nationalists, who then expediently allied themselves with forces on the Left, paradoxically bringing the Left to support the cause of regional autonomy. Such experiences in all three nations bolster the conclusion that political leaders excluded from national power tend to support regional rights. If excluded parties later participate in national power, frequently their regionalist enthusiasm wanes and their leaders embrace central solutions to political and social questions.

In sum, the evidence seems to bear out our proposition that the form of the state reflects the concerns of the elites who rule it. As regimes change and parties rotate through national office, new leaders shape and reshape the state in conformity with their views and purposes. Such structuring is, of course, influenced by historical traditions and prevailing institutions and ideologies, as we have illustrated.

CENTRALIZATION AND DECENTRALIZATION: LONG-TERM TENDENCIES

As our analysis has shown, center-periphery relations in these three nations are structurally and temporally more complex than a simple, unitary state model might suggest. Local and regional governments have been at times more dependent and less dependent on decisions made by the central administration. Often local notables are closely linked with central administrators in applying solutions to local problems. We believe that the complex and changing structure of organizational and interpersonal relations between central and regional institutions makes it difficult to advance simple generalizations about central-local relations. We noted that some scholars emphasize the complex interpenetration and osmosis of central-regional-local relations (Tarrow 1977; Mény 1984b), while others underline the burdensome excesses of central domination over local decisions (Suleiman 1974, 1978; Crozier 1982). The multiple emphases of these varied interpretations reflect a complex and changing underlying reality. In all three nations, strong forces for both centralization and decentralization have always coexisted and continue to manifest themselves.

We noted Birnbaum's (1982) work in which he suggests that historical shifts in the composition of the coalitions that comprise the power elite affect both the cohesion of the state and its relative pluralistic heterogeneity or elitist homogeneity over time. We suggested that the forms of the state may change in response to the goals of changing political elites, and we saw that all three nations have experienced alternating tendencies toward more centralized and less centralized state power as a result. Accordingly, the development of centralization or decentralization in a given nation does not follow any simple unilinear evolutionary pattern. Because of the variety of political and structural forces that favor both the perpetuation of central state power and, at the same time, the development of local and regional identities and demands for power sharing, we conclude that a dialectical pattern exists between central actions and regional reactions. Central actions provoke responses by regional elites and governments, which in turn prompt further central responses in an ongoing dialectical process. As Suleiman (1974, p. 17) writes, state and society respond to one another. This centralization-decentralization dialectic seems to capture best the complex and changing reality of central-regional relations in all three nations.

In Italy and especially in France, we saw how pressures for devolved decision making emerged as responses to the growing centralization and technocracy of the national state. In both nations, increasing central planning led to a growing central recognition of the need for an intermediate level of government, the region, to coordinate and rationalize state planning. While the region in France was originally conceived as an administrative convenience for the central state, it gradually developed into something more than a geographically defined administrative entity. Although some Italian, French, and Spanish regions had a developed sense of community, often centering around ethnic identity, others did not. Yet the creation of administrative regions enhanced the growth of local and regional identity. As a sense of community developed, the regions increasingly pressed for greater decision-making powers.

This dialectic of central action, regional response, and further central action continues in an ongoing cycle in all three nations. While devolution is more developed in Italy and Spain than in France, regional demands persist as an influence on central policies in all three nations. Although simple generalizations are not possible, the future of regional devolution will continue to be shaped by the developing social and political interests of the regions as they emerge from the dialectic process.

At the same time, many structural and political forces favor the enhancement of central power. We observed in Italy the centralizing nature of the national political parties that frame regional issues in ways that augment the partisan standing of the party nationally and thereby serve as a counter to regional autonomy. Furthermore, the central government itself rather severely limits regional powers in various ways, particularly by checks on regional financial autonomy. In France as well, a variety of forces undergird the centralized state. We addressed the <u>grandes écoles</u> and <u>grands corps</u> that comprise the state's institutional base for centralized political administration. Even the recent Socialist government with its ambitious political decentralization program left these important structural supports of centralized administration fundamentally unaltered. The historic Jacobin view that only the central state can represent the general interest of society as a whole retains its powerful influence among political elites and parties of both Left and Right. The centralized nature of such major French institutions as political parties, labor unions, corporations, and the like provide support for centralism. Although Spain experienced alternating periods of centralization and decentralization as regimes changed, the development of a viable central state in the face of strong regional autonomy remained a dominant issue. True, beyond the dialectical shifts in central-regional relations observed in all three nations, some evidence suggests a potential long-term trend toward a gradual increase in power by the central government at the expense of regional and local governments.

Thus far, we have noted two distinctive and rather incompatible tendencies: a dialectical process of reciprocal challenge and response, involving a seesaw struggle for advantage between centralizing and decentralizing forces; and a combination of structural, political, and societal pressures promoting gradual movement toward greater central control. In spite of dialectical shifts between centralization and decentralization, we have observed that regional decisions in both Italy and France are increasingly being developed within the larger framework of central government policy, and that a similar pattern of events may well be crystallizing in Spain. The continuing central influence over regional agendas suggests that regional devolution can perhaps best be understood as an attempt to provide local and particularly regional governments with an opportunity to participate in the exercise of political power, rather than as an effort to endow regional governments with clearly defined and inviolable areas of self-determination. From this perspective, even if regional devolution has not really altered the fundamental power structure of the unitary state, it has helped to ensure that regional and local governments have some input into central decisions.

Thus, as we see, a third possible trend that can be read into recent events is toward a form of cooperative federalism or intergovernmental relations (IGR), characterized by a continuous process of power sharing, cooperation, bargaining, and competition among central, regional, and local agencies and officials. The IGR model has gained increasing acceptance among American scholars (see Elazar 1976; Rosenthal 1980). A number of European scholars--for example, Donolo and Fichera (1981) and Fichera (1982), with their concept of "partial government"--have suggested, directly or by implication, that something corresponding to the IGR model may well apply to unitary systems as well as to federal systems. These insights pose the distinct possibility that a convergence may be taking place between systems of central-regional-local relations in various Western democracies. Such a convergence in decision-making styles and procedures would greatly reduce the significance of the legal and structural distinctions between unitary, federal, and regional-devolution systems.

The development of central state power has followed no simple, unilinear, evolutionary course. While strong forces have propelled the growth of the central administration, our dialectical analysis revealed that the expansion of central power has not gone unchecked. Periodic regional reactions have restrained and channeled the growth of central power and have compelled the central authorities to modify their methods and goals. The dynamic tension between center and periphery persists, making the progress of regional devolution a continuing story with no clear denouement in sight. Moreover, the internal divisions within both center and periphery; the complex and fluid relationships that have developed between central, regional, and local agencies and individual actors; the kaleidoscopic patterns of alliance and conflict--all of these phenomena warn us of the inadequacy of a simple center-periphery approach to the issues raised by regional devolution. Central-regional relations are marked by a curious blending of cooperation and conflict, aggregation and disintegration, and our models are hard-pressed to comprehend and dominate such a mercurial reality.

PROBLEMS FOR THE FUTURE

We have examined centralization, decentralization, and the progress of regional devolution in Italy, France, and Spain from a number of perspectives. These processes may be viewed as superficial aspects of an underlying struggle among competing elites; as part of a steady growth of central power at the expense of the periphery; as successive phases in a dialectic and never-ending conflict between center and periphery; or as formal categories, which tend to conceal the congruence between the system of central-regional-local relations in southern Europe and the IGR model accepted in the United States. We have not stated a clear preference for any single one of these perspectives. Each has its merits and limitations as a way of viewing a bewilderingly complex reality and posing problems for future research. In the years ahead, social scientists should have ample opportunity to employ these approaches, in comparing the systems of regional devolution in southern Europe, and to assess their relative usefulness in the field.

Before this can be done, however, some time must elapse. For the fact is, that of the three European democracies under scrutiny, only Italy has had an adequate span of institutional experience with regional devolution. As a result, the quantity and range of the Italian literature on regional devolution far surpasses what is available on the newly hatched experiments in France and Spain. Also, the empirical component plays a much more prominent role in the Italian literature. After all, without adequate institutional experience, one can hardly expect empirical studies to be produced in significant quantity. So one problem is simply to furnish the necessary underpinning for further theoretical progress. Obviously, this problem can only be resolved with the passage of time and the future availability of comparable empirical insights and data.

A second task is to develop new research strategies to conform to the new perspectives that seem to be gaining the ascendancy in the field of subnational politics. The IGR model cries out for some means of imposing order on a chaotic interplay of actors that respect no jurisdictional boundaries. It may well be that the intricate and ever-changing relationship among actors in subnational politics, with factions banding together to form temporary coalitions that, in turn, break up to form new factions, may require the application of factional and coalition theory in order to reduce a hopelessly confusing real world to comprehensible dimensions.

REFERENCES

Badie, Bertrand, and Pierre Birnbaum. 1983. The Sociology of the State, trans. by Arthur Goldhammer. Chicago: University of Chicago Press.

Birnbaum, Pierre. 1982. The Heights of Power: An Essay on the Power Elite in France, trans. by Arthur Goldhammer. Chicago: University of Chicago Press.

Bognetti, Giovanni. 1984. "Le regioni in Europe: Alcune riflessioni sui loro problemi e sul loro destino." Le Regioni XII (November-December): 1087-136.

Crozier, Michel. 1982. Strategies for Change: The Future of French Society, trans. by William R. Beer. Cambridge, Mass.: MIT Press.

Donolo, Carlo, and Franco Fichera. 1981. Il governo debole: Forme e limiti della razionalitá politica. Bari: De Donato.

Dye, Thomas. 1983. Who's Running America? The Reagan Years. Englewood Cliffs, N.J.: Prentice-Hall.

Elazar, Daniel J. 1976. "Federalism vs. Decentralization: The Drift from Authenticity." Publius: The Journal of Federalism 6 (Fall): 9-19.

Fichera, Franco. 1982. "Le Regioni: Dalla programmazione ai 'governi parziali.'" Democrazia e Diritto XXII (January-February): 93-102.

Leonardi, Robert. 1984. "Riflessioni conclusive sulle ragioni dello sviluppo del regionalismo nell' Europa occidentale." Le Regioni XII (May-June): 505-10.

Mény, Yves. 1984a. "Decentralisation in Socialist France: The Politics of Pragmatism." West European Politics 7 (January): 65-79.

————. 1984b. "La posizione delle regioni nello sviluppo e nella trasformazione dello Stato: Un' analisi comparata delle politiche di regionalizzazione in Francia, Italia, e Spagna." Le Regioni XII (November-December): 1137-65.

Putnam, Robert D. 1976. The Comparative Study of Political Elites. Englewood Cliffs, N.J.: Prentice-Hall.

Rosenthal, D. B. 1980. "Bargaining Analysis in Intergovernmental Relations." Publius: The Journal of Federalism 10 (Summer): 5-44.

Suleiman, Ezra N. 1978. Elites in French Society: The Politics of Survival. Princeton, N.J.: Princeton University Press.

⎯⎯⎯⎯⎯⎯. 1974. Politics, Power, and Bureaucracy in France: The Administrative Elite. Princeton, N.J.: Princeton University Press.

Tarrow, Sidney. 1977. Between Center and Periphery: Grassroots Politicians in Italy and France. New Haven, Conn.: Yale University Press.

Tocqueville, Alexis de. 1969. Democracy in America, trans. by George Lawrence. Garden City, N.Y: Doubleday.

Wright, Vincent. 1984. "Regioni e regionalizzazione in Francia, Italia, e Spagna." Le Regioni XII (November-December): 1166-80.

Index

absolute majority, 242
absolute monarchy: attempt to return to, 208; principle of, 207
absolutism, 155
administrative centralization, defined, 64
agrarian Centre party, 30
Algerian war, 166
ancien régime, 155–57
anticlericalism, 216
antiregionalist philosophy, 113
Aprile, Finocchiaro, 99
assessorates (regional executive departments), 109
association, freedom of, 65
Autonomic Pacts, 227, 229, 233, 248, 254
autonomous communities, 234, 242, 250; creation of, 229; restricted taking power of, 246; rule-making powers of, 238
Autonomy Statute (1972), 133

Balbo, Cesare, 93, 94
Basque Autonomy Statute, 214
Basque Nationalist Party, 211
Basque provinces, terrorist violence in, 226
Benso di Cavour, Camillo, 94
bilingual education, 255–56
bilingualism, 132
Birnbaum, Pierre, 61
Blanco, Luis Carrero, 217

block grants: for governmental operations, 186; for public works, 186
Bodin, Jean, 10
Bonaparte, Napoleon, 93, 157
bureaucracy, 51, 52; inevitable growth of, 53; Weber's analysis of, 54
bureaucratic blockage, primary sources of, 74

caciquismo, system of, 212
Calhaun, John D., 20
Calvo Sotelo, Leopoldo, 227, 233
Carlist Wars, 208–9
Carlos, Don, 208
Carlos, Juan, 218
Castilian hegemony, 204, 213
Castilian laws, extension of, 205
Catalan regionalist parties, 211
Catalan Renaissance, 210
Catholic Church, 208; disestablishment of, 160
Catholicism, 31
Cattaneo, Carlo, 93, 94, 100
center-periphery cleavages, 7
center-periphery interaction, 78–81
central government, relationship between Spanish autonomous communities and, 236
central government agencies, and opposition to centralization, 23

central hegemony, vs. territorial defense, 25
centralization, 8, 153, 268; alternatives to, 3, 31–34; consequences of in Spain, 206; factors favoring, 270; forces favoring, 22; historical and social factors favoring, 409; and military expansion, 5; peasant reaction against, 28; rationale for, 9–12; structural foundation of, 274; virtues of, 2
centralization-decentralization controversy, 2, 3, 272; historical and social factors of, 2
centralized state, domestic tranquilty and, 10
centralizing tendencies, under fascism, 97–98
central-peripheral relationships, 113
central-regional relationships, issue of, 222
Chamber of Deputies, 115
Christian Democratic party, 96, 100, 104, 105, 106, 252
circulation of elites, 45
citizen participation, decentralization and, 18
Civil War, the, Franco regime and, 215–17
class, defined, 51
class cleavages, 6, 16, 30
classical elitism, 44–54, 69
classical pluralism, 63–67
collectivités specialisées (specialized governments), 169
collegiality, 109
comarcas, 249, 250

Commission de développement économique régionales (CODER), 168
Committee for Economic Development, 60
Committees of National Liberation (CLNs), 98
Communist party, 163, 178, 222, 228, 252
community power, decision-making method for measurement of, 75
comparative political analysis, 85
competition, 83
comprensorio, 122, 123, 250
conciertos economicos (economic accords), 210, 215, 247
conditional grants, 119
Conference of Junta Presidents, 115, 116
conflict resolution, beneficiaries of, 59
Congress, middle level of power in, 58
Congress of Vienna, 93
Conservative party (Great Britain), 25
Constituent Assembly, 99, 100, 101, 163
constitutional permissiveness, 248
Constitutional Tribunal, 238, 239, 240, 241, 243, 248, 259
Constitution of 1978, 220–29
contemporary elite pluralism, 67
contemporary elitism, 54–62, 67
contemporary pluralism, 67–77
cooperative federalism, concept of, 118

corporation, 57
corporatism, 123
cortes (parliamentary assembly), 208
Council for Foreign Relations, 60
Crozier, Michel, 23, 73-75
cultural diffusion model, 11
cultural extinction, fear of, 29
cultural identity, emergence of, 181
cumul des mandats, 27

Dahl, Robert, 55, 75-77
decentralization, 33, 153, 268; Communist systems and, 21; cultural traditions and, 26; diversity and, 21; efficiency and, 21; forces favoring, 26; forms of, 2; motives for, 105-6; political, socialist embrace of, 180; political recruitment patterns and, 26; power and, 82-85; rationale for, 18-22; vested interests and, 28; virtues of, 2
decision making: beneficiaries, 59; researchers, 55
deconcentration, defined, 32
de Enterria, García, 227
de Gaulle, Charles, 62, 163, 166, 167
delegation of power, lack of, 120-21
democracy: defined, 63; side effects of, 64; Tocqueville's reservations about, 64, 65
Democracy in America, 63

democratic corporatism, in Scandinavia, 20
democratic era, in Spain, 218
democratic revolutions, impact of, 9
de Olivares, Dugue, 205, 206
dependency-marginality model, center-periphery relations and, 79
de Rivera, Primo, 213
despotism, 66
d'Estaing, Giscard, 62, 174
de Tocqueville, Alexis, 63-67, 82, 155, 177
devolution, political, 43
diffusion-isolation model, center-periphery relations and, 79
diputacion (deputation), 208
distribution welfare, policy of, 79
domestic tranquility, centralized state and, 10
Domhoff, William, 59-60
Dye, Thomas, 58-59, 82

economic backwater, 28
economic modernization, 176
economic nationalization, 179
Economic Planning Committee, 128
economy: crisis in France, 187; planning and the regions, 128-31; role of institutions, 46; spending patterns and disparities, 9
egalitarian distribution, of goods and services, 9
elections, manipulation of, 212
elite heterogeneity (pluralism), 61
elite homogeneity (elitism), 61; state autonomy and, 61

elite integration, 68
elite pluralism, 67
elite rule: desirability of, 68; inevitability of, 47, 58, 68
elites, political, function of, 69, 272-76
elitism, 61; defined, 60, 69
elitist power-concentrated model, 194
elitist theorists, emphasis of, 82
empirical data, scientific measurement methods in collection of, 67
Estado de Autonomías (State of Autonomies), 222
ethnic activism, political autonomy and, 182
ethnic activists, 189
ethnic identity, emergence of, 181
ethnic-linguistic issue, 131
ethnic minorities: protection of in regions, 131-34; self-assertiveness of, 257
European Coal and Steel Community, 165
European Common Market, Norwegian entry into, 25
European Economic Community, 30, 165
European nation-state, development of, 4
exclusive regional power, principle of, 237
executive junta, 107
expansionist wars, 5
extrapolitical centralization, 6

fascism, 271
Fascist era, 97
federal expansion, legal tradition of, 22
federal government, executive branch of, 57
federalism, 2, 7, 14
Federalist Papers, The, 10
Federal Republic of Germany, 235
federal systems, 32; formation of, 7, 14
federal union, establishment of, 7
Ferdinand VII, 208
feudalism, decline of, 28
Fifth Republic, the: Giscardism, 174-77; Socialism, 177-92
financial autonomy, lack of regional, 118
First National Economic Plan, 129
"flight from the Court," 114
foralidad, principle of, 249
foral rights, 206, 209, 216, 222, 247, 275
forced Italianization, program of, 97
forces vives de la nation, 29
Fourth Republic, the, 163-66
framework laws (leggi-cornice), 111
Franco, Francisco, 202
Franco-Prussian War, 159
Franco regime: campaign of suppression during, 216; Civil War and, 215-17; forced assimilation policy of, 217; terrorism in, 217
French administration, decentralization and, 74
French colonial empire, postwar dissolution of, 166
French democracy, 174
French political history, turbulence of, 192
French Revolution, 5, 6, 13, 152, 157

Index / 287

French state, centralized nature of, 152
fringe groups, 19
functional fragmentation, 123
functionalism, 68
functional interest group, 24
functional specialization, 16; at national level, 15
functional systems theory, 68
functional-territorial dichotomy, 81
fused hierarchy, prefectoral tradition of, 23

Gaullist party, political setback of, 170
General Planning Commission (Paris), 27
Gioberti, Vincenzo, 93, 94, 100
Girondists, 154, 158
Girondist tradition, 272
governing elite, defined, 45, 61
governmental centralization, defined, 64
governments, services provided by, 8
grandes écoles, 60, 74, 179, 190, 274, 278; study of, 190
grands corps, 60, 190, 274, 278
grant money, unconditional, 15
grants-in-aid, 15
grass-roots movements, 107

hegemonic power, 71
hierarchy, 81, 82
higher education, in France, 179
Hunter, Floyd, 55, 56-57

identity, crisis of, 78
industrialization, 13
industrial revolution, 16; impact of, 9
inequality, political and social, three-dimensional characterization of, 51
institutional discontinuity, 207
institutional elites, 57
intendants, 156
interdependent economy, 7
interest groups, 59, 71; interaction with parties, 124-26; middle level of power in, 58; role played by in policy making, 72; varying powers of, 67; as veto groups, 71
intergovernmental lobby, 15, 27
intergovernmental relations (I.G.R.) model, 279
Interministerial Commission for Autonomic Development, 244
internal colonialism, 79
Interterritorial Compensation Fund, 242, 245, 246
intraregional centralization, 121
iron cage, 53
iron law of oligarchy, 49
Italian cabinet, 102
Italian Christian Democratic party, 11, 31
Italian Communist party, 31
Italian Conference of Regional Junta Presidents, 243
Italian Constitutional Court, 103
Italianization, in Italian provinces, 97
Italian nationalism, 93
Italian parliament, 102

288 / Index

Italian peninsula, French occupation of, 92
Italian Republic, establishment of, 98-102
Italy, historical background, 92-98

Jacobin concept, 10
Jacobin-Girondist debate, 165
Jacobin ideology, domination of, 193
Jacobin orientation, Gaullists' ideological commitment to, 172
Jacobins, 154, 158
Jacobin tradition, 23, 26, 188, 189, 191, 272
Jefferson, Thomas, 19
judicial activism, 114
judicial review, 14; power of, 33
July Monarchy, 62
junta president, 107

Keller, Suzanne, 68-71
king, as primary institution, 156

Labour party (Great Britain), 25
landed aristocracy, decline of, 28
language: official, 255; co-official, 255
La Reconquista, 203
leadership recruitment, 49
legal tradition, of federal expansion, 22
leggine, defined, 129
legislative evolution, 187
legislative initiative, power of, 115
legitimacy, crisis of, 78
legitimation, third principle of, 52

Liberal party, 30
linguistic discrimination, in hiring policies, 256
linguistic minorities, and central government policy of benign neglect, 20
local administration, Napoleonic model of, 93
local authorities: conservatism of, 12; flexibility of, 12; lack of fiscal resources and, 11; lack of functional specialization, 12
local governments: and reduction of political power, 158; regions' relations with, 119-23
local oligarchies, subversion of, 25
local rule, political interference in, 184
Louis XIV, 155

Madison, James, 10
mancomunidades, 213
marginal groups, 19
Mazzini, Giuseppe, 93, 94
Michels, Robert, 48-51
Middle Ages, 13
military, 57
military expansion, centralization and, 5
Mills, C. Wright, 55, 57
Millsian tradition, 58
minority groups, decentralization as advantage to, 19
minority oppression, 64
Mitterrand, François, 178, 182, 191
Mixed Commission on the Transfer of Powers, 238, 239
models of regional government, similarities and differences between Italian and Spanish, 230-33

monarch, as primary object of allegiance, 13
Monarchists, 100
monocephalous state, 8
monopoly of power, moral principles and, 47
moral principles, monopoly of power and, 47
Mosca, Gaetano, 46-48
multiple officeholding, 191

Napoleonic empire, 153
National Assembly, 162
National Association of Italian Communes, 123
national economic plan, 17
national elites, 69
national policy making, ruling class domination of, 60
North Atlantic Treaty Organization (NATO), 165
Norwegian Conservative party, 25
Norwegian labor party, 25

occupancy-of-the-field legislation, 112
oligarchy, 68; defined, 48; iron law of, 49
oligopoly, 81
Organic Law for the Harmonization of the Autonomic Process (LOAPA), 228, 241, 259
overcentralization, 22, 96

Papal States, 92
Pareto, Vilfredo, 45-46
Parliamentary Committee on Regional Issues, 115, 116
participation: crisis of, 78; importance of, 18
participatory democracy, 121; as unattainable ideal, 110

parties, defined, 51
penetration, crisis of, 78
Philip IV, 205, 206
Philip V, 205
Piedmontese system, of local government, 94
pluralist power-dispersed model, 194
plurist theorists, emphasis of, 82-83
political autonomy, ethnic activism and, 182
political distance, decentralization and, 18
political opportunism, 275
political parties: changing of thinking on regional questions, 253; role of in regional devolution, 251
political philosophy, 1
political power, 1; institutional basis of in modern societies, 268
political revolutions, social and economic changes resulting from, 6
polyarchy, 59, 76, 82
Pompidou, Georges, 167, 171
Pope, the, 92, 93
Popular Alliance (AP), opposition force to autonomic pacts, 228
population growth, effect on centralization, 84
populist alliance, 80
pork barrel relationships, 24
Post-Franco period, 218-29
postindustrial society, 17
power(s): centralization of, 4-12; as continuum, 84; decentralization, 12-22, 82-85; decision-making approach to, 55; as dichotomy, 84; distribution

of, 1-2; empirical measurement of, 54; expropriations of, 114; institutional nature of, 62; positional approach to, 55, 57; principal centers of, 61; reputational approach to, 55, 56; separation and division of, 65
power and authority, nature of, 51, 52
power clusters, 76
Power Elite, The, 57
power elite, state's, as primary source of blockage, 73
power measurement, approaches to, 55
power relationships, conceptualization of, 71
power theories: classical elitism, 44-54; classical pluralism, 63-67; contemporary elitism, 54-62; contemporary pluralism, 67-77
preautonomy, principle of, 219
preautonomy formula, 219
prefectoral tradition, of fused hierarchy, 23
press, freedom of the, 65
productive alliance, formation of, 79
proletariat, class-conscious, 6
Protestant Reformation, 5
Provincial and Communal Act, 94, 97
public hearings, 107
public policy agenda, corporate boardroom decisions and, 77
public schools, creation of, 160
public spending, increase in subnational, 15

redistributive centralization, defined, 29
redistributive policies, 25
reformist orientation, of central government, 24
reformist program, 128
Regional Administrative Tribunal (TAR), 120
regional autonomy, 212-15; Communist supported, 101; investigation of problem of, 227; motives for, 105-6; movement toward, 3; pressure from grass roots for, 260; pressure from political parties for, 260; reasons for delay in granting, 104
Regional Control Commission, 112, 119
regional council, 107
regional devolution, 2-4, 33-34, 54, 70, 105, 120, 168, 180, 219; consequences of, 120; defined, 2; shortfalls of, 33-34
regional government, structures and basic processes of, 107-10, 233-36
regionalism: and ethnic issues, 254-57; revival of, 98; studies of, 175
regionalist movements, rise of, 210-12
regionalist resistance, historical and social factors favoring, 12-18
regional-local relations, in Spain, 247
regional prefect, powers of, 168
regional reform(s), 106; under de Gaulle, 169

regions: budgeting freedom and, 175; contributions of, 137; political authority and, 175
representative principle, 6
residui passivi, 119, 135
Resistance, the, 98
Resistance period, 98
Restoration Monarchy, 207
revenue sharing, 15
Riesman, David, 71-73
Risorgimento, 92, 93-95; defined, 93
Roman Catholic Church, 4
rule-making function, 110
rule-making powers, of autonomous communities, 238

Sardinian Action party, 97, 99
Sardinian junta, 103
security of tenure, 109
self-management, socialist ideology of, 182
separatist movement, 99
social composition of power, potential for shifts in, 62
social heterogeneity, 45
Socialist party, 101, 105, 106, 177, 178, 190, 222, 227, 252, 254
Socialist reform legislation, 178
social stratification, 51, 52
societal transformation, 21
solidarity principle, 245
southern blacks, oppression of, 10
sovereign state, as source of power, 46
Spanish-American War (1898), 209
Spanish constitution, ratification of, 202

Spanish Ministry of Education, 256
Spanish state: creation and consolidation of, 203-7; and question of legitimacy, 207
speech, freedom of, 65
special regions: autonomy of, 99; fiscal advantages of, 103; restriction of powers and, 103
spending patterns, economic disparities and, 9
state, as source of power, 45
state bureaucracy, 73
state formation process, 92
state political power, as source of power, 48
state transfers, regional dependence on, 119
status groups, defined, 51
strategic elites, 69
structural functional postulates, 70
Sturzo, Don, 96, 100
Suarez, Adolfo, 218
Südtyroler Volkspartei (SVP), 132
suffrage, expansion of, 96
Suleiman, Ezra, 60
Supreme Court, 14
system of recruitment, 127

taxation, powers of, 8
technocracy, at national level, 15
technocratic reformism, policy of, 79
territorial defense, vs. central hegemony, 25
territorial division of power, 2
terrorism, Algerian campaign of, 166
terrorist violence, in Basque provinces, 226

theoretical diversity, 83
theory of elitism, 46
Third Republic, 159–63
Third World, 7
tutelle, 184, 185, 186
tyranny of the majority, 64, 66, 82
tyranny of the minority, 66

unification, process of, 206
unitary systems, decentralization in, 32–34
United States: amorphous power in, 71; as military capitalism, 58; as pluralist, polyarchic society, 76; polyarchy in, 77
University of Lausanne, 45
Uomo Qualunque (Any Man) party, 100
urban commercial centers, 5

urban middle class, 5
urban renewal, examination of, 77

veto (rinvio), 113, 240
veto groups, theory of, 71
violence, political, 257
voluntarism, 65, 66, 67, 82
vote of no confidence, 107

War of Independence, 207
War of the Spanish Succession, 205
Weber, Max, 51–54, 82
welfare state, 8, 15; decentralist reaction to, 16
western Europe, state formation of, 4, 5
West German Bundesrat, 116, 232
World War I, 96, 97, 100
World War II, 132, 164, 181
world wars, expenses of, 8

About the Authors

MARK O. ROUSSEAU is an associate professor of sociology at the University of Nebraska-Omaha. Dr. Rousseau has published in the areas of social stratification and political sociology, including an analysis of decentralization in France in The French Review. He holds a B.A. and M.A. from Indiana University, Bloomington, and a Ph.D. from the University of North Carolina, Chapel Hill.

RAPHAEL ZARISKI is professor of political science at the University of Nebraska-Lincoln. He is the author of Italy: The Politics of Uneven Development and of a number of journal articles. He has published in the areas of subnational politics and comparative political parties. He holds a B.A., M.A., and Ph.D. from Harvard University, Cambridge, Massachusetts.